Tomáš Pospiszyl

An Associative Art History
Comparative Studies of Neo-Avant-Gardes in a Bipolar World

JRP|RINGIER & LES PRESSES DU RÉEL

Tomáš Pospiszyl

An Associative Art History
Comparative Studies of Neo-Avant-Gardes in a Bipolar World

Table of Contents

Sven Spieker *
Conditional Similarities: Parallax in Postwar Art from Eastern Europe

* Sven Spieker teaches modern and contemporary art at the University of California, Santa Barbara. His publications include *The Big Archive. Art from Bureaucracy* (MIT Press 2008) and *Destruction* (Whitechapel 2017). Spieker is a founding editor of *ARTMargins Online* and *ARTMargins Print*.

Czech art historian Tomáš Pospiszyl's essays, which were originally published between 2000 and 2014, focus on the history of neo-avant-garde art from the former Eastern Europe with the ambitious goal of finding "the place of Czech, Slovak, or, in general, Eastern European postwar art in global history." As such, they inscribe themselves into the efforts undertaken, over the last two decades, to rewrite the history of postwar art from Eastern Europe with the aim of establishing its place within the broader confines of the "global margins." However, if in the post-*Wende* 1990s such projects were largely compensatory and responded to a perceived need to give postwar Eastern European art its deserved place in the (Western) canon, nowadays the parameters have shifted perceptibly. A recent resurgence in scholarly interest in the nation has enabled the study of specific *national* trajectories of Eastern European neo-avant-garde art, including that of the former Czechoslovakia. These studies neither accept as a given the origin of the neo-avant-garde in a monolithically conceived Western canon, nor do they presume that art history can effortlessly shift gears from the national or regional to the global without taking into account modernism's often very specific local inflections. Studies such as Pospiszyl's assume, felicitously, that neither modernism nor its neo-avant-gardist contestations have a single point of origin or that they can, despite their often striking similarities, be understood universally. And while up to this point—outside, that is of the ambit of art from the former Soviet Union where Socialist Realism has recently been given the aesthetic and philosophical attention it deserves—studies of Eastern European postwar art have largely confined themselves to non-official art, now official art, too, is gradually coming into the purview of art historians from the region, a development explicitly welcomed by Pospiszyl.

As the late Polish art historian Piotr Piotrowski and others have argued, the geo-political position of the former Eastern Europe does not simply reproduce the relations between a colonial center and its colonies. Eastern Europe, even during the time of the Cold War when it was more or less hermetically sealed off from Europe's Western half, never ceased being part of the broadly conceived *Kulturraum* we call Europe. And yet the area's location on the margins of the continent; the peculiar demarcation, in the countries of the region, between official and non-official art; and the widespread insistence, in the face of art's pervasive politicization by the government, on the necessity for non-official art to operate autonomously, all mean that neo-avant-garde art functioned under circumstances that were only very conditionally in sync with related practices in the West. This resulted in an art production that, while it was phenomenologically close to these practices, at the same time remained removed from them in any number of ways.

The methodological problems raised by such "conditional similarity" lie at the very core of Tomáš Pospiszyl's concerns. Clearly he is right to point out that it is inadequate to anchor the specificity of Eastern European non-official art in its geo-political location alone; a temporal dimension is also at play. What we are dealing with is less a condition of belatedness—a charge often heard among scholars as they look at art from the former Eastern Europe—than the condition of being asynchronous. While Eastern and Western Europe may share a common *Kulturraum*, this space is riven by historical discontinuities, both internally and externally, a fact that complicates any effort to neatly align postwar art from either side of the Iron Curtain. And herein lies perhaps the most profound lesson of the case studies Tomáš Pospiszyl offers in this volume: while he acknowledges a "bipolar world" (East/West) in the book's subtitle, his analyses rarely succumb to the temptation of searching for the specificity of Eastern European art in the reversed optics familiar from postcolonial thinking. Where those optics—implicit also in the project known as "The Former West"[1]—turn on examining the center from the vantage point of the colony and remain, by the same token, firmly beholden to the center's (colonial) mindset, Pospiszyl approaches Eastern European neo-avant-garde art in an effort to develop what Piotrowski has referred to as "another way of writing art history." He argues that a radically "horizontal" art history cannot limit itself to revisiting the West from the vantage point of its periphery; it must also acknowledge the periphery at the center and examine the way in which the center's perception is underwritten by its periphery.

This is the point where Pospiszyl's interest in the unlikely presence of Czechoslovak artists Jan Kotík and Pravoslav Rada at the First World Congress of Free Artists, organized in 1956 by Asger Jorn and Pinot-Gallizio among others, acquires an almost emblematic significance. Ironically, despite the affinity of Kotík's thinking, in particular, to that of the congress's organizers, his presence there, according to Pospiszyl, highlights nothing if not the difficulties involved in transferring the rhetoric of revolution and transformation that animated the Western Situationists to the world of *real existierender Sozialismus* in Eastern Europe: "'Creating and living differently,' the old avant-garde slogan, which rolled off the tongues of leftist Western European intellectuals, could in Czechoslovakia only be pronounced with an ominous question mark at the end." One may, in this context, want to caution—as Pospiszyl also does—that the ranks of the so-called neo-avant-garde in the former

Eastern Europe were not by the same token, as is often falsely assumed in the West, filled with programmatic dissidents.

Indeed, what we might call the "apolitical leftism" of Eastern European neo-avant-gardists (a more committed version of Václav Havel's "nonpolitical politics" that does not automatically equate the private realm with the absence of politics), in addition to their belief in art as a way of remaking life, is perhaps the most important justification for using the term "neo-avant-garde" in relation to non-official postwar art from the region. Furthermore, if the Eastern neo-avant-garde is not to be written off as a mere "repetition of a repetition"—extending Peter Bürger's thesis regarding the Western neo-avant-garde as a repetition of the historical avant-gardes—it must additionally be placed in the context of the politico-aesthetic aspirations of the prewar and interwar avant-gardes both in Eastern and in Western Europe alike.

At first glance, the comparative approach Pospiszyl adopts in this book seems to raise many questions: after all, generally speaking, comparisons rarely take place on a truly equal footing. At best they function like a form of ideal translation: by appealing to a third, invisible universal, comparisons establish a relationship between an original word and its translated equivalent in the target language, with the understanding that the translated term will always be found to be lacking, insufficiently original, and derivative vis-à-vis its original. Pospiszyl avoids the pitfalls of such comparisons—which in art history unfailingly tends to affirm the superiority of Western trends over their counterparts elsewhere in the world—in several ways. First, by insisting on genealogy. When discussing, for example, the interest displayed by the American critic and doyen of modernism, Clement Greenberg, and his Czech counterpart, Jindřich Chalupecký, in the work of Marcel Duchamp, Pospiszyl notes that while that interest may superficially align both critics, in fact it arises from different circumstances rooted both in personal history and in the intellectual context of the nations in which both worked.

A second way in which Pospiszyl avoids the pitfalls of universal comparisons is by directly addressing the calamitous situation of anyone who wishes to write about postwar art from Eastern Europe: the absence of a meaningful descriptive vocabulary in which to write about that art. While in the official sphere Socialist Realism successfully ended all (art) historical periodization, the designation of Eastern European non-official art as "neo-avant-garde" keeps such periodization in play. And with good reason: to the extent that Eastern Europe, even during the time of its geo-political isolation, never stopped being part of the European *Kulturraum*, its cultural production at best partially inherits the function historian Dipesh Chakrabarty associates with "provincializing Europe," a term Chakrabarty uses to describe instances where events that originate on the periphery of a dominant culture resist being absorbed into that culture's central archive. In the case of Eastern Europe, however, there is no reason to assume that any part of its cultural production eludes historicization in principle. Since Eastern Europe was never in the position of the West's colonial Other, any efforts to "provincialize Europe" from the vantage point of the "East" must remain incomplete by necessity. As Pospiszyl writes: "It is the departures from the mainstream modernist canon and the changing relationships between the centers and the periphery that are most interesting."

That said, in the absence of any homegrown art historical terminology to describe Eastern European art, and given the factual, if problematic, universality of terms such as minimal, post-minimal, conceptual, post-conceptual, etc., how can the below-the-surface differences that divide Eastern Europe's art practices from those of Western minimalism, post-minimalism, or conceptual art be accounted for without essentializing such differences? In a famous 1979 article, Boris Groys addressed this problem with respect to Moscow Conceptualism by adding the qualifier "Romantic" ("Moscow Romantic Conceptualism") to his designation of artworks that, while they shared certain formal characteristics with their Western counterparts—such as the pervasive use of language and a diminished interest in visuality—nevertheless owed themselves to a wholly different set of social, political, and ideological circumstances. In several of the articles collected in this book, Pospiszyl tackles a related problem: how to account for the glaring similarities between, say, American minimal sculpture and the works of several Czech artists who were more or less contemporary with them, even though the latter worked in a completely different geo-political context?

In his efforts to respond to this issue, Pospiszyl follows a principle I will qualify as *parallax*. The word parallax, derived from a root related to the Greek *allos* = "other", refers to the effect whereby the direction or position of an object appears differently when that object is viewed from non-habitual angles. Parallax is a productive way of reframing an object in such a manner that it can reveal hitherto unknown qualities. As such, parallax challenges dominant normativity (for example, the Western canon) by accepting the dominant trend as no more than one among a host of other possible approaches, pluralizing in the process what remained, at one point in time, an unchallenged point of view. Parallactic vision, which shares certain characteristics with Piotrowsky's "horizontal art history," but which, unlike the latter does not limit itself to "viewing the periphery (the East) from the center (the West)" is very productive in Pospiszyl's work. A case in point is the triangle he constructs of the sculptures by Polish artist Alina Szapocznikow, Czech Eva Kmentová, and American Eva Hesse. Similar juxtapositions are common enough in scholarship on Eastern European art, and they generally aim to show that neo-avant-garde art from behind the Iron Curtain, despite its obvious morphological affinity to Western modernism, was wrongfully denied the place it deserves in the Western canon. Pospiszyl's strategy is quite different: his point is neither the redressing of the canon—at least not primarily—nor does he aim to "provincialize" the American artist in the manner of Chakrabarty. Instead Pospiszyl deploys Hesse's sculptures as a functional background for a comparative discussion of what separates Szapocznikow and Kmentová from each other. Methodologically, this parallactic manoeuver does not foreclose the consideration of Hesse as a reference point for her Czech and Polish counterparts; at the same time, neither does it install her as the "original" toward which the artists from the periphery aspire, contradicting the finding that Szapocznikow's and Kmentová's work must be considered a form of belated minimalism when compared to that of Hesse. Pospiszyl argues that both Eastern European women artists join Hesse in their desire to comment on the minimalist legacy from vantage points that are specifically their own, and that take into account the different national perspectives on the phenomenon. Parallax, in this instance, demonstrates that while Western European trends and art historical concepts are inevitable in a meaningful discussion of the Eastern European neo-avant-garde, this does not mean that the latter can be reduced to these concepts. In Pospiszyl's analysis, the Western artist (Hesse) is no longer in the position of a formal "gold standard"—and as such, representative for the Western canon as a whole—assuming instead the quality of a foil that helps give contour to the relations between different art practices *within* Eastern Europe.

It is, generally speaking, the dynamic relationship between an artist's life and his or her work that comes into view in Pospiszyl's analyses of Eastern European art. This does not mean, however, that Pospiszyl subscribes to a vague humanism unhinged from the material conditions in which artists live and work, or that his focus on "life" excludes politics by definition. On the contrary, it is the (inherently political) desire to reshape life—primarily one's own, but by extension that of everyone else—that animates the artistic practices discussed in his book and that legitimizes their qualification as neo-avant-garde. For Pospiszyl, the fundamentally asynchronous position of Eastern European postwar art vis-à-vis its Western counterpart is less a calamity than highly productive, implying the possibility that the private itself may be, or has to be, viewed as being political.

[1] The Former West was a large-scale, multi-year contemporary art research, education, publishing, and exhibition project (2008–2016).

Tomáš Pospiszyl

Foreword

The essays collected in this book were written in the years 2000–2014. Their central theme is the search for the place of Czech, Slovak, or, in general, Eastern European postwar art in global history. Thus, the texts document a certain historical phase of thinking on this subject. The first decade following the dismantling of Communist rule in the Czechoslovakian Velvet Revolution of 1989 was rich in projects devoted to the unearthing of previously little-known art from behind the Iron Curtain. After 2000, efforts to interpret that art in greater detail intensified. As Eastern European art entered the new millennium, it was seen, from an international perspective, as a "rediscovered" phenomenon. This perception, however, calls for a reading of it in the context of Western art, as well as that of other areas.

The underpinnings of the idea of Eastern European art in the latter half of the 20th century are far from distinct; the idea is more an ideological construct than a culturally anchored understanding. Despite its apparent homogeneity, the region has been subject to a series of historical discontinuities. In them, nevertheless, we can see certain shared traits: state socialism led to the socialization of art production, complicating relationships with local avant-garde traditions while disrupting international communication. The socialist state not only transformed traditional art institutions—museums, galleries, schools—but also institutionalized forms of historical and theoretical reflection on art.

Logically, for an understanding of Eastern European art, the theoretical discourse established in the course of Western art history suggests itself. Art historians, whether from West or East, can make good use of its long-standing conceptual apparatus and time-honored methodology. However, the limits of such resources may become apparent when they are applied in practice. Naturally, Eastern European art does not represent an isolated and impenetrable world; nonetheless, its distinct social and cultural contexts must be acknowledged. This approach is illustrated primarily in the first chapters of this book, conceived as a series of traditional comparative critical studies. It turns out that ostensibly similar forms of artistic expression originating to the east and west of the bygone Iron Curtain can neither be compared nor interpreted mechanically. Juxtaposing the artworks themselves, however, can shed light on these contextual distinctions.

In contrast to the 1990s, a great number of original studies that are reshaping the postwar art history of their regions are being produced in Eastern Europe today. A characteristic they share is the perception of global art as a decentralized system; sometimes they directly reference Piotr Piotrowski's concept of horizontal art history or other illuminating methodological models. The aim is no longer to make unproductive comparisons between the Eastern and Western neo-avant-gardes but to understand and interpret the specific circumstances in which particular artworks were created. Although some of the studies in the second part of this volume do compare East and West, another, clearly more fundamental aim is to study the channels of artistic communication, the migration of artistic motifs and approaches across historical periods, and the mapping of the personal genealogies of artistic evolution—an investigation into artistic dialogues across generations.

Side effects of the uncritical application of dominant theoretical frameworks are the imposition of Western values and the belief that other regions lag behind the West. The peripheries, as seen from the vantage of the centers, are not only far away; they are on the margins of time as well. Eastern European art is still assessed mainly through the institutions of Western art, which, understandably, concentrate on works that readily establish a dialogue with their culture's own artistic creations. A portion of what is produced locally—and, from a long-term perspective, perhaps what is most original—thus remains outside the main areas of global interest. This is true mainly of the field of "official art" before 1989, and I propose that the future of the study of Eastern European art lies there.

This volume contains a selection of texts that were originally included in two books published in Czech: *Srovnávací studie* [Comparative Studies] (Agite/Fra, 2005), and *Asociativní dějepis umění* [An Associative Art History] (tranzit, 2014). As may be gleaned from the editorial note, a number of the chapters originated as independent texts for a variety of catalogs, journals, or conferences and their proceedings. Exchanges with readers and listeners helped shape the texts for presentation in published book form and explored the interconnections between them. Like every author whose work is published again after some time—in this case, for a readership not necessarily conversant with the context of Eastern European art—I was tempted to rework what I had previously written. I resisted the temptation, however. Only where there were factual errors did I rewrite. In certain instances, I also eliminated contextualizing passages originally intended for Czech readers but redundant in the English translation. Conversely, particulars about some events I describe or the people I mention were added to facilitate understanding. The bibliography was not updated, for doing so would have required me to include relevant new materials and address texts written in a different historical time frame. Three new explanatory notes were added in cases where material that substantially expanded the original text or cast it in a new light was uncovered.

A Modernist Crossroads: Jindřich Chalupecký versus Clement Greenberg

I.

Modern art appears on the international stage in remarkably similar forms, but the transfer of ideas from artistic centers to the periphery causes certain shifts to occur. Numerous examples from the history of currents in modern art from both the 19th century and the first half of the 20th century attest to this. For instance, although Impressionist and Cubist paintings were created all over the world, there can be fundamental differences between works that at first glance seem similar. That is why, from the perspective of the Paris Cubists, certain works by Czech painters Bohumil Kubišta or Otakar Kubín seem like curious misunderstandings, like variations on the Cubist form that fail to grasp Cubism's special essence. While national modern art museums at a remove from the main cultural centers tell a similar story, in each case the protagonists are different, and so the modern painters and sculptors we may admire in museums and galleries in Vilnius, Barcelona, or Bucharest will usually not be found anywhere else. If we follow these shifts in 20th-century art history, we see that it is the departures from the mainstream modernist canon and the changing relationships between the centers and the periphery that are most interesting.

Without a doubt, Czech art in the second half of the 20th century was profoundly marked by the political events of the period. The Iron Curtain made it hard for people and ideas to travel freely in the years from 1948 to 1989. Aside from a few exceptional years, a great deal of essential international cultural exchange—including much connected with modernism—was restricted or deformed in Communist Czechoslovakia. The Czechoslovak artists during this period were not commonly exposed to the art scenes in Paris, New York, London, or even Moscow, and the distinct character of their artworks is naturally ascribed to this international isolation and internal repression, which did not tolerate certain forms of artistic expression and persecuted individual artists for their political views or family origins. Nonetheless, we should not be led to believe that the distinctive character of Czech art may be attributed solely to politics. Even before 1948 Czech art had emerged out of a specific context—one that is responsible for its uniqueness.

I think that from the beginning of World War II, Czech art stood out thanks not to its formal aspects but to a distinctive self-reflection carried out at a time when avant-garde art was squaring up against totalitarian regimes. The fate of artists, theorists, and critics in small nations appears to be a constant search for self-justification, meaning, and social utility—particularly at times when the very foundations of their cultures are under threat.[1] Debates concerning the national particularities of Czech art and its relationships to both the art of other nations and its own nationhood have a long tradition in Czech culture. We will find parallels in the cultures of other Eastern European countries as well. Such debates flared up at the time of the National Revival in the 19th century and gained new life with the rise of modernism at the turn of the 20th century. They returned in modified form when the nation's autonomy came under threat in the late 1930s. The exalted nationalist rhetoric characteristic of the 19th century was replaced with more general considerations about the relationships between art and society and the mission of modern art. It was in the context of such debates on the social role of art that I see the moment when the branch of Czech art began to separate from the main trunk of world modernism.

I shall try to account for these differing understandings of the significance and tasks of modern art in Czechoslovakia by comparing two conceptions of modernism represented by the thought of American theorist and critic Clement Greenberg (1909–1994) and his Czech contemporary Jindřich Chalupecký (1910–1990). The conceptual starting points of their work are remarkably similar; their theoretical conclusions, in contrast, are almost diametrically opposed. They differ as much as the work of the American Abstract Expressionists and the paintings of Group 42, a loose association of Czech writers, artists, and literary theorists founded in 1942 around the ideas of Chalupecký; they were determined to break down hierarchies of high and low art and to introduce elements to poetry that were deliberately and strikingly unpoetic, as well as to illustrate the importance of local conditions in the theory and practice of modern art in the mid-20th century. Chalupecký and Greenberg are to a certain extent reminiscent of identical twins raised apart after birth whose "mother"—their common intellectual background—was the interwar leftist avant-garde and the Marxist ideology that was undergoing a profound crisis in the late 1930s, in both Czechoslovakia and the United States. The thinking of both critics was formed and eventually distinguished by the differing political and cultural worlds they moved in. A full-fledged comparison of their work is complicated somewhat by the fact that, on the whole, Greenberg systematically derived his views on art and his evaluative criteria from a general theory of modernism that he was continually refining in each of his writings, whereas Chalupecký was first and foremost an essayist who had no ambition to develop a systematic theory of art. He would react spontaneously to his environment, and some of his essays contain observations and conclusions that he would go on to repudiate unequivocally just months later.

Jindřich Chalupecký and Clement Greenberg are also linked by the fact that in the countries where they were active, their thinking on art became authoritative. Even after their deaths, both theorists continue to impact debates on the art of the past and present. Even though more recent reactions to their ideas might be—and, for the most part, are—negative, rarely are people indifferent to them. Both had, for many years, the status of interpreters and legislators of fundamental artistic values. In their time, they enjoyed privileged positions from which they influenced not only the assessments of concrete artworks but also the fates of individual artists and entire movements. Their judgments could easily derail a promising career or lead artists to destroy works the critic deemed mediocre. Both Chalupecký and Greenberg gladly assumed their roles as arbiters of values and performed them well. No one stepped into their shoes when they died; eventually—with the arrival of post-modernity at the latest—homogeneous evaluative criteria were replaced by a variety of value hierarchies in which critics could no longer occupy such authoritative positions.

II.

In 1939 and 1940, within a span of just a few months, Jindřich Chalupecký and Clement Greenberg published the most important theoretical works of their early careers. Greenberg's "Avant-Garde and Kitsch," published in autumn 1939 in the American *Partisan Review*, and Chalupecký's "The World We Live In" [Svět, v němž žijeme], first published in the February 1940 issue of *Program D40*, deal with the relationship between the artistic avant-garde and society and the place of avant-garde art in modern times.

The two theorists, who were not yet well known, gained the attention of the general public at a time when Parisian Surrealism had lost its wind and was becoming a cliché. From a historical standpoint, it is perhaps more important that both essays appeared at a time that must have been particularly difficult and confusing for left-oriented critics. News of the Moscow political trials were spreading all over the world, and the German-Soviet Nonaggression Pact had been signed in 1939. Many Western leftist intellectuals who had viewed the Soviet Union as the land where a dreamed-of new society had become a reality felt deceived and betrayed.

Most avant-garde artists in interwar Czechoslovakia adhered to leftist ideals or openly professed allegiance to Marxism and supported the USSR. Nonetheless, by the end of the 1920s, the Marxist worldview had come into conflict with modern art, giving rise to many polemics. The rise of Klement Gottwald to the leadership of the Czechoslovak Communist Party in 1929 became an important milestone in the relationship between the artistic avant-garde and Marxism and signaled the departure of a number of avant-garde artists from the Communist political orbit. Relations between Czechoslovak leftist intellectuals and the USSR were further splintered in 1936–1937 by the controversy provoked by André Gide's *Return from the Soviet Union*. Disputes over events in the Soviet Union and the acceptability of collaborating with Stalinist Communist parties constituted one of the reasons that the Surrealist group fell apart in Czechoslovakia in 1938. Surrealist theorist Karel Teige spoke out against the curtailment of artistic freedom at that time in the Soviet Union. In contrast with poet Vítězslav Nezval, who was willing to countenance Stalinism along with its sway on the art world, Teige championed the autonomy of art from politics and would not condone what was happening in the USSR. We may characterize Jindřich Chalupecký politically as a socialist. Although he never joined the Communist Party, he remained true to his leftist ideals, not only between the wars but during the German occupation and after 1945 as well. In the postwar years, he actively took up leftist causes in the Czechoslovak art world until he was pronounced a "bourgeois critic" in late 1948 and was banned from public life.

In the United States the avant-garde artists began parting company with Marxist thinking in the mid-1930s, doing so in discussions carried out in the pages of New York's *Partisan Review*, where in 1936 poet William Carlos Williams contended that Marxism and American historical traditions were incompatible. The same year, a polemic was sparked between the director of the New York Museum of Modern Art, Alfred Barr, and Marxist art historian Meyer Schapiro. Barr claimed that modern art did not depend on its social context and developed exclusively on the basis of its own principles. Schapiro, in contrast, espoused the view that art is influenced fundamentally by the social conditions under which it arises. The definitive break between the American left-wing intellectuals around the *Partisan Review* and Marxism did not come until a few years later; nevertheless, the influence of Marxist dialectics on their thought was long lasting. In the early 1940s such critics found themselves isolated. Even though they had distanced themselves from the Stalinist Communists, they remained too radical and unpalatable for the American middle class. The only option that remained was a marked individualism.[2] In contrast, the European avant-garde and its theorists collaborated in a wide variety of ways with political organizations and movements. The danger represented by World War II called forth a wave of efforts to create a unified cultural front in which artists were supposed to come together not on the basis of a commonly shared aesthetic but as a collective defense against the swell of Nazism, Fascism, and their cultural politics.

Some Marxist theorists of modernism applied dialectical materialism to art in an attempt to shed light on the historical emergence of the avant-garde and its relationship with the different social classes. They wanted to determine whose interests were represented by the avant-garde. Most of the time they came to similar conclusions on basic issues. Karel Teige applied himself to these issues as well in the introductory chapter of his *Jarmark umění* [Art Fair], in which he described the avant-garde as a product of the bourgeoisie dating back to the time of its struggle against feudalism. According to Teige, however, the later art of the School of Paris could not be considered authentic bourgeois art because it was permanently opposed to official bourgeois ideology. In view of capitalist market relations and the commercialization of art, the artists of the School of Paris were bound to the bourgeois class through the collectors they were financially dependent on. Nonetheless, wrote Teige, in capitalist society there was another form of art as well: "the accursed poetry of the avant-garde,"[3] which was truly independent of the bourgeoisie and prefigured not only non-bourgerois culture but also a new type of social organization.

In his essay "Avant-Garde and Kitsch," Clement Greenberg saw the modernist avant-garde as a form of artistic expression originally produced by the bourgeoisie but eventually alienated from the class it had come from. However, the proletariat—the anticipated bearers of social changes to come, which was supposed to replace the bourgeoisie as the leading social force—was firmly in the thrall of kitsch, and for that reason avant-garde art was not associated with any social class. According to Greenberg, that did not significantly disadvantage avant-garde art; on the contrary, it made possible its independent development.

Greenberg wrote "Avant-Garde and Kitsch" in the summer and autumn of 1939. At the time, he was working in the customs office and, in addition, was interested in poetry, painting, and leftist politics. He was motivated to write the essay after reading an article on Soviet cinematography written by critic Dwight Macdonald for the *Partisan Review*.[4] Greenberg took issue with Macdonald's claim that the unsophisticated Russian peasants accepted Stalinist propaganda films whole cloth and did not demand avant-garde cinematography because they lacked education and were ignorant of higher cultural values. He sent a letter to the editors of the *Partisan Review* characterizing such a view as simplistic and laid out, in shortened form, his theory of kitsch and its function in modern society. According to him, kitsch represented a feeble rehash of real high culture with which the ruling class satiated the cultural needs of the proletariat.[5] He understood low culture and kitsch as the antithesis of high-culture values. Far more weighty than a distinction between high and low culture, he thought, was the fact that kitsch had struck out on its own and, in a boomerang effect, was undermining the higher spheres of culture it was derived from. The editors of the *Partisan Review* asked Greenberg to elaborate on his views.

Readers of Greenberg's article (the final version was printed in autumn 1939) were struck by its opening lines—it referred to the heterogeneity of modern Western culture: "One and the same civilization produces simultaneously two such different things as a poem by T.S. Eliot and a Tin Pan Alley song, or a painting by Braque and a *Saturday Evening Post* cover. All four are on the order of culture, and ostensibly, parts of the same culture and products of the same society."[6]

Unlike Charles Baudelaire, Greenberg found nothing in low culture that might be of any value. At the same time, he captured the paradoxical stance of leftist avant-garde intellectuals: on the one hand, they admired and defended an elitist cultural avant-garde that was incomprehensible to the wider masses; on the other hand, they advocated a revolution to establish a more just world to be led by the proletariat, who for the most part expressed no interest in such art. Greenberg was certainly not the first to notice such contradictions within modern culture. In *Art Fair* (1936), Karel Teige used almost the same words to describe the existence of a similar cultural divide: "In the capitalist era two different cultural worlds persist, one situated above the other: a lower one, which is an under-culture, a trash culture for the people; and a higher one, which was the real culture (with the exception of certain creative spheres such as poetry and art) during the capitalist boom."[7] However, Teige was not nearly as uncompromising in his separation of culture into high and low as was Greenberg, and as regards values, he perceived the two extremes first and foremost from the perspective of a Marxist worldview. Both Greenberg and Teige pointed to the capitalist system as the cause behind the existence of two such antithetical cultures within a single society—a system that might hold sway in most of the world but that would one day be overthrown.

Nevertheless, Greenberg did not anticipate an automatic resolution to existing cultural contradictions through this sort of revolutionary transformation. He argued that even in the Soviet Union, a land of workers and peasants, kitsch existed, and was a mass phenomenon to boot. A mere transformation of social relations in itself would not resolve the conflict between high and low culture, which is based on the very essence of cultural evolution: If art were not to stagnate and die out, it would have to evolve continually from lower to higher forms irrespective of concrete social conditions. According to Greenberg, the elitism of the avant-garde was one of the ways art as such could survive. He saw a solution in the deepening chasm between the avant-garde and folk art and in the uncoupling of art from everyday life. Like many 19th-century authors, he defended the hermeticism of modernism and saw in art's loss of contact with the masses its only protection from corruption by the mass culture of kitsch and entertainment. He saw the growing divide between the art of the masses and the art of the avant-garde in a positive light, as a defense against the trivialization of art. He drew attention to attempts by totalitarian regimes to present kitsch as official state culture: "The encouragement of kitsch is merely another of the inexpensive ways in which totalitarian regimes seek to ingratiate themselves with their subjects."[8]

In contrast, Jindřich Chalupecký viewed the breaking away of the avant-garde from the general culture at the turn of the 1940s with unease, as is evident in the introduction to his 1938 essay "On Art, Freedom and Socialism":

> There is no need to demonstrate that the undertakings of modern art have no relationship with the contemporary worker's movement and cannot be enriched by such undertakings […] The literature of the people is pulp fiction and not *U-Blok* [a journal published by an art association of the same name] […] Art placed in the service of socialism must be heedful of its mass efficacy; why, therefore, should it not seek the widest and safest efficacy where it has been tried and tested the most and not degrade its creative endeavors by catering to the present day with the psychology of romance novels, the drama and heroism of adventurous pulp fiction, the raciness of the operettas produced at the Tyl Theatre and the sentimentality of Czech blockbuster films? […] At any rate, it would probably be fanciful to insist on a sharp distinction between art and kitsch.[9]

Chalupecký saw the participation of art in social changes as its primary task. He believed that the decadence of mass culture was chiefly the result of the decline of the capitalist social system and not a general pattern by which culture evolves.

Even between the lines of "The World We Live In," we can sense an attempt on Chalupecký's part to link the artistic avant-garde with the mass public. That was also the basis of Chalupecký's critique of modern art at the time: by losing contact with the working classes, the avant-garde had lost its substance as well. It would once again be able to link up with working people and thereby serve the revolutionary struggle if it began making use of the resources of mass culture and even kitsch. For Greenberg, kitsch was an absolute evil that destroyed art. Writing in the early 1940s, Chalupecký believed it possible to cultivate decadent art and its public and then raise them to a higher level.

Both Chalupecký and Greenberg had remarked that the modern era was universal. For Greenberg, that premise entailed the danger that kitsch might spread all over the world, whereas for Chalupecký it meant the hope that art might once again occupy a more central place in society. In Chalupecký's essay "The World We Live In," the elitist avant-garde is seen as something that must be struggled against. The difference between high and low must be overcome, and avant-garde art ought to look for ways it might be embraced by the broad public, even if it has to abandon its avant-garde forms. "If art is to regain its lost significance in the life of the individual, it must return to the things people live among and live with."[10]

III.

In addition to highlighting the clash between high and low culture, both Greenberg's "Avant-Garde and Kitsch" and Chalupecký's "The World We Live In" showed that the transmission of content was being suppressed in modern art and traditional artistic genres were disappearing. According to Chalupecký, this was an alarming development. The danger was that a weakening of content in artworks would lead to the hypertrophy of poetic metaphor, which would in the end become the only subject art would be left with:

> The content of a poem is its form and that also means that the form of a poem is its content. Form and content blend into one another, proving to be one and the same thing. Hence the *non-thematic character* of modern poetry. It has no theme that transcends the poem (e.g., emotion, reflection); its theme is nothing less than acquiring poetic knowledge of the universe [...] Let us note that the same is true of modern painting. Even here the goal is to destroy the rational universe: Picasso's pictures smash their subjects, rethinking them into forms that bear more and more meanings. The individual thing disappears,

> leaving a painterly form corresponding to a world that is no longer made up of things.[11]

Chalupecký's passages claiming that the theme of modern art is nothing but art itself are reminiscent of Greenberg's arguments. According to Greenberg, however, art for art's sake is the only way to maintain a life-giving forward movement in culture under the conditions of capitalism.

> In turning his attention away from subject matter or common experience, the poet or artist turns it in upon the medium of his own craft [...] [Art and literature] themselves become the subject matter of art and literature [...] Picasso, Braque, Mondrian, Miró, Kandinsky, Brancusi, even Klee, Matisse and Cézanne, derive their chief inspiration from the media they work in. The excitement of their art seems to lie most of all in its pure preoccupation with the invention and arrangement of spaces, surfaces, shapes, colors, etc., to the exclusion of whatever is not necessarily implicated in these factors.[12]

If, for Greenberg, self-referential art—the main feature of modernism—is the only salvation from the potential degradation of modernism, for Chalupecký the same phenomenon is the cause of the decline and mutual alienation of art and society. Chalupecký's text appeals to artists to turn from a refined art for art's sake to everyday life and to draw inspiration from it. According to Greenberg, the inspiration of modern art originates solely from the medium of painting and from its expressive resources; the fact that the narrative content of painting disappeared over time is to be interpreted as a triumph of modernism. The idea that in turning away from content the artist turns toward the formal qualities of an artwork led, Greenberg thought, to the liberation of modern art from the need to tell a story. Here we come to an important shift in the thought of Clement Greenberg, a shift that prefigured his renunciation of Marxist positions and his turn toward a formalist theory of art. The basic premise remains that if art does not want to stagnate in academism or kitsch, it must keep moving forward. For leftist theorists, this movement earlier corresponded to a vision of social evolution from a lower level to a higher, more evolved level—to a classless society. However, Greenberg replaced the Marxist conception of social evolution with a Hegelian development of artistic forms themselves, from imperfect versions toward more perfected ones. By contrast with Chalupecký, Greenberg was convinced that the aesthetic and social contexts of art could not be separated. He went from being a critic who saw art from a Marxist—or, more precisely, a Trotskyist—perspective, to being an apolitical critic. He believed that being apolitical was the only way the avant-garde could retain its independence, which would enable it to continue growing.

Clement Greenberg had no interest in the subject matter or the social dimension and impact of art. He was mainly concerned with the evolution of forms; he sought to identify the specific laws of each artistic discipline, which in the case of modern painting he saw as an orientation toward abstraction and two-dimensionality as well as a growing interest in the inner principles of the painterly medium. Greenberg ascribed a single function to art: to continue in its own formal history and move constantly forward. According to Chalupecký, in contrast, it was the whole of society, not art, that should be marching forward on its journey from capitalism to communism. Art might reflect such a process or take part in the struggle directly, but in such a struggle it mattered little which weapon—whether kitsch or avant-garde expression—was used.

In his work, Greenberg expressed his faith in the inevitability of the future evolution of modern art. Whatever social conditions it might take place under, it could not be stopped. Chalupecký did not share his optimism. According to Chalupecký, modern art was hardly compatible with the mighty social forces that had been set in motion in the 20th century. He felt that the imminent changes that would do away with the previous divide between rich and poor would be quite fundamental, and he believed in their wake it would be senseless to seek lessons in the art of the past, which would only retain a historical significance. At least in his writing, Chalupecký renounced modern culture as something unnecessary; he sacrificed it in the name of socialism.

The idea that art ought to have a social function did not appear out of the blue in the thinking of Chalupecký.

The very opening line of one of his early essays, "Art" (1934), seemed to conflict with everything Greenberg would later maintain:

> I cannot believe that art has its own validity that is separate from the rest of the life of humanity, that the value of art lies in itself alone, that people approach pictures without practical interests, that the needs of art are the needs of some other world, a world of beauty, a refined cosmos where we go for relief from the stale air of our present life in search of the more refreshing and radiant winds of the spirit […] I cannot believe that in the absolute sovereignty human beings ascribe to images, there is nothing more than the perfection, richness, exceptionality and contemplative peace provided by the images.[23]

In his essay "Towards a Newer Laocoön" (1940), which appeared just after "Avant-Garde and Kitsch," Clement Greenberg was now entirely focused on describing his conception of the dialectical evolution of artistic forms and, in the case of painting, its tendency toward abstraction and its liberation from literary contents. Although the text made reference to German philosopher Gotthold Ephraim Lessing and his ideas on the specific traits of artistic disciplines, it had not yet rid itself methodologically of Marxist historical dialectics. Much as Marxists cast light on historical competition and the emancipation of individual social classes, Greenberg described the process of the emancipation of artistic disciplines toward a state in which they would let nothing but their specific, unmistakable expressive means speak for them. Greenberg evaluated art not on the basis of its relationship to life but on the progressive character of its expressive means alone. Its merit consisted in the extent to which, cut off from transitory everydayness, it cultivated its own forms.

IV.

New life was breathed into the topic of kitsch in Czech culture following World War II. The critic Otakar Mrkvička devoted a study to it in 1946 in which he characterized art and kitsch as irreconcilable antitheses and observed joyfully that the gaudiest examples of kitsch had been banned by the state.[14] He described kitsch as an infection that had come primarily from Germany: "Kitsch was brought about by fascism and deals itself in fascism."[15]

Jindřich Chalupecký, too, revisited the topic of kitsch after the war. However, his previous liberal stance toward mass culture, in whose gradual cultivation he had seen a way to overcome the conflict between the avant-garde and the masses, was radically revised under the new social conditions of the postwar period. This is evident in his brochure titled *A Great Opportunity: Notes on the Reorganization of Czech Fine Arts*.[16] In it, Chalupecký saw kitsch as an obstacle to improving the state of culture in society as a whole:

> We know, for instance, what a cultural danger kitsch is; but I do not believe we shall overcome it through preaching, lecturing, going to exhibitions, applying censorship and other such means […] The existence of kitsch is rooted in the general state of culture in society, in the entire lifestyle of the times […] Thus kitsch will not disappear unless society changes down to its most intimate structures and the struggle against kitsch can only be really successful in connection with the struggle to change the primary, most elementary social structures […] So, suppressing kitsch is among the great political tasks. It must be destroyed everywhere it raises its head: in books and magazines, postcards and calendars, posters and three-dimensional reproductions.[17]

The struggle against kitsch was part of the revolution. Chalupecký immediately suggested practical ways kitsch might be exorcized—namely, with the aid of ministerial surveillance and various committees.

Chalupecký added the following footnote to the passages on kitsch in his brochure: "Reading through my text, I hesitate regarding the demand for artistic censorship. After all, isn't censorship too dangerous a tool?"[18] It must be noted that these doubts did not last long in Chalupecký's mind. Along with many intellectuals with similar views, Chalupecký regarded the postwar period as a new start for

Czech culture and succumbed to the illusion that it would be possible to plan and steer it; he subsequently engaged himself actively in the process. In 1946 he became a member of the State Publishing Committee, which evaluated and approved publishing plans. In 1947 the committee prepared a document for the National Assembly—signed by the writers Václav Řezáč and Jan Drda and the publisher Václav Petr in addition to Chalupecký—that concluded by demanding the restriction of the freedom of the press in the Czechoslovak constitution, which was being drafted at the time.[19] The document suggested that publishers should only be allowed to print and distribute "valuable" works, and that a special state committee should determine whether they were print-worthy. The proposal was approved, and Chalupecký himself became a member of the committee. As part of it, along with Jan Pilíř, Ivan Skála, František Listopad, and A.C. Nor, he advocated taking a hard line on lowbrow writing, which was to be driven out of literature, with no exceptions. However, deciding what was lowbrow could not be anything but subjective and subject to the politics of the day.

It is symptomatic that Jindřich Chalupecký himself had already experienced censorship before February 1948. In 1947, part of the print run of T.S. Eliot's *The Waste Land*, which he had translated with Jiřina Hauková, was marked for destruction. The committee had judged the poem to be existentialist dross.[20] Chalupecký regarded the Communist takeover of Czechoslovakia in February 1948 with concern but remained a communist sympathizer. In March 1948, he was one of the organizers of the Conference of Young Czech Writers at Dobříš, which attempted to bring together the different currents of leftist literature in the name of the future of socialism. At around the same time, news began to arrive of new cultural purges in the USSR. Within a matter of months, Chalupecký and his friends, who had been publicly critical of Stalinism, had been—in the best of cases—shunted to the margins of the Czech cultural scene.

Greenberg had no ambitions to engage in censorship. Although he could not come to terms with kitsch, he did not fight it by smearing those responsible for it or by advocating distribution bans but, on the contrary, by advocating for the cultivation and isolation of high art while warning against using the forms of folk art. He wanted avant-garde art to be in constant motion and to constantly seek avenues for formal growth. He expressed his responsibility for the advancement of art in critical texts on specific exhibitions, which he published in various leftist journals, particularly the *Partisan Review* and *The Nation*. Even though he worked as an advisor to several galleries and museums and was involved in the promotion of American art abroad, he himself never had dealings in the art world or participated in the buying or selling of art. In March 1948, when Chalupecký was waking up from his communist pipe dream, he published an article titled "The Decline of Cubism."[21] In it, he criticized contemporary art in Paris and simultaneously proclaimed that American art was the most advanced in the world, declaring its independence from the European avant-garde. This self-assured declaration was not based on a real decline in Parisian art or the outstanding work of American artists; instead, it expressed the emancipation of American culture, a desire to stand out and take an active role in world culture. Jackson Pollock became the American representative of postwar modernism. His originality, individuality, and the formally "advanced" character of his art were celebrated. Pollock's paintings might have seemed incomprehensible to many, but Greenberg was able to argue convincingly that the painter had been acting in accordance with the evolutionary principles of modernism and was fleshing out what Claude Monet, Pablo Picasso, and Piet Mondrian had merely intimated. The cult of genius we see in Pollock's case was in keeping with more general ideas about American politics and ideology as well: he personified individuality and freedom, expressed the liberality of American society and its ability to absorb a wide spectrum of trends, and groom first-rate experts in all spheres of social endeavor.

At the time, Chalupecký rejected an exalted artistic individualism; it seemed elitist to him: "This is no longer a time of romantic individualism, a time of oversize personalities, titans, rebels, who once hurled their questions in the face of the silent heavens and finally in the face of the bourgeoisie [...] If I think of some sort of new modernity, I think not of a sort of art that would [...] rise up against the heavens or the bourgeoisie, but of an art that would believe in humankind instead; in those altogether everyday people, those altogether inconspicuous, altogether secret, altogether anonymous people."[22]

V.

Many artists in the countries where the essays "Avant-Garde and Kitsch" and "The World We Live In" were written made reference to them, chief among them the Seven in October group and Group 42 [Czech: *Sedm v říjnu* and *Skupina 42*]. Those who were active on the art scene during the Protectorate years or immediately after World War II turned from the revolutionary programs of the interwar avant-garde toward an anonymous, "naked" humanity—to-ward city life, the poetry of the periphery, and everyday events. In particular, the visual artists and writers affiliated with Group 42 clearly distanced themselves from Surrealism. Eschewing the traditional orientation toward France, they demonstrated an interest in Anglo-American literature and an inclination toward text collages and poetic chronicles of reality. A turning point came with *Prométheova játra* [Prometheus's Liver], a 1950 manuscript by Jiří Kolář. The painters in Group 42 were not able to find a comparably radical form. For them, the starting points were magical realism and expressionism, both formal doctrines that were far from binding and that tolerated the parallel existence of Abstract Expression.

Greenberg's essay captured the advent of a generation of American painters who, having started in the fields of surrealism and automatism, grew into what would later be identified as Abstract Expressionism. First and foremost, they were interested in the medium of painting itself and an unceasing progressive radicalization of expressive resources. Greenberg warned painters against using the expressive resources of other artistic disciplines, particularly literature. Pictures should not have contents that could be converted into literary form; they should express themselves abstractly, by means of visual images exclusively.

Obviously, American modernism and Group 42's Czech art did not arise because Greenberg and Chalupecký masterminded them. The critics simply postulated the programmatic significance of the art around them at a particular time. For America, the historical moment was far more propitious than it was for Europe. People were fleeing from

Europe and arriving in America; the center of avant-garde action had been relocated from Paris to New York. Over time, the divide between the thought of Clement Greenberg and that of Jindřich Chalupecký deepened. It was doubtless caused by both the direct experience of World War II and the different ways that experience was reflected in the United States and Czechoslovakia. The foundation for Greenberg's evolutionary theory of modernism was the continuity represented by modernist painting; in addition, he elaborated upon the formal genealogy—uninterrupted by World War II—of modern art. By contrast, in his 1946 essay "The End of the Modern Era," Chalupecký emphasized, in the spirit of Theodor Adorno, the fracturing of European culture provoked by Nazism and World War II. He called for a reaffirmation of the values civilization had held sacred up to that time and contemplated the decline of modern culture.

Even though Chalupecký broke with the radical leftist ideals of his youth after 1948, the relationship between art and society remained a key issue for him. Greenberg's formalism did not address such issues; his theory was based solely on an analysis of art and its expressive means. Thus, if we might label Greenberg a formalist, Chalupecký could be characterized as a moralist. According to Chalupecký, art was in the service of society; for Greenberg, art was related only to itself. Greenberg was interested in the rules that made it possible to create the perfect work of art. Chalupecký wanted to examine art's effects or, rather, the effects it ought to have. He lived in a country where there was censorship of avant-garde art; those who produced it were smeared—all in isolation from international developments in art. It is no wonder that under these conditions such expressions as "the authenticity of an artwork" and "the ability of art to 'transcend' its viewers" assumed key importance for Chalupecký. This approach allowed him to write with equal enthusiasm about both imaginative surrealism and body art. Greenberg, on the other hand, concentrated on an ever-narrower circle of artists.

The differences in the thinking of Clement Greenberg and Jindřich Chalupecký were also manifested in their appraisals of the work of Marcel Duchamp. For most of his life, Chalupecký was fascinated by Duchamp. For him, Duchamp represented the perfect embodiment of the 20th-century artist. He was already mentioned briefly in

"The World We Live In"—at a time when Duchamp had not yet gained the respect he would command in the 1960s. Chalupecký returned to his work all his life. They corresponded, and when the time was right, in 1968, Chalupecký was able to organize an exhibition for Duchamp in Prague. In the late 1960s, Chalupecký began writing a monograph devoted to Duchamp that he worked on intermittently for 20 years; we might even view it as his life's legacy. It is his only book on a foreign artist, which is remarkable considering that Duchamp's influence on Czech art—if he had any influence at all—was quite indirect. The content of the two-volume *Úděl umělce* [The Artist's Lot][23] extends beyond that of an art-historical monograph. Particularly in the second volume, Chalupecký summarizes his reflections on the fate of 20th-century European art. In addition to some outstanding passages in which he reconstructs Duchamp's intentions in his unfinished *The Large Glass*, Chalupecký presents a distinctive interpretation of the artist's work that flies in the face of most of the literature on Duchamp. The book says more about the writer's own views than the work of the founder of Conceptualism. For Chalupecký, Duchamp, the creator of the myth of modern art, tapped into the tradition of European spiritual culture as conceived by the German Romantics. He was fulfilling the artist's higher calling, which in modern society meant mainly providing consolation. Chalupecký read the playful and ironic work of the destroyer of artistic conventions in an almost religious light.

Although Greenberg declared many times, based on his theory of art, that Duchamp's work was marginal, he, too, often returned to the artist's work in order to explain his rejection in greater detail each time. We may consider all of Greenberg's later critical writings from the 1970s—even those that do not mention Duchamp explicitly—to be a polemic against Duchamp and those who at the time stood behind his work. In 1971 Duchamp became a central figure in Greenberg's seminar at Bennington College in Vermont. The texts used in individual seminars were printed in 1972–1979 in *Arts Magazine* and were later published in a critical edition.[24] Greenberg either could not or did not want to fully comprehend Duchamp's work. He considered his paintings outdated, asserting that they relied on traditional conventions of illusory painting. According to Greenberg, Duchamp never understood Cubism, and, perhaps more important, he lacked the taste and ability to attract interest through artistic means alone.[25] Greenberg may have regarded Duchamp's ready-mades as conceptually thought-provoking and even provocative to anyone interested in aesthetics. However, he thought Duchamp was unable to adequately express his ideas.

We can only regret that a direct debate between Greenberg and Chalupecký never took place. Although he had been interested in American modern culture, particularly poetry, since the 1940s, Chalupecký knew Greenberg's writings mostly from a rather late edition of *Art and Culture* (1961). Nevertheless, there is no record of what he thought of the American critic's work. Still, to a certain degree, the art each of them defended led to debates in many parts of the world on their behalf. Greenberg was surrounded by art. The sheer extent of the cultural offerings he encountered in New York studios and galleries forced him to apply strict standards and be selective, to think about art from a bird's-eye view and consider how it might be given direction. He did not see artists as mavericks or romantic heroes but rather as creative spirits answering to the higher calling of art.

Chalupecký also believed in art's higher calling; however, for him that involved not the formal evolution of art, but human society. He could not view artworks as mere fodder for formal analysis. Behind them he also saw the fates of individual artists and the living societies that produced them. For this reason too, particularly in the last decades of his life, he was drawn to forms of expression at the border between art and life, expressions that intentionally crossed the line and fulfilled a conception of art as therapy—or even as a possible substitute for religion in a modern secularized society.

[1] "A key problem which provided a general framework was the relationship between art and society." This is how the central theme of Czech art in the prewar period was characterized by the editors of an anthology of programmatic texts on Czech art of the second half of the 20th century. See *České umění 1938–1989: Programy, kritické texty, dokumenty* [Czech Art 1938–1989: Programs, Critical Texts, Documents], ed. Jiří Ševčík, Pavlína Morganová, Dagmar Dušková, Prague, Academia 2001, p. 15.

[2] The process by which the American artistic avant-garde distanced itself from Marxism is described by Serge Guilbaut in the introductory chapter of his *How New York Stole the Idea of Modern Art: Abstract Expressionism, Freedom, and the Cold War,* Chicago–London, University of Chicago Press 1983. But even in the 1940s and 1950s, certain artists in the United States advocated a socialist realism in the Soviet spirit.

[3] Karel Teige, *Jarmark umění* [Art Fair], Prague, Československý spisovatel [Czechoslovak Writer] 1964, p. 55.

[4] Today's historians also see in the emergence of Greenberg's text a reaction to contemporary discussions in the leftist German press—specifically, to "Discussions about Expressionism," an article by German Marxist Ernst Bloch printed in 1938 in *Das Wort*, a Moscow-based émigré journal. In it, Bloch opposed György Lukács and his essay "'Größe und Verfall' des Expressionismus" [Expressionism: Its Significance and Decline], which was a reaction, in turn, to Wilhelm Worringer and his vision of the historical development of expressionism.

[5] "In the West, if not everywhere else as well, the ruling class has always to some extent imposed a crude version of its own cultural bias upon those it ruled […] There is a constant seepage from top to bottom, and Kitsch (a wonderful German word that covers all this crap) is the common sewer." Quoted in Florence Rubenfeld, *Clement Greenberg: A Life*, New York, Scribner 1997, p. 51.

[6] Clement Greenberg, "Avant-Garde and Kitsch," in *Partisan Review* 6.5 (1939), pp. 34–49.

[7] Teige, *Jarmark umění* [Art Fair], p. 45.

[8] Clement Greenberg, "Avant-Garde and Kitsch," p. 74.

[9] Jindřich Chalupecký, "O umění, svobodě a socialismu" [On Art, Freedom and Socialism], in *J. Ch., Obhajoba umění 1934–1948* [A Defense of Art, 1934–1948], Prague, Československý spisovatel 1991, p. 54.

[10] Jindřich Chalupecký, "Svět, v němž žijeme" [The World We Live In], in *J. Ch., Obhajoba umění 1934–1948* [Jindřich Chalupecký: A Defense of Art 1934–1948], p. 73.

[11] Chalupecký, "Svět, v němž žijeme" [The World We Live In], pp. 69–70.

[12] Greenberg, "Avant-Garde and Kitsch," pp. 36–37.

[13] Jindřich Chalupecký, "Krásné umění [Art]," in *J. Ch., Obhajoba umění 1934–1948* [Jindřich Chalupecký: A Defense of Art 1934–1948], p. 24.

[14] See Otakar Mrkvička, *Umění a kýč* [Art and Kitsch], Prague, Orbis 1946.

[15] Ibid., p. 22.

[16] Jindřich Chalupecký, *Velká příležitost—Poznámky k reorganizaci českého výtvarného života* [A Great Opportunity —Notes on the Reorganization of Czech Fine Arts], Prague, Umělecká beseda 1946.

[17] Ibid., pp. 31–32.

[18] Ibid., p. 32.

[19] This is based on a study by Pavel Janáček, *Literární brak. Operace vyloučení, operace nahrazení* [Lowbrow Literature: Operation Exclusion, Operation Substitution, 1938–1951], Brno, Host 2004. According to Janáček, the proposed encroachments on the freedom of the press were similar to those found in the constitution of the Weimar Republic.

[20] Ibid., p. 225.

[21] Clement Greenberg, "The Decline of Cubism," in *Partisan Review*, 1948, n. 3, p. 369.

[22] Jindřich Chalupecký, "Umění musí myslit na všedního člověka" [Art Must Think of Everday People], in *Mladá fronta* 3, 1947, n. 255, November 1, p. 6. Cited in *Skupina 42. Antologie* [Group 42: An Anthology], ed. Zdeněk Pešat, Eva Petrová, Brno, Atlantis 2000, p. 343.

[23] The first volume has been published as Jindřich Chalupecký, *Úděl umělce: Meditations on Duchamp* [The Artist's Lot: Meditations on Duchamp], Prague, Torst 1998.

[24] Clement Greenberg, *Homemade Esthetics: Observations on Art and Taste*, New York–Oxford, Oxford University Press 1999. The differences between Greenberg's theory of art and the work of Marcel Duchamp are also the subject of a considerable part of Thierry de Duve's *Kant after Duchamp*, Cambridge–London, MIT Press 1996.

[25] Greenberg, *Homemade Esthetics: Observations on Art and Taste*, p. 55.

Paxism, Explosionism, and Aktual in the Struggle for Peace: Jan Lukeš, Vladimír Boudník, and Milan Knížák

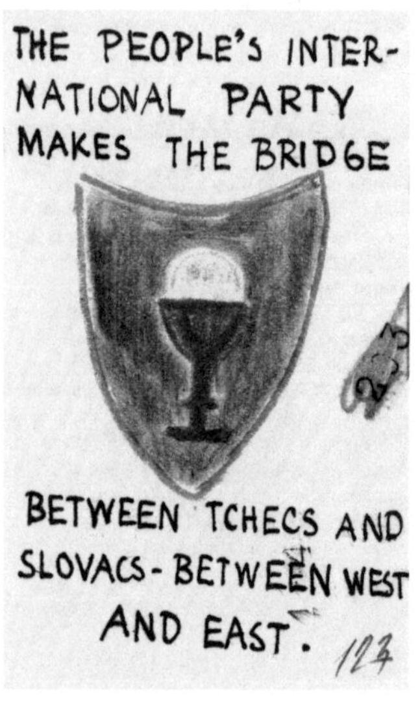

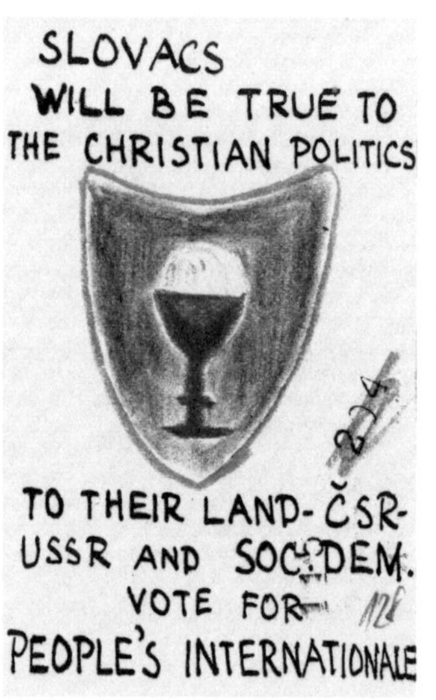

[ill. 1] Jan Lukeš, *Lidová internacionála míru* [The People's International for Peace], flyer from 1945 (Security Services Archive, record group 300, Country Security Division, Prague)

I.

The period after World War II saw some unusual pacifist activities in Czechoslovakia. At first glance, they seem less like artistic expressions than manifestations of quirkiness or even of psychopathy. The actors involved were viewed by most contemporaries as eccentrics or even crackpots. Today we consider some of them important representatives of postwar Czech culture. They did not limit themselves to traditional genres. They wrote no anti-war novels and created no peace-themed paintings; they wanted chiefly to reform society, to change people's lives. To this end, they wrote manifestos, printed flyers and letters, and distributed them to the media and to unsuspecting fellow citizens. At this particular moment in their lives, they thought the most important task before them was the seemingly self-evident one of fostering peace and understanding among different peoples.

The peace manifestos by the three Czech artists discussed here appeared in various years during the Cold War. The two world powers, the United States and the Soviet Union, were at a stalemate, keeping each other at bay by means of threats and shows of force, all in the name of peace. The word "peace" had been degraded; it had become an instrument in an ideological conflict of global proportions. The 1950s in particular saw a profusion of peace congresses and calls for peace. At mass events, signatures were collected across the Eastern Bloc in support of peace. A wide range of cultural figures from all over the world were recruited—or manipulated—to take part in calls for peace, including the modernist painter Pablo Picasso, who sided with the USSR and the Communist Party, even though a campaign against modernist art was coming to a head in the Communist Bloc. Whereas Americans marshaled the artistic individualism of abstract expressionism in their "struggle for freedom," the communists had Picasso and his doves of peace in their camp. Thanks in part to this political state of affairs, the illusion that modernism represented a homogeneous, universal global movement was definitively dispelled.[1]

We create posters or petitions and address unknown individuals when the usual channels of communication fail us. Some artists are not able to gauge what is going on around them realistically; such artists might stop listening and initiate long monologues comprehensible only to them. On the European continent after World War II, avant-garde artists felt a need to communicate that only increased in urgency as they began to discern the meager social impact of their work. Confrontations between artists and society escalated.[2] For many, making avant-garde art that in the end lacked social import was a frustrating endeavor. Certain artists felt such a fervent desire for their activities to have social repercussions that they were willing to abandon art itself.

II.

During the last weeks of 1945, inhabitants of the Vinohrady district of Prague saw some odd handmade flyers on street corners; some found them in their mailboxes. The flyers announced the existence of the Prague People's International for Peace, whose stated goal was to defend humanity against the new weapon race and the threat of the atomic bomb. Even though a scant few months had passed since the end of the war and there was hardly anyone who did not want peace, the inexpertly made leaflets seemed provocative. [ill. 1]

The author of the flyer was Jan Lukeš (1912–1977), a physician who remained entirely unknown to the public throughout his life. He spent his last years as a legally insane mental patient. In the past few decades, efforts have been made to shed light on Lukeš as an individual who enriched the fringes of Czech 20th-century culture. In the 1950s the peculiar case of Lukeš caught the attention of a professor named Jaroslav Stuchlík, as well as of the wider field of psychiatry, not thanks to his artistic endeavors but mainly through his articles and his unusual ability to create and use complicated artificial languages, an ability he had been cultivating and putting to use since childhood. Lukeš's literary and musical works remained unexplored and underappreciated for a long time. This was in part because they represented an amalgam of mental instability, Dadaism, pataphysics, and verborrhea that had no hope of official publication. Like many outsiders, Jan Lukeš created an elaborate parallel universe endowed not only with several artificial languages but with its own history and geography as well, from which he drew subject matter, "facts," and linguistic material for his novels and musical works. It is primarily thanks to editorial work by Vladimír Borecký that Lukeš's work has been made accessible.[3] In recent years, Lukeš's literary works have been published in stand-alone form as well.[4]

Jan Lukeš lived in seclusion for most of his life, and his campaigning for the People's Peace International in 1945 is not in keeping with any of his other activities. Most of the information we have on the People's Peace International (Paxism) or PPI(P) can be found in one of the letters he addressed to the academic Ivan Málek, dated November 7, 1960.[5] The lengthy text drafted in literary style contains, in addition to various biographical anecdotes, an account of the emergence of the Paxist movement and a related attempt at a coup d'état in 1945. According to the letter, Lukeš had committed the story of the PPI(P)'s emergence to paper and had sent it to the Central Committee of the Czechoslovak

Communist Party in the late 1950s. The committee did not respond. Lukeš, encouraged by the atmosphere of peace efforts after Kruschev's speech at the United Nations in 1959, began to promote the Paxist cause again in the early 1960s. He chose to address himself to Málek because of his engagement in the official peace movement of socialist Czechoslovakia. Lukeš wanted to draw the attention of the prominent Communist politician and party peace campaigner to the pressing nature of Paxism, which had originated 15 years earlier. He requested that his endeavors be recognized, at least retroactively, and, at the same time, requested that he receive rehabilitation and an increase to his meager disability pension. It is not clear, however, if Lukeš sent this letter to Málek or not.

According to Lukeš's lengthy letter, the roots of Paxism dated back to 1942, when he had been working in Dr. Olga Valentová's Lupus Institute at Motol Hospital. At Motol he met Franz Mudra, a Viennese catechist responsible for spiritual care at the hospital.

> At a time of mass executions of Czech patriots [...] in June 1942 Mudra confided to me his idea that after the end of this war it would be absolutely necessary to establish a mass global organization, the People's Peace International, or the "Paxist Movement," with the aim of achieving full and universal disarmament and working to prevent any new wars by means of mass referendums [...] Following several discussions we had on the subject on the nights of November 1 and 2, 1942, Mudra stated quite clearly that I should take part in the establishment and leadership of the PPI(P).[6]

The letter suggests that immediately after he had been entrusted with the task, Lukeš forgot about Paxism and his higher calling for a time. During World War II the recent medical school graduate worked in various health facilities in the Protectorate of Bohemia and Moravia. When one of his patients died because Lukeš neglected to tend to his severe injuries, Lukeš's psychological health was assessed for the first time. He was discovered to be mentally unfit and was gradually disbarred from professional medical practice.

In mid-1945 he was diagnosed with paranoid schizophrenia and eventually lost his job. In a letter to Málek he confided that in late May 1945 he had run into Father Mudra at U Fenclů, a Prague bookshop, and in the ensuing conversation had revived the idea of the Paxism international. Lukeš was reportedly entrusted by Mudra to visit prominent spiritual leaders, including the archiepiscopal vicar-general Theofil Opatrný, who offered his support for the fundamental ideas of Paxism.

Other events described come across as farcical. In June 1945 Lukeš decided to openly go into politics and began drawing up a manifesto he titled *Můj mír* [My Peace], which was the conceptual antithesis to Hitler's *Mein Kampf.* Written in the manner of a religious tract, in a quasi-Biblical style with numbered verses, it set forth the basic ideas of Paxism. The contrived style proved too much for the religiously tepid Lukeš, who ended up abandoning the unfinished text. But the dropping of the atomic bomb on Hiroshima on August 6, 1945, incited him to further activism. The attack roused him to write letters to Czechoslovak President Edvard Beneš, Prime Minister Klement Gottwald, and Secretary of State Jan Masaryk; he requested that all of them send letters of protest to the United States without delay. When he received no response, he himself addressed letters to Harry Truman, British ruler George VI, Général de Gaulle, and Pope Pius XII. When he received no response from them either, he quickly finished *My Peace* and set about campaigning.

Jan Lukeš writes that on the first Sunday in October 1945, he met with Rudolf Slánský, secretary of the Central Committee of the Czechoslovak Communist Party, who informed him that neither he nor Klement Gottwald had anything against the PPI(P) entering high politics. However, it would first have to obtain the support of the masses: "So, I began in October 1945 to draw and mimeograph promotional flyers with the help of two other physicians and the doorman of the Institute of Pathology (at Kateřinská 32) and one employee of the Ministry of National Defense. By the end of the year we had either hung on the streets of Prague or mailed out over 3,000 flyers, each of which bore at the top an emblem consisting of a red chalice with a white target in a blue field, which I chose as the definitive symbol of the PPI(P)."[7]

However, Lukeš was discouraged in the end, for the flyers did not meet with the reception he had originally hoped for. Still, he estimated the Paxism movement counted 300 regular members toward the end of 1945. A public people's camp and a general assembly of all the Paxists was convened on December 25, 1945, before Saint Vitus Cathedral, at Prague Castle. On the appointed day, the cathedral was surrounded by police. Of the approximately 50 Paxists present, 2 of them, named Mašata and Maywald, tried to make their way inside and deliver speeches, but they were silenced. Faced with the failure of the gathering, Lukeš left. He understood that Paxism had foundered. In a subsequent letter to Beneš, Gottwald, and Interior Minister Nosek, he renounced all his political activities.

It is obvious that Jan Lukeš's letter to Málek contains a series of fabrications. The course of events he describes and the personal meetings with Communist politicians are most probably figments of the author's imagination. The real extent of the Paxism movement will probably remain a mystery forever. Lukeš stated in later medical records that on February 5, 1946, he was arrested by the police and turned over to a psychiatry ward following several days of interrogation. The reason given was the hanging of the posters and the distribution of muddled letters. He spent six months in therapy, undergoing various types of treatments, including electric and insulin shock treatment.[8] But Paxism was not just one among the many figments of Lukeš's imagination. He elaborated on the idea of the movement in his later literary work as well, particularly in his novel, *Mariánské císařství* [The Marian Empire]. We cannot simply see Jan Lukeš as a forsaken lunatic, disappointed by everything, who wanted to call attention to himself. For we have his remarkable work, and in many ways his irony and Dadaist sense of humor resonate with the approaches used in the avant-garde art of his day. For example, among his musical works is the draft of *Bellica*, an opera composed for an orchestra reminiscent of one of John Cage's—twelve timpani, six drums, three machine guns, and six rifles—and a minimalist variation on Tchaikovsky's ballet entitled *Turtle Lake.* Readers of his letters to Málek would also find it hard to avoid the impression that the main reason behind his writings was not a desire for rehabilitation or money, but chiefly a compulsive, uncontrollable ambition that combined exhibitionism with artistic expression: a yearning to capture the Paxist movement literarily or even to embody it in an artistic text and share his creation with at least one reader—the recipient. He evidently had great fun writing them. "All Paxism, as I myself see it, was to a certain extent organized as a great opera, as a great utopian novel, as a grandiose dream."[9]

III.

Just a few years after Jan Lukeš, Vladimír Boudník addressed the public at home and across the world with his own peace manifestos. Today we think of Lukeš's work as that of an eccentric, and the future will probably concur. By contrast, Boudník is considered a classic figure of Czech art. During his lifetime, however, many people considered him a crackpot as well. Fighting against the dismissal of his work as the product of psychological pathology became a lifetime struggle for Boudník. For most of his life, he found that art critics and audiences showed less interest in him than psychiatrists did—a state of affairs that he was to ultimately accept as a fact of life. He himself sought out psychiatrists, and a portion of his work is preserved in their hands.

By contrast with Jan Lukeš, a wider spectrum of sources on Vladimír Boudník is available to us today. We have, in part, his correspondence and his journal entries; another invaluable resource are the notes that Vladislav Merhaut, a friend of Boudník's, made in the 1960s.[10] Nevertheless, it is not easy to come to an unequivocal view of Boudník's pacifist activities, which had a seemingly indirect relationship to his later graphic work. We must conclude that Boudník was the type of figure whose life and work are hard to separate with a clear boundary line. This is true especially of Boudník's manifestos, his numerous public appeals, and the countless letters he sent to people he both knew and did not know.

Before he formulated his well-known and oft-cited Explosionist manifesto in 1949, Boudník wrote and distributed anti-war appeals and letters. He sent them to various world organizations, the media, and famous individuals. In their naiveté, they might have seemed like the products of an ailing mind—most of the recipients of letters from a complete stranger calling for peace in the name of the welfare of humanity certainly got that impression.

Nobody knew Vladimír Boudník then. Called up for active duty during the war, he did not finish his higher studies in graphic design until he was 25. It is difficult to find direct parallels between his realistic and in essence mediocre artwork in the late 1940s, and his tempestuous activist and educational activities. In 1984 Jiří Valoch remarked that "more provocative than his graphic work were Boudník's early texts, manifestos, and appeals. Particularly his calls for peace, which quite directly reflected his personal experience with active duty in Dresden (probably chiefly digging up corpses from ruins following bombing raids), and painted a picture of him as an impractical dreamer, a utopian and, truth be told, a madman ..."[11] [ill. 2]

Boudník's peace manifestos and appeals have remained neglected by experts because of their unusual and unclassifiable character. Even the monumental monograph *Vladimír Boudník* (the last such work), published on the occasion of a retrospective of his work at Prague Castle's Imperial Stables in 2004, does not discuss the peace manifestos in any depth.[12] The silence surrounding the manifestos might also be meant to erase Boudník's reputation as a childish dreamer and a sufferer of mental illness. From the narrow perspective of the art historian, it is quite hard to add anything noteworthy on the subject. At least three samples created using drypoint and wood engraving have been preserved from the watershed years 1947–1948. They are calls to action or flyers, sometimes illustrated, sometimes consisting of text alone. The longest is a five-part proclamation from October 1947 beginning with the exclamation "Nations!" In it, Boudník tells the story of a tormented dog, warning against violence against humans at the same time. The extensive text is in a moralizing register and even contains generalized condemnations of humanity as a whole. According to Boudník, humanity's aggression and propensity toward violence is the greatest danger on the horizon. He calls for the eradication of selfishness, solidarity among peoples, and a generalized compassion. He urges humanity to avoid falling prey to warmongering at all costs and asserts that mothers have an important role to play in raising children to be pacifists and to oppose killing. "Do not forget that military weapons have not been liquidated. Do not be, as you have been so far, the murderers of your own children—think."[13]

Boudník belonged to a generation that had directly faced active military duty. During his service, he experienced Allied bombings that left him deeply shaken. His early existentially anguished graphic work, much like the work of his friends Hanes Reegen, Zdeněk Bouše, and Jaroslav Rotbauer, depicted ravages of war drawn from direct, specific experiences that could not easily be expunged from memory. "After the war the masses were tuned to the same wavelength due to its horrors,"[14] remembered Boudník in a letter to Zdeněk Bouše dated January 12, 1950. Of the circle of friends mentioned above, however, only Boudník transformed these experiences into both private artwork and public manifestos and calls to action, which he then distributed to fellow citizens and dispatched to world political organizations and media outlets.

From the end of the war onward, Boudník felt a responsibility for the world that did not wane with time. "There is within us a period of maturation, hope, joy, faith in a new world, a postwar, creative world; there is within us a consciousness of the capability of destroying millions and millions of people by a foolish act of war and at the same there are within us thousands of restraints to prevent us from committing any more senseless murders."[15] His desire to assume this responsibility for humanity found an outlet in his peace manifestos and letters. Many of Boudník's good friends were skeptical toward his peace proclamations in 1947–1948, considering them naive or demonstrations of abnormal behavior. Boudník went on fanatically proclaiming his truths; he wanted to rouse people from their indifference and turn their attention to something that he deemed of the utmost import. Contemporaries remember that "girls from his class [at the graphic design school] called him 'the missionary.'"[16] Among his friends—and all the more so among strangers—Boudník came across as an eccentric who sent confused declarations to heads of state and newsrooms both at home and abroad, missives to which no easy reply was possible.[17] At first, Boudník sent his letters and proclamations anonymously, until he was accused of cowardice, at which point he began signing his manifestos.[18] Beginning in 1952, he even began delivering the manifestos in person because he feared they would not be delivered through the post. In his correspondence, he states that he sent up to 1,200 letters to friends and editorial offices. When he included manifestos, the total number rose to an estimated 1,700 items. In another letter from the late 1950s, he claims that in seven years he sent his letters to 50 different addresses.[19]

Vladimír Boudník was serious about his calls to action and did not hesitate to risk being not only misunderstood but also persecuted by officialdom, much as Lukeš was. Boudník's manifestos, whether concerning peace or, later, Explosionism, could easily be interpreted as provocations or as criticisms of government policies. In 1949, during his military service, Boudník even tried to convince recruits who had never before come into contact with art to take up Explosionism and create art in an Explosionist spirit. But he did not limit himself to recruits. "I lectured on Explosionism to cultural workers + all ranks up to that of major," he wrote in a letter to Zdeněk Bouše.[20] However, we know of no documentary evidence indicating that the State Security showed an interest in him, even though he himself anticipated an encounter with the police, according to the testimony of Vladislav Merhaut.[21]

For Boudník, just as for Lukeš, public reactions to his anti-war appeals were immensely important; he did not understand the indifference of others. "I fear there might be a war, and the people I speak to, who are part of my vision, might perish. I want peace. I am afraid of war."[22] In a letter written only a few days later, he joyfully describes one of the rare responses to his pacifist appeals:

> Today I reproduced the original peace proposal "several times." As you can see, Expl. is not as shallow as you think. The proposal awakened a concrete official reaction in the press. However, *this time* people were disposed as *my friends* were and thought it was pointless—after such a war—to speak more widely about peace. Imagine how "magical" it was for me when I was referred to [in the newspapers] as a "haughty individual with a recipe for peace" […] Our dozens of manifestos + letters calling for pacifist

> laws may have been adolescent, naive, but they were heartfelt. We don't want war.[23]

Before 1948, initiating a society-wide transformation clearly took priority over his own artwork. He did not set modest goals for himself, and for the time being art could only help him indirectly. What was important was changing the world for the better, changing people's behavior, ensuring the coexistence of both nations and individuals, and clearing the way for people to understand the universe and themselves. Boudník's drawings and graphic work emerged on the side, as it were. Little by little, he developed his Explosionism, which brought together his theoretical, cultural, and artistic endeavors. Explosionism retained the agitative character of his peace manifestos; at least in the beginning, his art and his activism were so intermingled that it is hard to separate them. It would hardly be apt to limit the scope of Explosionism by defining it as a mere artistic style or art movement. It became and remained a way of viewing life, a set of beliefs with a society-wide compass in which the struggle for peace and human and creative freedom played important roles. The view that art should set itself more than aesthetic aims was one that Boudník held not only at the turn of the 1950s but throughout his lifetime. A few weeks before he died, he summed this up in a letter to Antonín Hartmann dated October 24, 1968: "[The] primary task [of today's artists] is to try to safeguard life on this planet."[24]

Although Vladislav Merhaut's notes on Vladimír Boudník were not written down until the 1960s, they shed valuable light on the motivation behind Boudník's peace activism in the late 1940s. One short passage from an entry dated September 24, 1964, deals with the issue of the manifestos directly. Boudník had forced his way into a lecture by psychiatrist Stanislav Drvota on Boudník's life and work. After Drvota's presentation, Boudník answered questions posed by the psychiatrists in attendance. When asked if he would do the same things then—i.e., in 1964—that he had done at the beginning of his career, he allegedly answered, "No, what I did was more or less bound up with the time. I wrote the manifestos and letters in order to break out of the narrow circle that surrounded me, to make contact with the most people possible, and thus be able to set my views against the views of thousands of other people."[25] Even though this is indirect testimony, and we may suspect that Boudník tailored his answer to the auditorium filled with psychiatrists, it is evident that although by this time he had distanced himself from his activism, he never renounced it. He continued to endorse the thinking behind it, though he was probably aware of its unviability and its dependence on the postwar atmosphere. This is also confirmed in a 1966 letter from Boudník to Jitka Hamzová that comes to us by way of a contemporary transcription by Merhaut:

> My manifestos in 1949–1952 must seem quite naive today. But to defend the authenticity of the idea, *there was no other way—I wasn't just writing for myself to shift the blame off my shoulders*! Before finding the courage to send one of the manifestos to Paris in 1949 with an imperfect foreword stitched together from phrases and sentences out of a French textbook, I sent it to dozens of places, to newspapers, the radio, the philosophical faculty, the academy, the university, etc.—and only when they saw I hadn't been charged with anything did the manifesto go abroad.[26]

Let us pause for a moment and consider Boudník's italics in the quotation. He is signaling here what is most important about the whole phenomenon of the peace manifestos. The very form of the manifesto—in the conditions of postwar Czechoslovakia they were reproduced by hand and distributed by post—was important. Boudník may have been groping in the dark artistically in the 1940s and having trouble combining his theoretical views with concrete artwork, but he did not have doubts concerning the form of the manifesto. It was a way to address the public, to communicate his ideas. The manifesto had fulfilled its mission once it had been sent to thousands of unsuspecting recipients, once it had become part of a process of communication, a process that also incorporated an institutional aspect, as the official mail had been used. Likewise, the chief significance of the street demonstrations Boudník carried out—in addition to his other activities in Prague beginning in the late 1940s—was that they were public. They bore fruit not in the form of permanent artworks, like the posters of the *affichistes*,[27] but rather in the form of both discussions with chance passers-by as well as distinctive expressions of personal artistic principles and social engagement.

IV.

Boudník remained alone on his creative journey until, in the 1960s, he discovered an artist who built on his ideas, whether knowingly or unwittingly. Milan Knížák (b. 1940)—like Boudník, but ten years later—staged artistic performances in the city streets and addressed the public by means of written anti-war appeals in the mid-1960s. He too wanted to elicit change in people's lives. His artistic methods were quite new in Czechoslovakia at the time, and for most people, they were incomprehensible too. He wrote manifestos, organized walks and games, and accosted passers-by on the streets by installing assemblages. The windows of his Prague's home on Nový Svět Street were plastered with calls to action; soon a community of young people fascinated by his ideas and his persona gathered around him. Most considered him a troublemaker; to others he was a guru. Even when cultural politics began opening up during the 1960s, Knížák, with his art and theories, was unable to make any official public appearances. One might ask to what extent he himself would have actually desired a different state of affairs. For him, gallery exhibitions were a symbol of an antiquated approach to art; in contrast, he proposed activities that were closely tied to everyday life and yet set themselves apart from it. He was expelled from art school, the samizdat editions he published reached a limited range of people, and the official newspapers and cultural revues showed no great willingness to provide him with a forum for his ideas. Before long, Knížák began using the mail to disseminate his ideas and to address the public.

In the 1960s, the mail was used as a medium for artistic activities on an international scale, primarily by those movements whose artistic activities bordered on political activism and on efforts to directly transform social life. The Fluxus movement, for example, created a correspondence network for its needs, in part because its members and supporters were scattered around Europe and North

America. Through this network members sent one another packages, multiples, and printed materials. The mail also offered an opportunity to carry out a variety of pranks and seditious activities. In February 1963 George Maciunas, the leading figure of the Fluxus movement, made a call to clog up the postal system by sending thousands of packages loaded with weights to newspaper offices, galleries, and artists. The unsolicited packages were to bear the addresses of other newspaper offices, galleries, and artists as return addresses. Such strategies did not always meet with understanding within the Fluxus community itself. Maciunas's *Fluxus News-Policy Letter* number 6, dated April 6, 1963, caused great controversy within the movement, for it openly called for political activities and provocations aimed against traditional society. The sharply negative reaction of certain artists in the Fluxus circle eventually forced Maciunas to provide a supplementary explanation: the calls had been intended only as a means to provoke further theoretical debate. Nevertheless, Maciunas's 1963 Fluxus manifesto, distributed by post, was never accepted as the movement's official manifesto.[28]

In 1965 Milan Knížák sent out his *Dopisy obyvatelstvu* [Letters to the Population]. By his own account, he sent 1,000 letters to randomly selected addresses with provocative anonymous appeals: "Walk non-stop along Národní třída [National Avenue] for 24 hours! Burn all the pictures in your flat and hang up dirty laundry instead. Masturbate in the presence of your mother, father, husband, wife, lover, son, daughter, friend!" The letters ended with the question "Does art mean teaching people how to live?"[29] Regrettably, we have no authentic records documenting the reactions to the appeals, only Jindřich Chalupecký's terse recollection that the recipients mainly felt offended by the letters and the obscene passages in them, which was to be expected.[30] Whatever the reactions may have been, Knížák carried on in a similar vein over the following years.

In 1966 Knížák and Jan Maria Mach organized an ambitious event that transformed a randomly chosen building and its inhabitants into involuntary participants in an art intervention. According to their own reports, they filled hallways in the building with furniture, clothing, and live carp. In addition, they sent individual inhabitants packages with different objects, letters with instructions (to "Get a cat," for example), and envelopes with cinema tickets. The inhabitants, however, considered the intervention a breach of their privacy; fearing for their safety and their property, they eventually called the police.

Even though the incident was investigated for some time by the State Security and Knížák was forced to explain his intentions at a meeting of tenants with the police in attendance, he did not abandon such public methods of accosting his audience. In 1967 he organized another large-scale event titled *Manifestace pospolitosti* [Keeping Together Manifestation], whose aim was to promote world peace and disarmament. Knížák sent out letters and flyers to foreign embassies in Prague, newspaper offices, the authorities, the military, and foreign governments. He declared March 1967 to be "Togetherness Month" and called on all he addressed to promote tolerance among nations and individuals.

An undated letter reportedly sent to unspecified military officials, challenging them to "personally demilitarize," has been preserved, along with another letter addressed to embassies, and yet another unaddressed appeal. The recipients were requested to inform other military representatives and, if possible, embassies, of the worldwide Keeping Together Manifestation. The headquarters of the Aktual group on Nový Svět Street was listed as the return address. Two unsigned flyers from the same year related to the same peace campaign have also been preserved. The first is an invitation to the worldwide Keeping Together Manifestation. Readers were enjoined to take responsibility for the call to action and to send out similar letters. The tone of the second is noticeably sharper, in a brisk anarchist spirit: "Assassinate all who prepare for war! We call on everyone to demonstrate against wars, against all violence, against unfreedom, against lies and hypocrisy."[31] Similar letters, according to its author, had been set to magazines; department stores were called upon to decorate their shop windows with togetherness slogans.

The subject matter of the Keeping Together Manifestation was different from that of Letters to the Population and *Událost pro poštu, veřejnou bezpečnost, obyvatele domu č. 26 A, pro jejich sousedy, příbuzné a přátele* [Incident for the Post, State Security, the Inhabitants of Building

No. 26 A and Their Neighbors, Relatives and Friends] (named after the event). It was not straightforwardly shocking or provocatively playful but contained "reasonable" calls for disarmament and the improvement of interpersonal relationships. Knížák's calls for peace and disarmament were at first glance surprising, coming from a nonconformist artist who consistently rejected all conventions. Judging by his date of birth (1924), his impressions of World War II must have been indistinct; he had probably not been traumatized by it in the long term, as Vladimír Boudník had. "All I remember of the war was tiny planes on the horizon, the licorice in the little shop across the street, beautiful and horrible bomb shrapnel, air raids, and being so scared during one of them that I wet myself."[32] In the early 1960s the official fight for peace was an overworked topic, a mainstay of socialist propaganda. At the same time, the mid-1960s saw the emergence of the hippie peace movement in the West. For young people, soldiers and generals became symbols of evil and of an antiquated model of society. They believed the world of the future should belong to the sun, love, and peace; in the light of their ideals, war was seen as something absurd, calling for an equally absurd reaction. For example, the first issue of the magazine *PROVO*, published in 1965 by the eponymous Amsterdam-based counterculture movement that inspired Knížák, displayed a sharply antimilitaristic tone. However, at the same time, it contained instructions for the production of explosives. This provocative strategy was popular with the public. The original print run of 500 in early 1965 had become 20,000 by a few months later.

The topic of peace in Knížák's letters spoke to everyone (though his calls for the burning of paintings and the massive consumption of alcohol, less so). The same was true of Boudník's letters. Nevertheless, Knížák's proclamations were all the more provocative in that they were sent as letters. Did Knížák really think that his letters would make the military officials to whom he wrote cast aside their pistols and devote themselves to the establishment of a peaceful society without weapons and war? More likely, the Keeping Together Manifestation satirized the absurd practices of political regimes that exploit peace propaganda in order to unleash violence; they announced, loudly, that the emperor had no clothes. The Aktual movement's Keeping Together Manifestation was one of its first international activities. The Prague call to action, which had been translated into English, was distributed by the artist Ken Friedman at an American version of the event he organized on the West Coast of the United States.

The police became interested in Knížák's letters right away, which did not bode well for him; nonetheless, he was able, in a highly clever way, to raise the question regarding the means individuals in modern society have available if they want to fight for something as uncontroversial as peace. Could someone possibly be persecuted for such a pursuit? What could better express the hypocrisy of the socialist regime and, more generally, the perversity and absurdity of modern civilization? Knížák did not take the struggle for peace too seriously; it was no more than an opportunity to satirize an official government line. This tongue-in-cheek approach is evident in the songs lampooning rock music and avant-garde art written for Knížák's musical group, Aktual. Peace and war were the subjects of many of them, with Knížák advocating both in alternation.[33]

Knížák's work, which comprises a large number of later notes and remarks, has been studied by art historians only in a piecemeal manner. He has included documents relating to the Keeping Together Manifestation in books and catalogues published over the past two decades. However, there is a lack of independent commentary, testimonials, or research situating them in the context of Knížák's other activities before his departure for western Bohemia in 1967 and for the United States in 1968.

We also see Knížák using the mail in *Přátelství se stromem* [Friendship with a Tree], a piece from the late 1970s. In it, participants chose a tree and acted toward it as if it were a friend. They visited it, talked to it, got it clothing or presents, sent it letters. This was meant to help participants increase their awareness of interpersonal relationships and the relationships among things in general. It was a game for adults or anybody willing to take part in it. The important thing was following the piece through in all thoroughness and not simply taking it as a thought experiment. Knížák's seriousness was borne out by his own attempts at corresponding with a tree. In the summer months of 1980, he repeatedly tried the patience of the German mail when he requested that his letters be delivered to a clothed tree that postal workers were supposed to find based on a little map on the envelope where the address should have been. When the letter was returned to the sender as undeliverable, Knížák just drew a more detailed map and sent the letter off again. The piece was a game, an absurd gesture, and the incomprehension of the postal service, which could not or would not deliver the letter to the tree, played an important role in it.

Perhaps even more than Boudník, Knížák considered his artistic activities an instrument to teach people about life. Boudník saw his street pieces as ways of kindling the imaginations of random passers-by and drawing them into discussions on the topics of modern art or creativity; he thought that anybody could become an artist. Knížák, too, saw his activities as a service to others, as a way to open their eyes through art, to "expose nerves," to teach them how to find a path to a more worthwhile humanity within modern society. The impact of this "school" and the way the randomly selected "students" related to its teaching methods remained a problem, however. Knížák's ideas regarding human coexistence had markedly social and utopian traits, and most of society thought they were either unreasonable or downright repugnant. From addressing a random group of people in as wide a circle as possible, Knížák gradually went on to focus his activities on a narrow group of sympathizers; in practice, he attempted to create an ideal community with them in the western border village of Krásné.

V.

How are the above three cases of peace activism by Czech artists to be interpreted? In certain respects, they are remarkably similar; in others, they are diametrically opposed. They coincide not only in their almost identical contents but also in the way they were propagated and in the way the protagonists, who inspired suspicion in observers, behaved. Nonetheless, in comparing them we must remain as cautious as possible.

Let us begin with the simplest similarity from a graphic point of view: Lukeš's flyers, Boudník's manifestos, and Knížák's letters coincide in the primitive, ineffectual forms of their thrown-together, cheaply created communications. There are no efforts to recreate graphic schemes or to captivate readers with typographical design; everything is amateurish, improvised, and roughly prepared in the simplest, most straightforward way. Jan Lukeš distributed his calls to action using a mimeograph. Vladimír Boudník chose simple lithography and Knížák a typewriter and carbon paper. By his own account, Lukeš's *Můj mír* [My Peace] took the form of a religious treatise, and Boudník's truculent and abrasive moralizing was redolent of a personal messianism. Aspects of Knížák's letters suggest official notices; the envelopes include return addresses and sometimes even a stamp. A scant few of Lukeš's peace flyers have survived in state police archives. There are several exemplars of Boudník's calls to action in the possession of his friends. The only extant copies of Knížák's letters are in the artist's archive; he himself introduced them into the context of the art world by incorporating them in his exhibitions and books.

The fight for peace meant different things for each artist. For Lukeš, although Paxism was probably an important component in the parallel world of a psychotic's boundless imagination, it was one among many. Knížák was probably not even all that concerned with the peace-related contents of his declarations themselves: he would never revisit any similar campaign for nonviolence. More important for him was the act itself of addressing large numbers of people, whether anonymous or carefully selected. His letter-writing campaigns from the late 1960s were among the few ways he could occupy the position of a "teacher" so that he might influence—at least by correspondence—the world around him and point out its absurdity. Of the work of the three artists under consideration, Knížák's letters and manifestos come closest to a well-thought-out art project. In the early work of Vladimír Boudník, he was apparently most sincere about the peace manifestos, which played a central role. They became the essence of his vision for the future of humankind, a goal everyone should aim for.

Calls for disarmament and world peace in the form of an individual's appeal invite comparison with futile attempts to construct and patent perpetual motion machines. With hindsight, Lukeš would satirize his Paxism (without, however, relinquishing his belief in its principles); years later

Boudník would acknowledge his own naiveté; and Knížák wanted mainly to provoke, to inject disquiet into the status quo. Nonetheless, none of them hesitated to send out their manifestos and letters at a critical moment, fully aware of the police persecution that might ensue. None of them gave up, either, and all of them took responsibility for their actions, despite the potentially unpleasant consequences. The only one imprisoned for his artistic endeavors was Milan Knížák, though it was not for anything directly related to any Keeping Together Manifestation.

Lukeš, Boudník, and Knížák all aggrandized their activities and overstated their impact. All of them tried to present their peace activities as wide-ranging mass movements. The core of Aktual was made up of four people; the only real Explosionist was Boudník; and although we have no information about how far Paxism spread among the populace, its impact most probably fell short of Lukeš's least optimistic estimates. Nevertheless, all of them gave their thoughts the spin of a mass political doctrine: their calls to action were written in the plural or at least tried to instigate a universal or even a worldwide reaction. At the same time, their activities betray at first glance their political dilettantism and outsider status.

All three artists suffered from the feeling that they were unappreciated. They often attempted to convince others that it was they who had come up, years beforehand, with aspects of art and culture which their contemporaries held in high regard. They reacted touchily to the dissemination and success of the ideas they considered their own. In one letter, Boudník complained:

> I wrote hundreds of essays, thousands of letters, and today I can find analogues in my own earlier thoughts and manifestos for practically all the motivating forces coming from official places [...] The cultural revolution being promoted today overlaps roughly with my period from 1949–1950, when in addition to abstraction, I strove to interest artists more in spectators. In recent days I amused myself by sending newsrooms my "revolutionary" writings with underlined passages and a note calling attention to the date of my essays.[34]

This letter is from the same time as those of Lukeš to the academic Ivan Málek; the contents of these communications —to wit, the evaluation of the artist's own work up until then and references to previous activities that had suddenly become topical—are basically of a piece. Both addressed officialdom with bitter rebukes, while calling attention to their own priority.

Lukeš even believed that Professor Stuchlík, perhaps the only person who took him seriously, would become rich and famous on the strength of Lukeš's name and story. Boudník suffered from the impression that the Laterna Magika theatre owed its success to him because he had conceived its principles on his own years earlier, and the international renown of the Prague theatre was a heavy load for him to bear. Boudník also took a critical stance toward some of Knížák's activities. He thought the younger artist superficial and lacking a creative edge and regarded his works as nothing but pranks, ways of drawing attention to himself; he felt Knížák's work stood in need of a greater degree of personal responsibility. Also significant was Knížák's alleged irreverence with regard to values and principles Boudník himself had formulated.[35] Milan Knížák, too, felt that he was underappreciated and even that he had been robbed of his due. In the 1980s he considered himself the inventor of punk fashion, which in his view had been ripped off by rebellious young people from the West.[36] None of the three artists desired to fall in with the mainstream art community, and they all set great store by their own originality and exceptionality and defended it with a jealous intensity.

Also characteristic of all three were their later interpretations of their own work, which at times bordered on mystification. Lukeš cast the whole story of Paxism—largely made up, in all likelihood—as the grandiose tragicomic tale of how he had foundered on the shores of life. Boudník, too, nonchalantly made unverifiable claims involving the mailing of thousands of letters and the numbers of people who saw his demonstrations, as well as their reactions.[37] The same appears to be true of Knížák, who later embellished surviving documents relating to his Keeping Together Manifestation with footnotes and supplementary information.

Judging the psychological health of artists is outside the purview of the art historian; nonetheless, it is an art historian's responsibility to note any psychiatric or psychological circumstances that might have a bearing on an artist's work. Graphomania and recipes for world peace are symptoms of psychological instability—hence the need for this digression. Jan Lukeš really did suffer from mental illness and was declared legally insane. Vladimír Boudník also received psychiatric treatment for many years. We have no reason to question the psychological health of Milan Knížák, however. He did without psychological care at a time when it might have spared him, at least partially, from state repression.[38]

Last, but not least, the cases of Lukeš, Boudník, and Knížák all involve the practice of unhinged letter writing. Employees of the Office of the President of the Republic, the Patent Office, or the Academy of Sciences deal with such letters on a regular basis. Their often quite indefatigable authors demand recognition for their inventions, warn the human race against the threat of flying saucers, and propose recipes for universal bliss. Even though such letters for the most part are ignored, their authors can be quite persistent. The very institution of the Czechoslovak postal service, a traditional state organization with the stamp of Austro-Hungarian gravity, possibly played a seductive role as well. Putting letters into a mailbox was a bureaucratic act that was nonetheless anonymous. There was no risk of any immediate confrontation with recipients. Sending a letter set things in inexorable motion. It was possible for the most nonsensical of letters to become an official bureaucratic document—and with an official stamp, to boot.

The three cases involving unusual peace manifestos illustrate the historical mutability of the clichés that real artists are mad and that those who are mad can, under certain circumstances, become extraordinary artists. The Romantic period saw the emergence of the stereotype of the mad artist; madness was taken to be a virtue. "In any case, the Reason-Madness nexus constitutes for Western culture one of the dimensions of its originality; it already accompanied that culture long before Hieronymus Bosch, and will follow it long after Nietzsche and Artaud."[39] Let us note here that for a large portion of his life, Antonin Artaud, too, wrote various world figures open or private letters that flouted the rules of ordinary correspondence. In the 1920s he addressed, in the form of intentionally shocking letters, the Pope, the Dalai Lama, and rectors of universities, among others, that were eventually published in Surrealist reviews. It is unclear whether they were really delivered; it is quite certain, however, that Artaud's letters to Hitler from 1939 were sent off; he wrote them at a psychiatric clinic and challenged the recipients to safeguard world peace. Art history provides other examples of artists who were on the edge of normality; some of them even engaged themselves politically, with different degrees of success.[40] Nevertheless, we find very few really significant world artists who would take an interest in such peace manifestos.[41]

A manifesto is always against something, always charged and loud; it proclaims to the world not only the author's ideas but his or her existence and the particularity of his or her views on a state of affairs. Almost all manifestos are written in the plural, because they are meant to express the ideas not only of their authors but also of at least one potential reader, whom they call on to become engaged.

The significance of the art manifesto grew from the late 19th century on and probably reached its peak with the Futurist manifestos preceding World War I. The Symbolists published their proclamations and principles in art reviews; the first of Marinetti's Futurist manifestos appeared in the form of a paid advertisement on the front page of the French newspaper *Le Figaro* on February 20, 1909. It was not only the ideas in the manifesto—a rejection of tradition and the pronouncement of the apotheosis of the modern technological world—that were influential but also its declarative form and its publication in a familiar and widely read newspaper. Vladimír Boudník was already acquainted with the Futurist manifestos in the late 1940s. It is not hard to imagine that had it been technically and financially possible, he would have published his Explosionist manifestos himself as newspaper advertisements. Even the Aktual group, which spurned all conventions, expressed itself through manifestos, despite their ostensibly being an outdated form of artistic proclamation, and allowed them to be published in an official journal such as *Tvář* [Face]. They were essentially the last manifestos of their kind in the Czech lands, the terminal offshoots of interwar avant-garde art.

For modernism, formulating and disseminating the views of particular movements and artists is just as important as the artists creating their own artworks, for the aim is nothing less than the transformation of life—or, in the words of Giacomo Balla, "reconstructing the universe." In contrast to the interwar avant-garde, artists after World War II had murky visions of what such a reconstruction would entail. Perhaps this is why they tended to make general proclamations calling on individuals to experience fuller, more authentic lives or why they waged serious (or ironic) struggles for peace.

[1] Many European intellectuals found themselves in quite a schizophrenic predicament at the time. A piercing analysis of the contemporary situation in France is set out in Serge Guilbaut's "Postwar Painting Games: The Rough and the Slick," in *Reconstructing Modernism: Art in New York, Paris, and Montreal 1945–1964*, ed. Serge Guilbaut, Cambridge–London, MIT Press 1990, pp. 30–84.

[2] Jochen Schulte-Sass, "Foreword: Theory of Modernism versus Theory of the Avant-Garde," in Peter Bürger's *Theory of the Avant-Garde*, Minneapolis, University of Minnesota Press 1984, p. 11.

[3] Vladimír Borecký, *Zrcadlo obzvláštního*, Prague, Hynek 1999. See also Borecký's journal study "Záhadný pacient profesora Stuchlíka" [Professor Stuchík's Mysterious Patient] in *Technický magazín* [Technical Magazine] 28, 1985, no. 11, pp. 44–49, "Pandemie kosmofrenie" [A Pandemic of Cosmophrenia], in *Analogon*, 1996, no. 13, pp. 82–89, "Nevšední případ nevyléčitelné kosmofrénie" [The Extraordinary Case of Incurable Cosmophrenia], in *Revolver Revue*, 1999, no. 39, pp. 242–299, and others.

[4] To date, the following works by Lukeš have been published: *Co byl paxistický puč v Praze o vánocích 1945 aneb Osudy jednoho českého bojovníka za mír* [What Was the Paxist Putsch in Prague on Christmas 1945 or The Life Story of a Czech Crusader for Peace], Prague, Pražská imaginace 1991; *Z knižnice iškovské kultůry* [From the Library of Iškov Culture], Prague, Garamond 2000; Car Osten [= Jan Lukeš], *Dekadentův lós* [The Decadent's Draw], Brno, Petrov 1999; *Můj život v hudbě* [My Life in Music], Brno, Petrov 2003.

[5] The original letter is to be found as part of Lukeš's literary estate, preserved at the Museum of Czech Literature. The following excerpts are taken from the cited edition of Lukeš's *What Was the Paxist Putsch in Prague on Christmas 1945*.

[6] Ibid., p. 12.

[7] Ibid., p. 17.

[8] Note from 2017: At the time this text was written (in the summer of 2003), we could only speculate as to the true extent of the idiosyncratic peace movement and its organizational base, and the possibility that it was another instance of Lukeš's mischief could not be ruled out. Now, however, we are sure that Paxism really did exist. In 2014, the Security Services Archive of the Institute for the Study of Totalitarian Regimes discovered a file that demonstrates the extent of Lukeš's Paxism activities. The file contains the originals of various leaflets and letters distributed in 1945–1946 to both important personalities and random individuals. Paxism parodically combined elements of Communist, Christian, and national-revivalist propaganda, and the movement quickly attracted the interest of the authorities. According to the interrogation records, Lukeš began distributing the leaflets and letters in October 1945, sending them to at least 100 people, including cabinet members and the Soviet and American ambassadors. Jan Lukeš was identified by police as the sole author of the Paxism materials. After a brief investigation, he was hospitalized in a psychiatric clinic and eventually released for home care with his parents.

[9] Lukeš, *Můj život v hudbě* [My Life in Music], p. 59.

[10] Vladislav Merhaut, *Zápisky o Vladimíru Boudníkovi* [Notes on Vladimír Boudník], Prague, Revolver Revue 1997.

[11] Jiří Valoch, "Vladimír Boudník: Exhibition on the Artist's 60th Anniversary, Which He Did Not Live to See," in *Vladimír Boudník: Grafika* [Vladimír Boudník: Graphic Work], Brno, Dům umění města Brna [Brno House of Art] 1984, p. 1.

[12] *Vladimír Boudník. Mezi avantgardou a undergroundem* [Vladimír Boudník: Between the Avant-Garde and the Underground], ed. Zdeněk Primus, Prague, Gallery 2004.

[13] Vladimír Boudník, proclamation made on May 12, 1948.

[14] Vladimír Boudník, *Z korespondence I (1949–1956)* [From the Correspondence I (1949–1956)], Prague, Pražská imaginace 1994, p. 21.

[15] Vladimír Boudník, *Z korespondence II (1957–1968)* [From the Correspondence II (1957–1968)], Prague, Pražská imaginace 1994, p. 30.

[16] Jaroslav Rotbauer, "Vzpomínka na dva spolužáky" [Memories of Two Fellow Students], in *Revolver Revue*, 1995, no. 29, p. 125.

[17] Jan Koblasa also remembers a similar first meeting with Boudník; he was a recipient of one of his letters, and before becoming acquainted with Boudník and his work, he apparently attached no importance to them. In a note dated November 12, 1958, he writes, "went to see Boudník for the first time—before now I'd only known him from his letters, which he sent me before the wedding with Tekla—explosionist manifestos—extraordinary surprise—shock—beautiful abstract graphics!!!—he spoke excitedly into the night—." See Jan Koblasa, *Záznamy z let padesátých a šedesátých* [Notes from the 1950s and 1960s], Brno, Vetus Via 2002, p. 120.

[18] "If you should know, I undertook the peace manifestos and proposals for a mass peace movement—including the spreading of the idea of an improved movement in 1947–1948—anonymously or under a code name." Boudník, in a letter to Jiří Svoboda dated September 5, 1958, as cited in Boudník, *Z korespondence II (1957–1968)*, p. 23.

[19] Cf. Boudník, *Z korespondence I* and *II*.

[20] Boudník, *Z korespondence I (1949–1956)*, p. 17.

[21] "When he wrote different letters, he thought he would be locked up, he was constantly prepared for it, he always went around freshly washed, shaved, wearing clean socks, his things in order at home, even though he lacked space." Merhaut, *Zápisky o Vladimíru Boudníkovi* [Notes on Vladimír Boudník], p. 137.

[22] Vladimír Boudník, *Jedna sedmina* [One Seventh], as cited in *Pocta Vladimíru Boudníkovi* [In Honor of Vladimír Boudník], ed. Josef Hampl, Vladislav Merhaut, Ladislav Michálek, Prague, Přátelé Vladimíra Boudníka [Friends of Vladimír Boudník] 1974, p. 5.

[23] Boudník, *Z korespondence I (1949–1956)*, p. 63.

[24] As cited in the samizdat edition *Pocta Vladimíru Boudníkovi* [In Honor of Vladimír Boudník], ed. Vladislav Zadrobílek, Věra Boudníková, Prague 1988. Evidence that Boudník continued to devote himself to pacifism is a poem dated October 25, 1958: "Hiroshima is a warning // It should not happen / that above the clouds / ghosts of death should fly // It should not happen / that innocent people / should be turned into shadows / and that in a million years / walls should be transported into museums / where children will visit / with their teacher / who will speak / half as if about a fairy tale / that scientists believe / that on these walls unknown artists / using unknown techniques / created silhouettes."

[25] Merhaut, *Zápisky o Vladimíru Boudníkovi* [Notes on Vladimír Boudník], p. 126.

[26] Ibid., p. 264.

[27] *Affichisme* was an art movement associated with French New Realism. As early as 1949—that is, in parallel with Vladimír Boudník—its representatives were making images directly on poster-saturated surfaces. Later, they transferred the method to the studio, and their works became traditional gallery artifacts. Among the most well-known

affichistes were Jacques de la Villeglé, Raymond Hains, François Dufrêne, and Mimmo Rotella.

[28] "Purge the world of bourgeois sickness, 'intellectual,' professional & commercialized culture, PURGE the world of dead art, imitation, artificial art, abstract art, illusionistic art, mathematical art,—PURGE THE WORLD OF 'EUROPEANISM'! PROMOTE A REVOLUTIONARY FLOOD AND TIDE IN ART. Promote living art, anti-art, promote NON ART REALITY to be grasped by all peoples, not only critics, dilettantes and professionals. FUSE the cadres of cultural, social & political revolutionaries into united front & action." As cited in Hannah Higgins, *Fluxus Experience*, Berkeley–Los Angeles–London, University of California Press 2002, p. 76.

[29] As cited in Milan Knížák, *Akce, po kterých zbyla alespoň nějaká dokumentace, 1962–1995* [Actions That Left Behind at Least Some Documentation], Prague, Gallery 2000, p. 71.

[30] Jindřich Chalupecký, *Na hranicích umění* [On the Frontiers of Art], Prague, Prostor–Arkýř 1990, p. 95.

[31] See Knížák, *Akce, po kterých zbyla alespoň nějaká dokumentace, 1962–1995* [Actions That Left Behind at Least Some Documentation], p. 136.

[32] Milan Knížák, *Cestopisy* [Travelogues], Prague, Radost 1990, p. 141.

[33] Let us recall the titles of songs like "Zab pro mír" [Kill for Peace] or "Zastavte všechny války" [Stop All Wars] and compare the lyrics "trample flowers, destroy the earth" from the song "Against Hippies," with the first stanza of the song "Mrdej a neválči" [Fuck and Don't Go to War]: "Getting beaten up in the pub / catching your sweetheart sucking someone else's cock / committing suicide with triphenydyl // all that is better than war." See Milan Knížák, *Písně kapely Aktual* [Songs of the Aktual Group], Prague, Maťa 2003, p. 145, and others. Let us also recall that toward the end of 1964, The Fugs were forming in the circle of owners and customers of the alternative Peace Eye Bookstore in New York. Its members were avid peace activists. The Fugs's second, officially untitled album is commonly known under the title "Kill for Peace," based on the eponymous song from the album with the chorus "Kill, kill, kill for peace."

[34] Vladimír Boudník, in a letter to Jana Čížková dated May 6, 1959, in Boudník, *Z korespondence II (1957–1968)*, p. 26.

[35] Letter from Vladimír Boudník to Jindřich Chalupecký dated March 25, 1967, manuscript, private collection.

[36] "When someone asks you where Punk came from, say in the Czech Lands. In the 1960s. A large percentage of current trends (from '63–'65) are discovered 10 or 15 years late by world punks. (And not only them.) Wild rock that wasn't actually rock anymore, just as the Aktual group played it beginning in 1968, is repeated exactly in the newest music of the most underground Punk bands. It's repeated in such an exact form that it's hard to believe it arose spontaneously." Knížák, *Cestopisy* [Travelogues], p. 180.

[37] In this regard, the sober recollections of Zbyněk Fišer (Egon Bondy) of Boudník's street demonstrations, which he himself participated in, are demythologizing. See *Vladimír Boudník. Mezi avantgardou a undergroundem* [Vladimír Boudník: Between Avant-Garde and Underground], pp. 56–57.

[38] Knížák as an interesting case did not escape the notice of psychiatrist Stanislav Drvota, who was interested in the relationship between psychological difficulties and artistic creativity. He summarized the results of his many years of research in the book *Osobnost a tvorba* [Personality and Creativity], which was published in 1973 by the Avicenum publishing house. From today's perspective, Drvota's speculative conclusions are not as interesting as his case descriptions of Czech artists who were prominent in the 1960s.

[39] Michel Foucault, *Madness and Civilization: A History of Insanity in the Age of Reason*, London, Routledge Classics 2005, p. xiii.

[40] To name but one, Johannes Baader (1875–1956) was probably the most radical member of the Berlin Dadaist group. An artist a generation older than his other Dadaist friends, he considered himself, with no irony, to be Jesus Christ and was declared legally insane. In 1916 he sent Prince Wilhelm Friedrich a letter in which he demanded the immediate suspension of military battles on his authority as a "commander of a spiritual kingdom." In 1919 he managed to interrupt a meeting of the parliament of the Weimar Republic, where he demanded that power be handed over to him. In 1920 Baader set out, along with Richard Huelsenbeck and Raoul Hausmann, on a Dadaist lecture tour of Czechoslovakia; unexpectedly, however, his friends lost sight of him just before the Prague lecture. Due to Baader's unpredictable and quite deranged behavior, the Dadaists themselves eventually turned their backs on him.

[41] In addition to the cases I have already mentioned, I shall mention that of Öyvind Fahlström. In one of the 11 points in his 1966 manifesto titled *Take Care of the World*, he calls on humanity as a whole to disarm. See *Theories and Documents of Contemporary Art: A Sourcebook of Artists' Writings*, ed. Kristine Stiles, Peter Selz, Berkeley, University of California Press 1996, pp. 304–305.

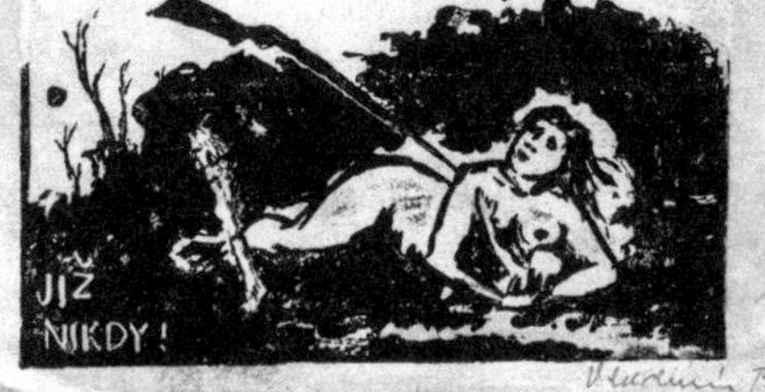

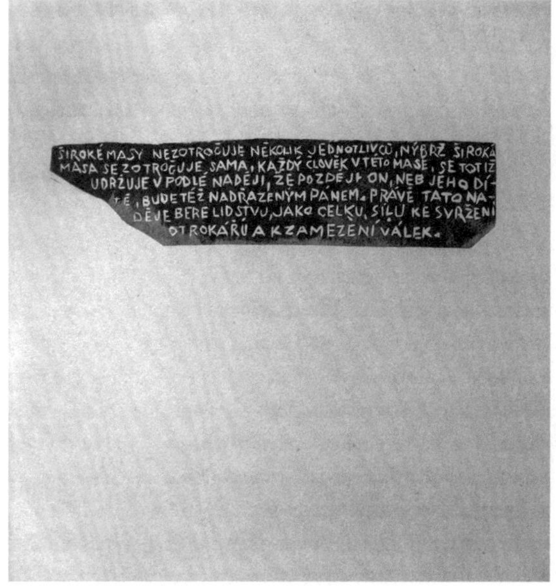

[ill. 2] Vladimír Boudník, *Appeal to Nations*, 1947
Linocut on paper, print dimensions 20 × 12.5 cm and 3.8 × 16 cm
Courtesy of Ztichlá Klika Gallery, Prague

The Fates of the Free Artists: Czechs and the Situationists

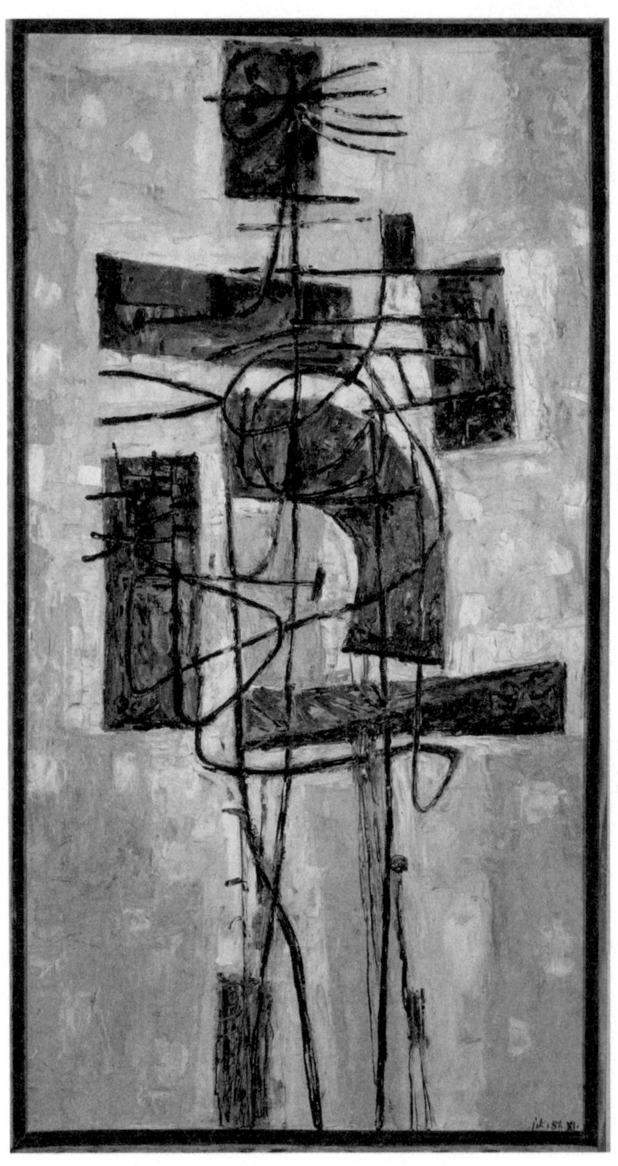

[ill. 1] Jan Kotík, *Benjamin, muž ze železa* [Benjamin, Man of Iron], 1956
Oil on canvas, 116 × 62 cm
Location unknown

I.

In September 1956, the First World Congress of Free Artists met in the Italian town of Alba. Representatives from several wellsprings of the European postwar avant-garde came together there, both old friends and artists who had never before met. A representative of the Letterist International arrived from France, and artists who had formerly been part of COBRA came as well. Upon its dissolution, some of them formed the Movement for an Imaginist Bauhaus, whose ideas were popularized in the Milanese journal *Eristica.* The organizers of the congress later claimed with pride that artists of eight nationalities had been present. However, the total number of participants hardly surpassed a dozen; the meeting itself was more like an informal gathering of friends than anything else. The significance of the gathering certainly did not lie in its international scope or its orderly organization. For art historians, of far more significance is that it was the first meeting of the artists and theorists who would go on to found the Situationist International less than a year later. The Situationist International has an alluring reputation as the most radical avant-garde of the 20th century. It left behind almost no artworks but rather theoretical declarations and manifestos influenced by Surrealism, Marxism, and far-left ideologies. The Situationists, like other related 20th-century avant-garde groups, did not want to change art but change life itself—to an unprecedented degree. They prefigured or influenced action art, utopian urbanism, new realism, Fluxus, and postmodernism, and their critiques of modern architecture, the mass media, and consumer society are in many respects still valid and appealing to this day.

The First World Congress of Free Artists left a written record in the form of a resolution signed, among others, by two artists from what was then Czechoslovakia: Jan Kotík and Pravoslav Rada. How did their names find their way onto such a resolution—particularly in 1956?

II.

Pravoslav Rada (1923–2011) belonged to a generation of artists whose lives were impacted by World War II. Until 1943 he studied at the school of stone sculpture in Hořice before transferring to the Academy of Arts, Architecture, and Design in Prague, which at the time did not yet have university status and therefore had remained open to students during the war. He studied sculpture and ceramics in Jan Lauda's sculpture workshop. After 1945 a new, robust generation of painters and sculptors came to the Academy. But Pravoslav Rada became increasingly drawn to ceramics, though his interest was far from merely artisanal. He appreciated its varied expressive resources and the possibilities it offered for working with surfaces and a wide chromatic range. He approached clay as a sculptor would. In 1947 Rada received a residency scholarship from the Danish government and spent half a year in the ceramics workshop of Nathalie Krebs at the Academy of Industrial Arts in Copenhagen. Scandinavian ceramics were well known across the world at the time; Danish designers had managed to fuse the demands of production and commerce with modern forms and theory of design. In Copenhagen, Rada rented a room in a house whose landlady also ran a nursery school. She knew that the father of one of the children at the nursery school was also an artist and mentioned the young Czechoslovak artist to him. His interest was piqued, and he met with Rada. The Danish artist's name was Asger Jorn.[1] The meeting probably took place sometime in early spring 1947. Within a few days they had established a friendship that lasted, albeit at a distance, until Jorn's death in 1973. In postwar Copenhagen they did not have much time for each other. Rada only spent six months in Denmark, several weeks of which he spent traveling through Scandinavia. In 1947 Jorn spent time in Normandy, Holland, and Belgium; in the second half of that year, he set off for the Tunisian island of Djerba to spend a few months there with his family. In 2003, after over half a century, Rada did not remember having visited Jorn's studio; he only knew his work from the period based on graphic art prints. As a farewell gift, Jorn had given Rada his book and a collection of lithographic prints, which Rada later donated to the National Gallery, Prague.

Jorn's friendship with Rada was hardly his only contact with Czechoslovak art. As early as May 21, 1947, he sent a letter to the Ra Group and invited it to take part in an art review that was prepared but never published. He corresponded with Ludvík Kundera, who years later remembered, "I heard from Asger Jorn, a painter but also a remarkable theorist and a connoisseur of folk art from around the globe. He quickly became our [our?—indeed, here Ra and *Blok* join forces] Scandinavian expert number one. We printed an article and a reproduction for him, and we had further plans."[2] In October 1947 an International Congress of Revolutionary Surrealists took place in Brussels , organized by the poet and Surrealist renegade Christian Dotremont. Alongside Jorn and other European artists, Josef Istler and Zdeněk Lorenc from Czechoslovakia also participated. Afterward, Lorenc recalled his unforgettable contact with Jorn in a text written for the catalogue to Jorn's 1995 Prague exhibition.[3]

After 1948 and the ensuing political and social transformations in Czechoslovakia, the opportunities for international cooperation quickly underwent a sea change. As late as 1948, the Brno revue *Blok* printed Jorn's and Dotremont's texts and reproductions; however, the promising relations between the Ra and COBRA were broken off due to the closing of the Eastern bloc's borders. As late as 1949, Istler was slated for inclusion in an exhibition of the COBRA group in Brussels and Amsterdam. Nonetheless, the organizers were only able to exhibit graphic prints that Istler had left in Brussels two years earlier during his trip to the congress. During the 1950s in Czechoslovakia, avant-garde artists were driven underground. Following the forced dissolution of the Ra Group, Istler forged closer ties to the Surrealist group around Karel Teige and later Vratislav Effenberger. Officialdom regarded the activities of the Surrealists as not only unwelcome, but categorically subversive.

During the period when the dictates of social realism held sway in Czechoslovakia, some avant-garde artists were able to work in the applied arts. The relationship between fine and applied arts was far too complicated in the early 1950s for us to see the gravitation of certain artists toward artistic crafts, design, or the organization of exhibitions as only an escape route from an oppressive sociopolitical situation. In the spirit of Bauhaus, the chief temptation was the possibility of influencing the tastes of the wider public. Pravoslav Rada had decided on ceramics long before the new circumstances made free artistic expression difficult and ultimately impossible. Even so, he was not spared hardships. The tableware he designed may have won him various awards, but the nationalized factories refused to produce it because of its unusual character; they saw no market for it. In addition to his industrial designs, Rada was able to carry out small-scale studio work, producing small animal figurines that recalled the stylized blown-glass animals that had brought fame to Jaroslav Brychta in the 1930s. Rada's figurines were expressively wild, and their stylized colors and forms were clearly modernist. His fish and cats were imbued with a peculiar sarcasm, acidity, and irony. In the 1950s, owing to the utility of ceramics, the display of works containing elements of modernist art was permitted. Working with textiles and typography offered similar opportunities.

During the prewar period, Rada had been introduced by his father, the painter Vlastimil Rada, to the stimulating and—in contrast to the Mánes Union of Fine Arts—tolerant atmosphere of the *Umělecká beseda* [Artistic Circle]. Its members included not only traditionalists such as Václav Rabas and Vojtěch Sedláček but also the modernists Josef Šíma and Jan Zrzavý. The last two large-scale exhibitions organized by the Artistic Circle before the war were *Staré umění na Slovensku* [Early Art in Slovakia] in 1937 and *Pražské baroko* [Prague Baroque] the following year. Both showcased first-rate art along with the work of often-anonymous folk artists and artisans. In the 1950s, socialist realism was the only acceptable normative aesthetic, which in the field of applied arts meant (in addition to the obligatory admiration for all things Soviet) the elevation and appropriation of folk art. This respect for folk art forms built on the interwar modernist tradition, which also sought inspiration in traditional folklore.

As early as the 1920s, Vlastimil Rada had been friends with the painter Pravoslav Kotík,[4] and in time Pravoslav Rada, too, met and became friends with Pravoslav Kotík's son, the painter Jan Kotík (1916–2002). Kotík was a member of Group 42, and when in 1948 its future direction was being decided, only he, along with Jindřich Chalupecký, took a firm stand against embracing socialist realism; after February 1948, Group 42 disbanded. But before that, Kotík had developed an interest in the practice and theory of the applied arts. In his case too, the interest was lifelong and not simply a way of making a virtue of necessity. Owing to his activities in the Communist resistance during World War II, Kotík worked for the Central Committee of the Communist Party of Czechoslovakia immediately after the war. Before long, however, he must have developed serious scruples about the political orientation of the day. Kotík abandoned his collaboration with the Communist Party in an original manner. He voluntarily enlisted for military service, which he had not been able to perform during the war, and found someone to take his place permanently in the party apparatus. After a few months of boot camp, he discovered the Center for Folk Art Production [Czech acronym, ÚLUV], an organization that functioned as an advisory and technical center for folk artists, and began working there as an organizer; at the time he also began writing an essay on the theory of industrial production. As a result of his position in the ÚLUV, he promoted his own design work, and in the 1950s, at a time when the dictates of socialist realism were at their most heavy-handed, he regularly worked with abstract designs.

Kotík was a Marxist for whom the Communist Party became life-threatening in the 1950s. Nevertheless, he did not give up on the idea of communism as a historically advanced and just way of governing society. Unlike many of his contemporaries, he had actually read Marx. From today's perspective, it is hard to imagine Kotík's plight at the time. Ideologically, he was a communist, but at the same time, among his communist friends, he criticized the totalitarian regime and urged a revision of its political trajectory. He was a member of the Central Committee of the Union of Czechoslovak Visual Artists, which upheld socialist realism, but at home he painted abstract paintings that clashed with the aesthetic norms prescribed by the Communists and thus had no hope of ever being exhibited. A freethinking communist and functionary, Kotík also found respect among visual artists who had retreated underground in the 1950s. In 1951 even the Surrealist group took him in; he participated in the creation of one of the collections from the *Znamení zvěrokruhu* [Signs of the Zodiac] cycle. Following difficulties with the police resulting from these contacts, Kotík left the ÚLUV and joined the editorial board of *Tvar* [Form], a journal devoted to the theory and practice of industrial design. This proved to be a good choice for both Kotík and Czech culture. *Tvar* was published by the Ministry of Interior Trade, so it could print views that censors at the Ministry of Culture would certainly have not let pass.

Rada and Kotík also concerned themselves with applied arts in a theoretical context. Pravoslav Rada's *Kniha o technikách keramiky* [Book of Ceramic Techniques] was published in June 1956. In addition to providing an overview of ceramic techniques, it offered an excursus into the history of ceramics worldwide. Soon thereafter it was published in several translations and is still in publication to this day. Jan Kotík wrote *Tradice a kultura československé výroby* [The Tradition and Culture of Czechoslovak Production]; in 1954 the book was published by the state-owned publishing house Orbis. Behind the rather stiff title lies a remarkable synthetic study of both historical and contemporary design in Czechoslovakia. At the same time that Asger Jorn was expressing admiration for Scandinavian folk art and Viking excavations, Jan Kotík, independently, but in a similar spirit, was including images of medieval ornaments, lace, painted coffers, and abstract textile patterns in his book. He also printed a passage that was de rigueur at the time on "Stalin's brilliant analysis of the economic problems of socialism,"[5] even though, among friends during the same period, he referred to Stalin as a mass murderer.[6]

The theory of design, industrial design, and production was not a substitute pursuit for Kotík; instead, it evoked the tradition of the leftist avant-garde, with its yearning for a better, more equitable, more practical, and more beautiful world order.[7] With hindsight, he characterized his political stance at that time—to a certain extent typical of an entire generation that had been shaped by leftist ideology—as follows:

> As a young man I was a confirmed Marxist. I may have refused to join the Communist Party in 1937 because I did not believe that the party discipline Stalin demanded could be combined with creative work, but in the resistance I got into the party automatically, as it were. There was another parallel development here, though: the more I became acquainted with contemporary science and developed an interest in philosophy, the clearer it became that mechanistic thought with its linear mono-causality did not correspond to the reality of the world or the state of existing science, either. Long before the war I had come to suspect that the term "dialectical realism" was actually a contradiction *in adiecto*. At the same time, though, the mishmash of preconceived ideas, the wreckage of old mythology, and the intellectual errors of the lowest variety that Nazism represented pushed us into an antagonistic, traditionally rationalist position. But after the war the dictatorship of the self-styled communist mouthpieces constantly manifested the unsustainability of the degenerated mechanistic rationalism of the 19th century.[8]

III.

The correspondence between Asger Jorn and Pravoslav Rada tapered off after 1948 but never completely died out. Jorn informed Rada of his exhibitions and sent him catalogues and journals. Pravoslav Rada, too, sent Jorn letters, to Denmark and Switzerland. A number of them have been preserved in the Jorn archive at the Silkeborg Museum.[9] The earliest, dating from December 1953, contains Rada's reaction to a letter from Jorn that had apparently reached him after a great delay. In it, he weighed the possibility of exchanging art journals (and thereby avoiding expensive subscriptions), informed Jorn that the journal *Blok* had gone out of existence several years earlier, and promised to reestablish the interrupted contact between Ludvík Kundera and Josef Istler.

The early 1950s were not the happiest of times for Jorn. He struggled to make ends meet and, in addition, fell seriously ill with tuberculosis, spending most of 1951–1953 in hospitals and sanatoriums. While on a health-related stay in Switzerland in 1953, he was contacted by the sculptor Max Bill, who tried to recruit him for the Hochschule für Gestaltung [School of Design] in Ulm, Germany, which he had founded in an effort to revive the interwar Bauhaus movement. Although Jorn had worked briefly for Le Corbusier in 1937–1938, in the early 1950s the idea of a school based on the principles of scientific functionalism was quite foreign to him. He spoke out against a rational-functional model of architecture and art, which he thought led to enslavement. Inspired by Johan Huizinga's book *Homo Ludens*, he wanted to see art become a game, a means for inducing general creativity. He was on guard against the danger of standardized thinking that might result from a mechanically applied functionalism. His organizer's disposition led him to contact various European artists and bring them together in the Movement for an Imaginist Bauhaus, as an intellectual counterweight to Bill's school in Ulm. It was not a traditional association of artists but a network of kindred creative souls.

In June 1954, Asger Jorn, with the help of Italian painter Enrico Baj, acquired a house in the town of Albisola on the Italian Riviera, where he lived intermittently until his death in 1973. Over the years, he and gardener Umberto Gambetta transformed it into a bizarre palace onto which he projected his ideas of a type of architecture that might spur the imagination. In the early 1950s Jorn's painting changed. Instead of making the neatly arranged and carefully fashioned compositions inspired by Paul Klee or by children's drawings, Jorn began wildly smearing paint on canvas. The results were half-abstract, half-figurative tableaux unshackled from the rules of any painterly style whatsoever. At Albisola, Jorn found himself among Mediterranean artisans and in their company began to work regularly in ceramics. He had already developed an interest in industrial design, and, in light of the potential for industrial production, he understood it as a way to effectively influence social life. As before, ceramics was not an escape from painting or an easier way to make money but, rather, an outlet for his need to make things with his hands, freed from the growing forms of automated production. Jorn's ceramic figures recall the shapeless and eccentric figures of his expressive paintings. In 1954 Jorn organized an international meeting of ceramists in Albisola. Participating were old friends from COBRA, such as Karel Appel and Corneille, the Italian avant-garde artists Enrico Baj and Lucio Fontana, and the Surrealist-inspired painters Roberto Matta and Wilfredo Lam. The results of the successful ceramics symposium were later exhibited in Turin.

In 1954 Jorn acquired his first copy of *Potlach*, a journal published in Paris by the Letterist International, which in 1952 had broken away from the Lettrist group founded in 1946, also in Paris. Its principal members were Gil J. Wolman, Michèle Bernstein, Guy Debord, and Ivan Chtcheglov. They had turned away from literary and film work toward a "living cultural revolution." They would organize a variety of games and situations that nonparticipating observers considered to be scandalous provocations: they called on their supporters to wander about town with painted faces and clothes, acquainting themselves with chance passers-by, picking fights and admiring subversive slogans on walls, such as the popular slogan "Never work."

Jorn was enthusiastic about the journal of the Letterist International and immediately wrote its chief editor, Guy Debord.[10] A friendship formed that would be solidified through mutual visits to Paris and Albisola and that would last, despite various disputes, for two decades.

Jorn also organized a ceramics symposium in 1955. Its participants were instructed to decorate ceramics created by children. As luck would have it, at a local bar named Lalla there was an exhibition of the work of the painters Giuseppe Pinot-Gallizio[11] and Piero Simondo,[12] who lived in Alba, a town about 60 kilometers away.

Jorn quickly befriended them; Pinot-Gallizio later described the meeting as sparking a fundamental turn in his approach to art and enabling him to move toward unbridled creativity. In September of that year, Jorn visited his new friends in Alba; at Pinot-Gallizio's studio in a closed monastery, they founded the Experimental Laboratory, a studio and center of avant-garde art. In contrast to traditional ways of creating artistic artifacts, they aimed to take advantage of industrial production and produce art on a mass scale, much like factory products. Here the idea of organizing a congress of free artists with the financial support of Pinot-Gallizio and through the network of Jorn's contacts was also born; eventually the idea acquired an international scope. Jorn traveled tirelessly between Alba, Albisola, Paris, and Silkeborg in Denmark, making contacts with like-minded artists and inviting them to Alba in September 1956.

IV.

Sometime in January 1956, Pravoslav Rada, Jan Kotík, and Josef Istler received a written invitation from Asger Jorn to attend a meeting of artists in Alba. In a letter dated February 7, 1956, Rada, thanking him for the invitation, reminded him that travel abroad for Czech artists was practically impossible; only official delegations could travel abroad. Nonetheless, in 1956, during the slow political thaw that followed the deaths of Joseph Stalin and Czech Communist leader Gottwald, travel to Western Europe began to seem like a real possibility. In spring 1956 Rada presented the invitation letter from Jorn to the relevant authorities and requested permission to travel abroad. Even though the meeting in Italy had prudently been termed a ceramics symposium, after several months Rada still had not been granted permission to travel. Kotík had more luck; at the last moment, he obtained a passport, and in September 1956 he set off for Italy. From the time of anti-Fascist resistance during World War II, he had known Vladimír Koucký, a member of the wartime Fourth Illegal Central Committee of the Communist Party of Czechoslovakia and later the chief editor of *Rudé právo* [Red Justice], the official newspaper of the Communist Party, as well as a longtime member of the Central Committee of the Communist Party of Czechoslovakia. Koucký's intercession was enough to secure Kotík free passage abroad.[13] Rada did not get permission until his father, the venerable artist Vlastimil Rada, interevened, and with a delay of several days, he set off in Kotík's wake. Istler, who had neither party cadre credentials nor influential relatives, remained in Prague.

The First World Congress of Free Artists took place at the town hall in Alba from September 2 to 8, 1956. In addition to the organizers Asger Jorn and Giuseppe Pinot-Gallizio, the participants in the congress were Gil J. Wolman, representing the Letterist International; painter Enrico Baj of the Milanese Nuclear Art movement (though he was expelled from the conference after the first day at the request of Wolman and Jorn); Constant Anton Nieuwenhuys, better known as Constant, and the musician Jacques Calonne (who had both been active with COBRA); and Piero Simondo, Ettore Sottsass Jr., and Elena Verrone, all of the Movement for an Imaginist Bauhaus. The Turinese artists Sandro Cherchi, Franco Garelli, Charles Estienne, and Klaus Fischer were also present as observers. Christian Dotremont, originally put forward as president of the congress, did not take part in the meeting due to poor health; in view of the tensions between Dotremont and the Letterist International, the congress participants considered this nothing but a diplomatic excuse. The artists and theorists present at the congress agreed on the need for a unified approach to ensure the transformation of art and the whole of society. At the same time, they were cognizant of the utopian character of their schemes. They wanted to achieve their large-scale goals not by means of isolated artistic works but with the help of a total urbanism—specifically, through goal-directed changes to the natural environment. At the close of the stormy proceedings, they signed a six-point statement, known as the Alba Platform, which was formulated to a large extent by the Letterist International representative Gil J. Wolman.

Another event was taking place at the same time as the Congress of Free Artists in Alba, a symposium and exhibition titled *Futurist Ceramics, 1925–1933*. Jorn and Pinot-Gallizio had made the acquaintance of a local Futurist veteran by the name of Farfa.[14] The exhibition of his ceramics took place at the local town hall, as did the congress.

Because of the delays in obtaining their authorizations to travel, Jan Kotík and Pravoslav Rada left Czechoslovakia so late that they arrived in Alba after the congress had already dispersed, with Rada arriving several days after Kotík. Most of the delegates had gone; however, Jorn and Pinot-Gallizio were waiting for them. The Czechs were at least able to add their signatures to the closing statement. In addition to Jorn, Constant also stayed in Alba after the congress ended and tried to implement his first utopian city planning project, which represented the principal means for the transformation of art and human society for the Lettrists, the Imaginist Bauhaus, and later the Situationists. In Alba, Constant devised a mobile architectural scheme for a small group of Romani living on land owned by Pinot-Gallizio. His model for the Gypsy encampment consisted of a circular building with a system of moving walls that made it possible to vary the dimensions of the space according to the needs of the community at any particular moment. Constant had been interested in architecture, at least theoretically, as early as 1953, when he wrote *For an Architecture of Situation*. In it, he called for an architecture that would impel a transformation of human life and gave voice to some of the ideas of Lettrist Ivan Chtcheglov.[15]

Rada and Kotík spent about two weeks in Alba. They worked at Pinot-Gallizio's Experimental Laboratory, creating both ceramic sculptures and ceramic items that were only fired after their departure. An exhibition of the ceramic products of the Experimental Laboratory apparently took place in the local cinema sometime in October. Represented were Constant, Pinot-Gallizio, Garelli, Jorn, Kotík, Rada, Simondo, and Wolman. Kotík had brought some of his drawings from Prague, and he and Jorn discovered, to their surprise, that even though they had never met before, their ideas on art were quite similar. Kotík also painted in Alba, as confirmed by a surviving photograph of the interior of the laboratory at Alba that shows an unfinished painting by Kotík on an easel.

Both Jorn and Kotík were staunch leftist intellectuals whose interests were hardly limited to art. They had fiery discussions, particularly late in the evenings when it was time to go to sleep. We can gain a sense of these discussions from the recollections Kotík noted forty years later: "Regarding paintings, there was talk not of composition but of structure. The idea of structure as a field of relationships was connected with an interest in topology, whose universality Jorn tried to convince me of over an entire afternoon at Albisola."[16]

After two weeks in Alba, it was time for the Czech artists to return home. Rada headed straight for Prague; Kotík would stay with friends in Vienna for another few days. He brought home a ceramic relief Jorn had dedicated to him in Italy.

V.

The year 1956 awakened hopes for the relaxation of political relations. Before leaving for Alba, Pravoslav Rada had seen information in a foreign ceramics journal about the International Ceramics Academy in Geneva. He convinced Otto Eckert, a former professor and chair of the applied arts branch of the Union of Czechoslovak Visual Artists, that it was imperative for them to affiliate themselves with the international institution. For Eckert, a high-ranking official, it was not difficult to arrange a trip abroad. So, just a few days after his return from Alba, Rada set off for Western Europe for a second time, this time to Geneva. Traveling along with Eckert and Rada was Emanuel Poche, then the director of the Museum of Decorative Arts. Upon their arrival in Switzerland, they learned of the Hungarians' attempt to overthrow their Communist government and of the ensuing invasion of the Red Army, which swiftly and bloodily suppressed the uprising. It became clear that the political thaw would have its limits. Nonetheless, there were attempts to quickly take advantage of the narrow opening in the state's cultural politics. As can be seen in a letter from the literary estate of painter Mikuláš Medek, in November 1956 Jan Kotík had already tried to organize a large exhibition with the participation of proscribed artists such as Istler, Medek, and Robert Piesen. However, nobody had yet managed to actually bring off such an open and freethinking exhibition.[17] Around this time, Jan Kotík met Vladimír Boudník, who until then had remained aloof from the Czech visual arts community. Kotík was one of the first to recognize the quality of Boudník's work and started to promote it both at home and abroad. Thanks to Kotík, Boudník was to have his first exhibition abroad, in Brussels in 1958.

From surviving correspondence, we learn that with the help of Jorn, Rada had planned an exhibition of his work in Albisola in 1957 and that Jorn wanted to come to Prague in the spring of 1957. Neither of these trips ever took place, however. Jan Kotík also exchanged several letters with Jorn after returning from Alba; four of Kotík's letters are preserved in Jorn's literary estate. In them, Kotík addressed him as his "Dear comrade." In March 1957 Kotík planned a trip to Paris and asked if his friend could arrange accommodations for him. Before he left, an important event occurred in Prague: on March 1, his exhibition at the Czech Writers Gallery opened—one that today is considered a landmark of Czech postwar art. Following a period of several years during which only recognized classics of Czech 19th-century art or works acceptable from the standpoint of socialist realism were granted permission to be exhibited, the first official exhibition of nonfigurative art took place. In it, Kotík showcased paintings he had begun to sketch out in Alba during the previous summer. The title of one of them, *Benjamin, Man of Iron*, had even been invented by Asger Jorn. The exhibition elicited extensive discussions in newspapers and cultural journals. Kotík's abstraction was harshly criticized in the pages of *Rudé právo*; in other periodicals, his nonfigurative form of expression was conscientiously defended. Kotík informed Jorn of the exhibition and the ensuing controversy. He ascribed a great importance to the debate, not only as a discussion concerning abstract art, but as a more general exchange of views on the role of art in social life.[18] After the opening of the exhibition, Kotík travelled to Paris for a short while, and in a letter dated June 8, 1957, we learn several interesting particulars—among them, that Jan Kotík met Guy Debord on the trip. It appears that the meeting was not exactly harmonious. "Do you think the words I said to Debord annoyed him?" asked Kotík of Jorn. "He is quite strict and rigid. His problem is he makes up for a lack of character with dogmatism." [ill. 1]

VI.

Jan Kotík spoke with Guy Debord during the period when the Situationist International was coming into being. After the successful conference at Alba in September, the Movement for an Imaginist Bauhaus was already organizing an exhibition in Turin in December 1956 that the Lettrists were to take part in. The artists from Czechoslovakia did not come this time. In Paris in May 1957, Debord published the Report on the Construction of Situations and on the International Situationist Tendency's Conditions of Organizing and Action, which gave an account of the preparations for the eventual fusion of the Imaginist Bauhaus and the Letterist International. It contained summaries and transcripts of the discussions held by Debord, Jorn, Constant, and Pinot-Gallizio during the previous years. The general thrust was that culture reflected and simultaneously influenced the organization of social life. In the future, aesthetic work would mainly be generated in the fields of architecture, poetry, and cinematography. It would be based on the creation of unusual life situations, the invention of varied and natural stimuli, and the building of a diversified natural environment. New games for adults, divested of competitiveness and tied to aspects of everyday life, would emerge. On July 28, 1957, in a small bar owned by a relative of Simondo in the Italian village of Cosio d'Arroscia, the Letterist International fused with the Movement for an Imaginist Bauhaus to form the Situationist International. The conference lasted about a week, during which most attendees were perpetually drunk. When the time came to vote on the creation of the common group, five were for and two against.[19]

Even though the Situationists later repudiated practical artistic activities, at the turn of the 1960s there were several painters and poets among them who attempted to translate Situationist theory into artistic practice. Giuseppe Pinot-Gallizio, who was interested in the intersections between free art, crafts, and industry, experimented with new materials and tried to substitute ceramic clay with synthetic resin, to no great success. Together with his son, Giors Melanotte, he made industrial paintings consisting of canvases up to 90 meters long covered with wild, expressive painting. The industrial painting was to be rolled up and sold by the meter in markets or shops; it could then be used to make clothing or to decorate interiors.

Among the most inspiring aesthetic ideas put forward by the Situationists was their theory of *détournement* and the related practice of *la dérive*, which with the advent of postmodernism would become one of the basic strategies used in contemporary art, even up to the current day.

In 1959 Asger Jorn worked on a series of paintings titled *Modifications*, which in their original form had their origins in the theory of *détournement.* He bought about 20 mediocre 19th-century realist paintings at a junk shop and then partially painted over the romantic landscapes or wistful portraits with his own figures—or simply spattered them with paint and exhibited them as his own works. He thus appropriated and radicalized traditional kitsch. At the time, however, the core members of the Situationist International began to turn away from art in search of some sort of "art forms that […] could not produce art but only a new kind of life." Although Jorn was later expelled from the Situationist International, he did not cease to provide financial support for it. The Situationists used the proceeds from the sale of Jorn's paintings to finance the printing of their publications.

VII.

Most of the time, the Czech artists Jan Kotík and Pravoslav Rada had far more prosaic worries. A competition was being held in Prague to design the Expo 58 pavilion in Brussels. The winning design by architects František Cubr, Josef Hrubý, and Zdeněk Pokorný,was thoroughly functionalist in spirit. Rada and Kotík were involved in the interior design. The pavilion represented a perfect synthesis of applied and fine arts, a *Gesamtkunstwerk* joined up with a common architectural form that still surprises viewers. Rada created a series of glass ornaments, and Kotík made a large-scale stained-glass window that gave the impression of being a three-dimensional, light-emanating abstract painting. Both traveled to Belgium in 1958 to install their works. Coincidentally, Asger Jorn also exhibited work at the exposition, although according to Rada they did not meet there.

When the Expo pavilion was brought to Stromovka Park in Prague in 1960, Rada's ceramic bird sculptures were arranged before it. These, along with Olbram Zoubek and Eva Kmentová's children's playground in Nad Královskou Oborou Street and a few sculptures by Vladimír Janoušek and Zdeněk Palcr, for example,[20] were among the first truly modern sculptures set in public spaces in postwar Czechoslovakia. They were neither tamely post-Cubist nor based on sublimated organic shapes in the style of Henry Moore. Their radical yet playful style was reminiscent of the sculptures of Joan Miró or Niki de Saint Phalle. However, Rada's birds did not remain at Stromovka for long—only 14 days, to be exact. The director of what was then known as the Julius Fučík Park of Culture and Recreation had received a letter from a group of outraged workers who deemed the sculptures a provocation and an affront to good taste. Alarmed, he ordered them removed.

In the late 1960s, Rada sought out Jorn during several opportunities he had to travel to Western Europe (to Paris and Italy), without success. They continued to correspond sporadically. Jorn sent Rada catalogues, Situationist materials, and the catalogue for his *Modifications* containing, among other things, reproductions of a famous painting of a girl with a moustache and the inscription "the avant-garde never gives up" painted in.

Kotík never saw Pinot-Gallizio—one of the other participants at the 1956 Alba conference—again, but he never forgot him or his work. Ten years after their only meeting, Kotík named Pinot-Gallizio alongside Jackson Pollock as an artist who, in his estimation, had influenced world art with the idea of an image that appears to be continuous beyond the edge of the format.[21] The friendship between Kotík and Jorn persisted; they continued to meet at various large European exhibitions they took part in. Kotík visited Paris at least three times in the 1960s, and Jorn presented him with one of his paintings.

Kotík fondly remembered how during one visit to Paris, Jorn's children asked him to draw them a pony. When he granted their wish, the children showed theirf ather the drawing, reproaching him for not being an artist because he could not draw like that. Even though Jorn began accumulating his first international successes in the 1960s, he was never well off. It was during one of Kotík's visits to Paris that Jorn found out that a collector from Copenhagen was interested in his paintings. Nonetheless, he did not have the money to make the trip to Denmark and show him his works. Even though Kotík had brought with him nothing more than the paltry sum the Czechoslovak system of foreign exchange allowed, he lent Jorn the money for the train. In Copenhagen the transaction was successful, and Jorn was ultimately able to repay the money.

Kotík remained in contact with Jorn until the mid-1960s and followed the activities of the Situationist International, at least from a distance. When the Venice Biennale took place in 1964, he tried to organize a meeting between artist and poet Ladislav Novák—who was interested in the movement—and its members, particularly Guy Debord,[22] but in the end they never met. In 1965 Rada and Kotík, in part under the influence of Jorn's exhibition at the Van Loo Gallery in Munich, were inspired to organize an exhibition for Jorn in Prague and wrote to him several times to this effect. The exhibition was to be based on works from the collections of Rada, Kotík, and Istler. Kotík wrote that art historian Jiří Padrta was interested in Jorn's work and wanted to write a study for the journal *Výtvarné umění* [Visual Arts] on the prospective exhibition. Padrta was interested primarily in Jorn's theoretical work, and Kotík provided him with all the written materials he had acquired from Jorn over the years. Jorn's health worsened in the late 1960s. Having closed himself off increasingly from his surroundings, he did not respond to the offer of an exhibition in Prague. Similarly, he did not take part in the celebrated ceramics symposia that took place at Bechyně, despite several invitations from Rada. Much of his personal correspondence, including a number of the letters Rada and Kotík had written him in the late 1960s, remained unopened until the end of his life.

VIII.

Certain of the Situationist International's ideas came back to life during the 1968 student protests in Paris. Nonetheless, this did not save the movement, led as it was by doctrinaire Guy Debord. The group had fallen apart quietly in the early 1970s. The Situationist critique of the media and its rebellion against capitalist society were revived at the turn of the 1980s. Malcolm McLaren, the music producer behind the media success of the Sex Pistols, both admired and drew inspiration from Situationism. More generally, the fashion, typography, and poses of the punk movement had been prefigured by Situationism.

From a commercial standpoint, the most successful participant of the Alba congress would be the designer Ettore Sottsass Jr., a short-term fellow traveler of the Situationists who was able to transform the coffee-shop talk of revolution into commercially viable products. His designs of office interiors enabling each worker to create his or her own workspace out of modular and mobile furniture according to the needs of the moment were directly based on Situationist architectural theory. Sottsass found success with investors largely by virtue of the claim that workers would be more productive in such changing and playful environments. His postmodern furniture from the 1980s had a sculptural quality to it—and was priced accordingly.

The two Czech artists are hard to fit into such a varied biographical mosaic. They found themselves at the Congress of Free Artists mainly as friends of Jorn from a time when it had still been possible to travel and make international contacts. Rada never deepened his interest in art theory, devoting himself to making ceramics and organizing international gatherings of ceramicists instead. He became a world-renowned ceramicist, repeating the success he had garnered in Brussels by creating a set of large ceramic sculptures for the roof of the Czechoslovak pavilion in Montreal world exhibition in 1967. However, during normalization in Czechoslovakia, such assignments dwindled. It is ironic that the work he considered his best, the 1974 decoration of the atrium of the Koospol Building in Prague, met its fate with the advent of freedom in 1989, when a new owner arrived and renovated the atrium, ridding it of its ceramic decorations.

In contrast, theoretical thinking was an integral part of Jan Kotík's creative work. In his texts, we often find passages that the Situationists could in all likelihood have adopted as their own.[23] However, despite these parallels, Kotík would have vehemently spurned the Situationist label. In view of the "experiments" Czechoslovak society as a whole had been subjected to after 1948, the rhetoric of the Situationists probably seemed both dangerous and rather puerile. Radical talk of vital transformation sounded different in France than in Czechoslovakia, where over several years the status of individuals in society, the ownership of the means of production, and the working conditions of artists changed profoundly. "Creating and living differently," the old avant-garde slogan, which rolled off the tongues of leftist Western European intellectuals, could in Czechoslovakia only be pronounced with an ominous question mark at the end.

In 1968 Kotík emigrated from Communist Czechoslovakia[24]; nevertheless, he remained a confirmed leftist intellectual until his death in 2002. Years later, in an undated note, he summarized his stance toward the figures of the Situationist International: "All of them were revolutionaries. However, most of them fell out with political revolutionaries. Sooner or later. Debord thought of himself as a Trotskyist. Jorn, probably based on his experience in the Danish resistance, thought it was enough to be radically left-wing. The idea of personal freedom as a prerequisite for the development of creativity, and thereby of self-construction and self-actualization, stemmed from surrealism and was thus very close to existentialism: but chic Saint-Germain-des-Prés was quite suspect for the people of COBRA—they did not belong there."[25] Similarly, Kotík did not belong among the idealistic radicals who populated the studiously unkempt cafés. He had had his own experience with efforts to steer human society toward a brighter future.

Moreover, art in Western Europe and in Czechoslovakia had long been developing under different conditions. As early as 1957, Jan Kotík described in one of his letters to Asger Jorn the difficulty while traveling abroad of explaining events in the Czech art scene and of defending the values people espoused at home. He did not blame the difficulties solely on the political situation during the 1950s, which distorted art and thinking about art. He thought they had already been noticeable in the specific character of the interwar avant-garde, which had ignored abstract artists like Kandinsky and Mondrian and had instead developed under the "dictatorship of Picassism and Dalíism." Kotík put it concisely when he said that in Czechoslovakia there had always been prejudices against the "non-literary imagination," which made a flourishing such as the one experienced by modernist abstract art in Western Europe, and particularly in the United States, unlikely if not impossible. Postwar artists in Czechoslovakia devoted their energies to struggling against the anti-modernist reaction in the form of socialist realism and tried tardily to take up the formal charge of the avant-garde abroad. For many of them the relationship between the modern artist and society had remained an open and perpetually unresolved affair.

Situationism did not find fertile ground in the Czechoslovak reality of the 1950s and 1960s, not because its proponents had to work underground during the harsh totalitarian years but simply because refusing to fulfill work obligations would have exposed them to punishment. Despite the adverse conditions, there were several nonconformist movements, such as a Surrealist group and an association united around samizdat publishing ventures such as Egon Bondy and Ivo Vodseďálek's *Půlnoc* [Midnight]. Individual artists also proposed alternatives to the official aesthetic line. Most of them, like Vladimír Boudník, were artists on the social fringes who contended with an inability to address a wider public. A radical-left avant-garde could not take root in Czechoslovakia at the time, chiefly because it did not have a programmatic approach. Both the interwar avant-garde and the Situationist movement grew out of a critique of the capitalist system and a communist-influenced vision of how to change that system. Although a communist utopia did not emerge in Czechoslovakia after 1948, capitalism was effectively dismantled. With the advent of totalitarianism, the avant-garde in the prewar sense ceased to exist, and there was nothing to take its place.

[1] Asger Jorn (1914–1973), the most important Danish artist of the 20th century, led a nomadic life divorced from the usual social conventions. He was an untiring organizer in the sphere of European avant-garde art. In 1946 he met Constant Nieuwenhuys, a Dutch painter and architect (later known simply as Constant), who became one of the most thought-provoking artists in the Situationist International circle. In 1947 Jorn came into contact with the Belgian Revolutionary Surrealist Group founded by poet Christian Dotremont (1922–1979). Jorn became the spiritual father of the COBRA group (1948–1951), which was officially established in November 1948 and informally grouped together about 50 artists from 10 countries, including Czechoslovakia. COBRA arose from the Surrealist critique of modern civilization, which it saw as repressing the creative forces of both individuals and society. Its members rejected the dogmatic doctrines of socialist realism and abstract art and advocated expressive art influenced by folklore and the artistic expressions of children.

[2] Ludvík Kundera, "Ra memoáry" [Ra Memoirs] in *Skupina Ra* [The Ra Group], Prague, GHMP 1988, pp. 50–51.

[3] Zdeněk Lorenc, "Věci doličné o Cobře, Asgeru Jornovi, revolučním surrealismu a mnohém jiném" [Exhibits concerning COBRA, Asger Jorn, Revolutionary Surrealism, and Much More], in *Asger Jorn. Grafické dílo* [Asger Jorn: Graphic Work], Prague, Národní galerie [National Gallery] 1995.

[4] A reminiscence from the time has survived, according to which Pravoslav Kotík and Vlastimil Rada went to an exhibition by Kurt Schwitters in Dresden in 1923. His collages and assemblages excited them so much that both artists started spontaneously doing somersaults in the gallery. See Marcela Pánková, *Pravoslav Kotík 1889–1970*, Prague, Národní galerie [National Gallery] 1991, p. 70.

[5] Jan Kotík, *Tradice a kultura československé výroby* [The Tradition and Culture of Czechoslovak Production], Prague, Orbis 1954, p. 96.

[6] Ruth Kotíková explained the origins of the passage in question in a letter dated January 24, 2005: "The sentence on Stalin stuck in Kotík's throat like a fishbone. It was like this: Kotík wrote the book and agreed with Orbis that they would publish it. He submitted the text and the illustrations, and to his great surprise he found out that he had to add what Kotík called a 'libation to the deity.' He didn't say no, but he knew he couldn't write it. He met Karel Hetteš (a glassmaker and editor, he was secretary to the minister of interior trade for a while) and told him what had happened and that he absolutely couldn't write it. Hetteš just laughed and asked him how long it had to be. He brought it the following day. It was a solution, but Kotík always commented on it with the words: 'But I figure as its author.'"

[7] Kotík was interested in theoretical issues concerning the applied arts his whole life. This is evident not only in his books and articles from the 1950s and 1960s but also in his lectures for the "second Bauhaus," the Hochschule für Gestaltung in Ulm, written after he had emigrated to Germany in the 1970s. In them, leaning on Marxist philosophy, he deals with the theory of production and the role of industrial design. See more in Jan Kotík's *Tři přednášky o užitné hodnotě, výrobě a návrhu* [Three Lectures on Applied Values, Production, and Design], Prague, Silikátový svaz [Silicate Union] 2003.

[8] Jan Kotík, in a written response dated January 4, 1986, to questions posed by Bedřich Utitz for a Czech broadcast of the Deutschlandfunk. The manuscript belongs to Ruth Kotíková.

[9] The letters in question are a series of 12 that Pravoslav Rada wrote to Asger Jorn in 1953–1971. The Jorn Archive at the Silkeborg Kunstmuseum also houses five of Jan Kotík's letters and one of Jorn's letters to Rada. Through the friendship between the Czechoslovak artists and Jorn, the museum's art collections acquired 6 etchings and watercolors by Kotík made between 1956 and 1960, 3 lithographs by Rada made between 1968 and 1972, and 31 graphic works by Josef Istler made between 1941 and 1968. The Kunstmuseum organized a solo exhibition for Istler in 1987.

[10] Guy Debord (1931–1994) was a poet, writer, filmmaker, and above all a theorist of modern culture and society. He was a member of the Lettrist group and the Letterist International. His critique of capitalist society was shaped by Marxist ideas. In 1957 he was present at the creation of the Situationist International and soon occupied its leading position. Debord's principal theoretical work was the book *The Society of the Spectacle* (1967). He committed suicide in 1994.

[11] Giuseppe Pinot-Gallizio (1902–1964) studied pharmacology. He was an amateur archaeologist, ethnologist, producer of food essences and caramels, chemist, anti-Fascist partisan, factory owner, leftist politician and, above all, an eccentric artistic personality.

[12] Piero Simondo (b. 1928), painter and editor of the journal *Eristica*. Along with his wife, Elena Verrone, he was a founding member of the Situationist International in 1957; however, he was expelled not quite half a year later. In the 1970s he tried to establish various experimental art associations; in 1972–1996 he was part of the teaching faculty of the University of Turin. In 1997 he prepared a publication on the First World Congress of Free Artists at Alba. (*Una Mostra. Jorn in Italia. Gli Anni Del Bauhaus Immaginista 1954–57*, ed. Sandro Ricaldone, Moncalieri, Edizioni d'Arte Fratelli Pozzo 1996.)

[13] Thanks are due to Pavla Jerusalemová for this information.

[14] Farfa's real name was Vittorio Osvaldo Tomassini (1881–1964).

[15] Constant's thinking on utopian architecture and later on Situationist architectural theory was inspired by *City*, a science-fiction novel by Clifford Simak. See Henri Lefèbvre in conversation with Kristin Ross in *October*, 1997, no. 79, Winter, p. 75. In it, we read a description of a future in which there will be no need to work. For a society freed from work, suddenly the central question becomes what to do with free time.

[16] From an undated manuscript note by Jan Kotík in the possession of Ruth Kotíková.

[17] See Mikuláš Medek, *Texty* [Texts], Prague, Torst 1995, pp. 398–399.

[18] In addition to this general discussion, Kotík's exhibition might have given rise in many artists to a rather disturbing settling of accounts with their own pasts. Ruth Kotíková wrote on January 24, 2005: "People asked how it was that so many artists and even former members of Group 42 could have come unstuck after 1948, when there was evidence that even under duress it was possible to paint otherwise than in the spirit of socialist realism."

[19] The Situationist International existed officially from 1957 to 1972, publishing the journal *Internationale situationiste*. From 1962 on, its members abandoned art and began devoting themselves solely to theory, propaganda, and agitation. The group, led autocratically by Guy Debord, became famous for the frequent expulsion of its members.

[20] Olbram Zoubek ascribes the greater share of the authorship of the playground to Eva Kmentová. A considerable portion of it has been preserved and was restored—though not in a completely appropriate manner—in 2003.

[21] Jan Kotík, "Pohled zpátky" [A Backward View], in *Výtvarná práce* [Work in the Visual Arts] 14, no. 2, 1966, p. 4; printed

in České umění 1938–*1989: Programy, kritické texty, dokumenty* [Czech Art 1938–1989: Programs, Critical texts, and documents], ed. Jiří Ševčík, Pavlína Morganová, Dagmar Dušková, Prague, Academia 2001, p. 287.

[22] This is stated in a letter by Jan Kotík dated May 16, 1964, housed today in the Jorn estate at the Silkeborg Museum.

[23] "It almost seems as if interpersonal relations in all their forms […] were dangerous. It seems as if the only legitimate relationship people could have was with institutions, with offices. The only things that are 'reasonable' are reasons of state. Society is interchanged with the state, and whatever does not belong in politics or serve toward the accumulation of capital is considered to be private nonsense." See Jan Kotík, *Tři přednášky o užitné hodnotě, výrobě a návrhu* [Three Lectures on Applied Values, Production and Design], Prague, Silikátový svaz [Silicate Union] 2003, pp. 46–47.

[24] "I went abroad in the first place because I was convinced that neither psychologically nor physically would I be able to relive the state I had experienced once before in 1939–1945 and then again in 1949–1958." See chapter 1, note 6.

[25] From an undated manuscript note in the estate of Jan Kotík.

Eastern and Western Cubes: Minimalism in Dispute

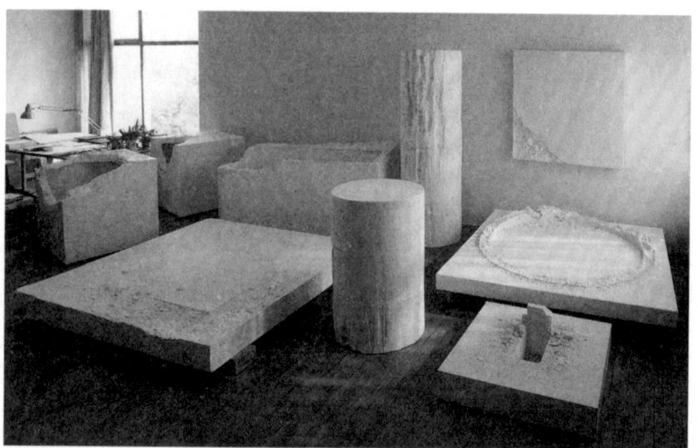

[ill. 1] Hugo Demartini, artist's studio, 1980s
Courtesy of the artist's estate

I.

In a photograph of Hugo Demartini's studio from the mid-1980s we observe something like a minimalist ruin—a cluster of white cubes reminiscent of the sculptures of David Smith or Robert Morris that look as though they have suffered violence from an unknown attacker. They have battered edges and punched-through openings. We cannot say when the attack took place, but the scarred white cubes seem almost like articles on exhibit in a historical museum, where a degree of wear and tear would count as a sign of age and authenticity. These modernist ruins are not simply a sort of formal exercise but rather the recollection of an avant-garde that by the 1980s was little more than a nostalgic memory.

We can even look inside Demartini's cubes. They are visibly hollow, and we can gauge the thickness of their walls.

There is only empty space inside; as a result we do not perceive them as mere abstract surfaces. We might wonder whether they had served to conceal a message or contain something that escaped at some point, as if from Pandora's box.

Minimalist sculpture—at least as it evolved in the United States—represented the peak of modernism; after this peak, modernism was ripe for a necessary revision. In essence, there was a reaction to the formalist and developmental theory of Clement Greenberg, who never embraced minimalist artworks because he did not consider them to have aesthetic value. What minimalists created did not bring him aesthetic gratification. Minimalist sculpture tried to refine the essence of sculptural expressive means by drastically reducing sculptural forms, which meant abandoning any literary or metaphorical contents, among other things. Literature and theater are for telling stories; minimalist sculptures exert their influence through nothing but their shapes, volumes, and interrelationships. They have no content; they consist only of forms in space. Most of the time they are produced with an emphasis on precision and meticulousness, and thus it is difficult to tell when they were made. After all, their raison d'être is to manifest an abstract idea on the development of sculptural forms, and idea-based concepts cannot exhibit any external traces of aging. Minimalists sought to ensure that their works would always look the same as they did at the moment they received their finishing touches. To their dismay, though, the materials used in their sculptures inevitably began to age, and once-polished surfaces became covered with blemishes.

Even though Demartini's cubes are empty, we can find content in their inner spaces: they are expressive and metaphorical—even eloquent. From the perspective of American minimalism, they may be unacceptable. But does that make them unsuccessful works of art? [ill. 1]

After the fall of the Iron Curtain, most Eastern European countries were faced with the task of reinterpreting—or, on an official level, interpreting for the first time—their own history, including art history. The traditional art-historical model studies the spread of formal innovations in time and space and follows the ways they evolve and are modified. In particular, modern art is often presented as a kind of Darwinist evolutionary system in which it is hard to concentrate on isolated species without, at the same time, investigating the entire evolutionary lineage. Given the isolation of Eastern European art from the main "continent" of modernist evolution, unique conditions, like those of a remote archipelago, developed in the former Eastern Bloc, where artists had to fend for themselves, lacking opportunities to regularly exchange ideas or present their work at international exhibitions. Within the archipelago, the situation was not universally seen as tragic; there were voices to be found that saw the isolation in a positive light, as an opportunity to create different, better art. In 1980 Jindřich Chalupecký wrote:

> It is surprising that this state of affairs [international isolation] is what became the stimulus for such remarkable development. Whereas elsewhere in the world modern art was providing modern artists with opportunities for success—that is, for fame and fortune—here artists could not count on success, or at least not success of that sort; and whereas elsewhere artists adapted their work to the conditions for such success, artists here did not even have anything to adapt to. And so, whereas in the rest of the world a sort of standard modernity took hold—mostly under the influence of new North American art, which, if judged by its consequences, might quite justifiably be termed a "new academism"—here modern artists remained free within their studios. They answered to no one but themselves or to the inexorability that had led them to art.[1]

Who knows if this stance was just an expression of the desperation of the day or of Chalupecký's leanings toward art as an aesthetic, semireligious activity firmly anchored in daily life—a context in which international exchanges played only a negligible role, if any at all.

However, others—not only Eastern European artists and art historians—saw the isolation as a handicap, and still do to this day. For instance, German art historian Hans Belting writes:

> In this part of the world modernism soon became an unofficial culture and, being an underground movement, had no access to the public. The loss of modernism was particularly traumatic for those countries for whom it served as a gateway to European culture (and Western art history) because their domestic art, if there was any worth discussing at all, had been understood as a product of Western colonization […] Eastern European art viewed in retrospect was, compared with the art of the West, delayed most of the time; on another level of development it served a different social role arising out of its historical lack of contact with Western modernism. It could always vindicate itself by arguing that it opposed official state art and thus avoided the permanent crisis of modernism, remaining in a state of innocence.[2]

Views similar to those of Hans Belting, whose books on the end of art history have been quite well received in the Czech Republic, sound distinctly arrogant to most Eastern Europeans. Why is that?

In 1989 the isolated archipelago was suddenly rejoined to the continent of the world. In the West, a series of exhibitions were held to showcase this heretofore unsurveyed territory. To the surprise of both sides, it turned out that not only had obsolete art forms been preserved in the East with a remarkable degree of authenticity, but new forms reminiscent of the Continental ones had also developed independently. Exhibitions aimed at a Western public and mostly organized by Western curators presented Eastern European art as part of a narrative that paralleled that of Western modernism. In Eastern Europe the history of postwar modernism had not yet been written, and there was little choice but to use terms and categories originating in the West to describe and analyze it. This approach probably caused the greatest confusion in the case of the application of the theory of American minimalism to Eastern European sculptural forms reminiscent of minimalism. We find similar cubes on both sides of the Iron Curtain. Is it nothing but a coincidence brought about by similar circumstances? Would the archipelago cubes withstand new mutations and maintain their specific traits under the new conditions?

Would they survive on the continent, and vice versa? Could the cubes enrich each other? To what extent were the phenomena really similar in the first place?

For artists and art historians from the East, it is not easy to understand American minimalism. In Eastern Bloc countries, independent culture had a political subtext, even if that subtext was merely opposition to the official art, as Belting noted above. Art without content or message was almost unimaginable in the East. For American minimalists, on the other hand, the Eastern European "minimalism with emotions" was objectionable. They thought it antediluvian and regarded it with mistrust.

There have been few attempts to write the history of modern art in Eastern Europe using categories other than those that arose in connection with the development of Western art; in the future such attempts may, in hindsight, seem like quixotic ventures.[3] Nonetheless, they deserve our attention. Why not risk disapproval and attempt something similar in the Czech Republic? Such a pursuit should not be limited to a simplified, nationalist-tinged search for Czech particularities. Instead, it should be an effort to define the space of a particular identity, which is, especially in Eastern Europe, complex and variable. The aim of the analyses that follow is quite specifically to show how Czech art is different and distinctive, which may, in the end, link it to certain forms of Western art, and American minimalism in particular.

II.

At first glance it seems that Stanislav Kolíbal's *Labil* [Labile] (1964) and *Jedno podpírá druhé* [One Supports the Other] (1965) invite comparison with Richard Serra's *One Ton Prop (House of Cards)* (1969). The principle behind the pieces and their execution are almost identical. Nevertheless, each comes out of a different tradition; they emerged in different contexts and, despite apparent outward similarities, show themselves to be distinct upon closer examination.

In the first place, there is the age difference between the artists. Serra is 14 years younger than Kolíbal. Moreover, their careers have followed different trajectories: whereas Serra's interest in experimental forms dates back to his early artistic career, in the late 1960s—among his first works were installations with live pigeons and a hare—by the same time, Kolíbal had already spent a decade doing figural sculpture that harkened back to the interwar avant-garde. Kolíbal gave up figures in connection with his architectural work; in his own words, for a long time he would distinguish between similar projects and free-form art and would hesitate to integrate pure geometry into his sculptural work. He was concerned about excessive decorativeness, however. It was with the help of the motif of lability—defined as a ready tendency toward, or capability for, change—with which he "expressed the being"[4] or feeling of something, that he overcame those worries. His breakthrough work came in 1964. Once he gave up figures, Kolíbal began assembling his works using several parts. This articulation imbued them with the theme of time. We apprehend them as a grouping of individual elements; each piece captures the state of things as selected by the artist and frozen in time (e.g., *Table*, 1965; *Target*, 1965), which might change in the future. Kolíbal's primary material remained plaster; if he had had the opportunity, he would have cast his works in metal.

In the 1960s American avant-garde sculptors were trying to unencumber their discipline from everything they thought superfluous, including symbolic content. Minimalists became increasingly aware of the space where their work would be exhibited; they cast aside pedestals, and the artwork itself could not even be considered without taking into account the surrounding spatial field in which the interaction between the work and the viewer took place. In other words, even the specific room where the work was being exhibited became part of it. This conception of the sculptural work meant that it could not be fixed and transported—it had to be installed afresh every time, in view of the conditions specific to the location. What was at stake was not simply a formal transformation of the manner in which an artwork was exhibited—using a new picture frame, for example—but one of the definitions of minimalism.

From this perspective, the installation of Kolíbal's first solo exhibition at Nová síň in Prague in 1967 was not minimalist: a relatively large number of works, including two older figurative sculptures, were set in the space on pedestals, and the individual works were independent entities that were not directly related to one another. The mutual relationships among elements in a space, so underscored in American minimalism, was only featured in *Table*, which stood right by the entrance to Nová síň. On its stylized top, two hemispheres are set next to one another—not, however, in the viewer's space but confined to the dimensions of the tabletop. In minimalism, the viewer enters an installation as does an actor on a stage; what is important is his or her interaction with the objects that are present. Works by Kolíbal like *Table* or *One Supports the Other* are like models the viewer must lean over and perceive from above, from the stance of an observer, not of a participant.

In Serra's case, we can oversimplify somewhat by saying that his work from the late 1960s is a reaction to Jackson Pollock and the minimalism of Donald Judd and Robert Morris. *One Ton Prop* is based, as is Pollock's painting, on the assumption that the viewer will be able, after the fact, to reconstruct the artist's actions and relive them. At the time, Serra's artworks were adumbrated in textual form; several verbs would appear one under another, such has "fold," "wind," "prop up," or "cut off." The works that followed could be understood as spatial instantiations of those verbs. Serra worked with materials differently than Kolíbal did. He used raw industrial materials such as lead, rubber, and neon. In this creative phase Serra could not have imagined working with models of his pieces or giving them their final form by casting them in plaster or another material.

Kolíbal's *Labile* was, in contrast to Serra's work, aesthetic; it made an impression based not only on its lability but also on its abstract forms and measured proportions, as well as its decorative character. *One Ton Prop* is intended to engage the viewer, to shock with its lability and the real possibility that the whole structure might fall. This feeling is not elicited by an optical illusion or trick (hence the title of the exhibition, *Anti-Illusion*, in which it was first shown); it really was unsteady, threatening to fall over at any moment. It is an actual unsteadiness, not a metaphorical reference to Kolíbal's existence and how it depends on balance; it straightforwardly calls attention to the force of gravity and the possibility of collapse. The drastic and literally dangerous impression made by Serra's sculptures contrasts with Kolíbal's artistic thematization of lability; in *Labile* it is no more than metaphorical, abstract. Kolíbal's *Pád* [Fall] (1967) is a sculpture of a fall, not a real possibility, and *Mizející tvar* [Disappearing Shape] (1967) depicts the process of spilling by means of modeling. In contrast, Serra's *Casting* (1969) is the result of a real, and consequently effective, splashing of molten lead onto the juncture between floor and wall. Such a work has no literary or metaphorical meaning; we cannot express its content better than as a description of the process by which it was created. It does not portray the outer world or a human situation; it does not relate to anything but itself.

It appears that Kolíbal's manner of working with space changed in 1969, when he started to set some of his pieces directly on the floor. Nonetheless, they still have a dimension that is private, turned in upon itself. The 1969 installation *Na tomto místě* [At This Spot], consisting of two irregular plaster objects lying on the floor, brings to mind a model of two islands. The withdrawn, intimate dimension is set off by the hand-drawn chalk circles enclosing them and demarcating their territories. Using a length of rope, Kolíbal highlighted and made visible the relationships between the elements of his installations. He also started working with untreated, simple materials; nevertheless, his works did not lose their strong literary subjects, which were often expressed in their titles (*Kam, není kam* [Whither, There Is No Whither], *Pouto* [Shackles], *Nedostatečně vymezený prostor* [Insufficiently Demarcated Space]). Kolíbal himself wrote, "then all my pieces became more and more metaphorical."[5] The works of Serra and his fellow travelers, in contrast, are connected to the body. The processes by which they are created border on performance. They attempt to enter into a direct dialogue with the physicality of the viewer—even through such tactics as eliciting the fear that a heavy, unstable construction might fall.

Richard Serra's works from the late 1960s led to the contemporary works in which—once again, put very simply—he tries to form and bend space and bring the viewer into unusual, stirring relationships with space.

Kolíbal's work over the last 30 years has gone through several stages. Among other things, he has devoted himself to reliefs and illusory spatial perspectives. His *Stavby* [Structures], dating from the last decades of the 20th century, imply a third dimension with a series of geometric drawings. They are characterized by spatial-textual contradiction: despite the title, we cannot enter into the structures themselves, or enter the drawings either; we can only observe them from different external vantage points.

Aside from the different ways they conceive space with respect to the viewer, I think the main difference between the work of the two artists is Serra's intentional emptiness with regard to content. This is in sharp contrast to the literary quality of Kolíbal's work—the ability of his artworks to convey not only forms but also dramatic content and a spiritual message. A void of content would have been unacceptable for Kolíbal.

III.

In the catalogue for a solo exhibition held in Litoměřice, Czech art historian Marie Klimešová compares Eva Kmentová's work to that of Alina Szapocznikow, Kmentová's Polish classmate who lived the last years of her life in Paris (until her death in 1973), as well as to that of American sculptor Eva Hesse.[6] Since the works of these three artists share certain traits, many people even ask, quite justifiably, why Eva Kmentová's work does not have a similarly decisive or even cult status as that of Eva Hesse in the United States or Szapocznikow's standing as a central figure of postwar art in Poland. However, upon closer examination, we find that the bodies of work of Kmentová, Szapocznikow, and Hesse, though they sometimes use identical or related formal approaches, are surprisingly different and constitute the three vertices of an imaginary triangle. In the center is a common territory we might characterize as the use of non-traditional, primarily soft-sculptural materials that radically transformed the expressive capacity of their works and that related them in a new way to reflections on the body in postwar art. However, the Central Europeans Kmentová and Szapocznikow, both ten years older than Hesse, were reacting to a different artistic tradition than the American one.

When Jindřich Chalupecký tried to describe the arc of Eva Kmentová's oeuvre, he wrote that, like others in her generation, "she went from academic realism to free abstraction."[7] This assessment is not only overly broad but, from the perspective of abstract American sculpture, also untrue. Of course, the accuracy of this conclusion depends on how we define Chalupecký's term "free abstraction." The corporeality that distinguishes Eva Kmentová's work, which is often, moreover, explored in the form of cast body parts, can really only be labeled free abstraction in the Czech context. Kmentová never deserted the figure; on the contrary, she continually found new methods to portray the human body with ever greater urgency. Her methods cover a broad temporal and dimensional range, from the monumental *Pupek* [Belly Button] (1972) to the minute, delicate, two-dimensional *Hrudník* [Chest] (1979). Even the different versions of *Sloup* [Column] (1979) and *Výhonek* [Offshoot], from the same period, take the human body as a theme.[8]

Primarily, Chalupecký's summary description was meant to express the idea that Czech art in the late 1950s had first to shake off the ideological heritage of socialist realism—and the concomitant imposition of a program of realist figurative sculpture—of an entire decade in order to reconnect with the Czech tradition of modern art and attempt to react to what was going on in sculpture abroad.

Eva Hesse did not have to come to terms with any such experience, even though the element of rejecting the past played a significant role in her work. She rebelled against orthodox minimalism—against what we might describe as the highest stage of modernism—as the most abstract of abstractions. I believe a strictly evolutionary and genealogical conception of art history founders when it comes up against the work of these two sculptors; both of them made postmodern art, in the sense that they were not interested in finding a general formal perfection in the discipline of sculpture; rather, they focused on the emotive contents of their sculptures. In the United States, Eva Hesse feminized and humanized minimalist sculpture; Eva Kmentová brought the immediacy of corporeal contact back to Czech sculpture.

Moreover, we also see a remarkable variety of personal approaches among them. Kmentová considered

Szapocznikow's works too literary and dramatic; Hesse might have had similar grievances with the work of Kmentová. Hesse used sculptural materials in a thoroughly nonmetaphoric manner: she did not use metal, latex, or laminated plastic to create the semblance of something else, as Kmentová or Szapocznikow did. Using different materials, Kmentová cast real sheets or curtains and thereby gave them solid sculptural form, an approach that would have been alien to Hesse, who would never have "imitated" or made impressions of sheets; she would have put the sheets themselves on display. However, that does not imply that one approach was better or more legitimate than the other.

In 1970 Kmentová made *Agresivní krychle* [Aggressive Cube], which, like several previous works, juxtaposes casts of the human body with a geometric shape. In this case, fingers protrude from the sides of a cube. The piece gives the impression that hands imprisoned within a geometric shape are groping out toward the surrounding world and trying to escape from the limiting form of their cage or prison. Fingers, the main bearers of the sense of touch, appear quite often in Kmentová's work, as do lips, another part of the human body that is highly touch-sensitive due to dense concentrations of nerve endings. In view of the political situation in Czechoslovakia in 1970, *Aggressive Cube* calls for a political reading. As soon as the sense of touch breaks through the boundaries of its confined space, the cube—which the title informs us is aggressive—stiffens and prohibits the fingers any further free movement. What then happens within the cube is hidden from view. But since the fingers are protruding, we can guess that it will not be pretty. [ill. 2]

Let us now compare Kmentová's *Aggressive Cube* with Hesse's *Accession*, several versions of which were created between 1967 and 1969. Each version consists of a metal cube with sides consisting of lattices of holes through which rubber tubes have been passed. The cube is topless, which enables us to contrast the interior of the sculpture with its exterior. On the outside, it looks like a carefully organized system—like a precisely woven basket. Inside, however, the tube ends generate an indistinct chaos; the tube shoots invite parallels with some sort of unknown biological system or even the human body. In an interesting parallel with Kmentová's *Aggressive Cube*, it is worth noting that some American critics saw the tube ends inside *Accession* as representing fingers.[9] Hesse chiefly wanted to express a tension between exterior and interior, outside and inside. She showed that outwardly precise minimalist geometric structures have inner lives and followed a path from geometry to organic form. Both sculptors gave geometric cubes an inner life, both by means of fingers or body parts; nonetheless, they differ in the way they used their sculptural materials. Kmentová cast real fingers in plaster; Hesse achieved a similar effect without resorting to an explicit corporeal image.

Eva Hesse, an emotional, psychologically fragile being, was the daughter of Jews who emigrated from Germany following a pogrom in 1939, when she was not quite four. In 1964 and 1965 she was deeply influenced by a trip to what was then West Germany, where she broke away from painting and began experimenting with reliefs and sculptures. She found a deep connection with "European culture" in general. The psychedelic optimism typical of 1960s American culture was alien to her; behind the period's enchantment with breaking old taboos and the ostensible advent of a new age and a new civilization, she felt a vague darkness. In an interview not long before her death, she said, "If I am related to certain artists it is not so much from having studied their works or writings, but from feeling the total absurdity in their work."[10] In the same interview, she revealed that her favorite artists were Marcel Duchamp, Jasper Johns, and the writers Jean-Paul Sartre and Samuel Beckett. We would be more likely to expect a selection of such names uttered somewhere in Central Europe than in the United States.

The works of Kmentová quite often express absurdity and dark humor, and not just in sculptures like *Terč-muž* [Target-Man] or the empty gesture in *Opuštený prostor* [Deserted Space]. Particularly with works from the mid-1960s, we might see some as cruel visual jokes, especially in view of their titles, *Proč* [Why] or *Co se nepovedlo* [What Didn't Work Out]). In addition to a straightforward sexual symbolism, a group of works, including *Velká škvíra* [Large Slit], *Díra* [Hole], and *Štěrbina* [Aperture], invite a deeply existential reading. Kmentová herself later ironized them in *Velká hostina* [Large Feast]: the originally dramatic gesture of slits cut out of paper was repeated in paper trays for hot dogs, thus transforming them into the ironic sigh of a person who has no choice but to see her fate as a tragic farce.

Despite the similarities noted so far, we would certainly not confuse the works of the two artists at a group exhibition. The very materials they use would help us distinguish them: Eva Hesse works with raw laminated plastic, metal, and latex, whereas Eva Kmentová works with more traditional plaster or paper. Kmentová expresses herself through the human body, which she models either in whole or in part or directly imprints into the materials she has chosen. Hesse creates objects that are related indirectly to the human body or to realistic representations of it. In the end, what most connects Eva Kmentová and Eva Hesse is the significance each one has for her own artistic community. They each offer what to some might seem like a poorer alternative to the "robust" expression of male sculptors. Their approach, however, was more convincing and personal than if they had expressed themselves through bronze or marble.

IV.

Many works of Eastern European sculpture that show evidence of a sort of delayed minimalism in reality represent post-minimalism or conceptual art. Their creators often did not want to build on minimalism but instead to critique it, or even to parody it. In this approach, they did not differ from their Western counterparts.

We may assign Jiří Kovanda's *Věž z cukru* [Sugar Tower] (1981) to this category. One day, when Kovanda had set off to the park at Vyšehrad in Prague (the site of a historical fort overlooking the Vltava River), he had nine sugar cubes with him, which he arranged into a small stack by a low wall. He then documented the installation and left the park. In a close-up photograph, *Sugar Tower* looks like a typical minimalist sculpture: in its simplicity it suggests the brick artworks Carl Andre made in the 1960s. Their additive principle is identical; Kovanda just applied it vertically rather than horizontally. Although both works were made using existing, ready-made materials, the impression they make is strikingly different, and not merely because of the difference in scale. Andre's bricks are neutral, commonly used construction materials. Though sugar cubes may in some respects be similar to bricks, their chief characteristic is that they are sweet; the material itself, regardless of whether it is exhibited in a public space, thus conveys a powerful metaphor. Sugar is nourishment, an energy reservoir. Andre's brick installations, according to eminent critic Arthur Danto, blur the distinction between what is art and what is not. Whether we consider arranged bricks to be works of art depends only on our knowledge of art history and the circumstances under which we encounter them, much as with Warhol's *Brillo Box* (1964). If we are in a gallery and are familiar with minimalism, we know that what we have in front of us is art. Perceptually, however, it is nothing but carefully arranged construction materials.

Kovanda's sugar cubes are different. The way they have been set down and arranged means they cannot be confused with something else, like a forgotten stash of sugar or an ant trap. If we found them in the park, we would wonder how they had gotten there. We would probably approach them as if they constituted a secret message, as if they conveyed information in an unknown sign system. *Sugar Tower* takes the hermeticism of contemporary art as its theme; we imagine the tower has some significance, but it is difficult or impossible to say what it is. What is at work here is not simply an additive principle, as used by Carl Andre, but, rather, the secret significance of the addition. If we can characterize Andre's works, in keeping with minimalist theory, as particular objects, we might say that Kovanda, rather than creating objects, creates a particular situation in *Sugar Tower*, which chance passers-by stumble upon and must then come to terms with. The work cannot be called a sculpture; it is related more closely to Kovanda's previous work, which involved expression in the form of performance art. Whereas Andre's pieces are always exhibited in galleries and could, in theory, be recreated with everyday bricks, Kovanda did not exhibit in galleries in the 1980s. His works would be performed on the street, or he would set up his installations in public spaces or in his own home. His work is not a pointed response to art theory; Kovanda is responding to a social state of affairs, which he comments on not from afar but by introducing himself into his works.[11] [ill. 3]

V.

The history of art in Eastern Europe before 1989 was influenced by the political situations in each individual country. There was either official history, which had to conform ideologically to government policy, or unofficial history, which was a reaction against the oppression of the state. In either case, the story of modern art by necessity became a struggle for freedom of expression. When writing new histories of art, authors are tempted to emulate existing histories of Western art, with their definitions, categories, and periodizations. Many Eastern European art historians have not been able to resist adopting those categories and grafting them onto the art of their countries. In such cases, traditions of Eastern European art are mostly engulfed by the Western context, in which they cannot hold their own. Adopting foreign terminology leads to searches for domestic minimalists, abstract expressionists, or pop artists.
The works of some Eastern European artists were derivative of what—in a different place and under completely different circumstances—the likes of Robert Rauschenberg or Yves Klein might have done. But many key artists in each country fall to the wayside in the critical narrative, because none of the categories of Western art applies to their work.

Eastern European "minimalism" shows that there is no way to take in global culture as a single, all-embracing whole. A systematic transplantation of artistic terms that originated at a particular time in a particular cultural context must necessarily end up confining the significance of the "other" and thereby converting it to "colonized art." Nonetheless, the worldwide system of exhibitions and art markets dominated by the economic and political might of the United States and Western Europe *is* a single, all-embracing whole. If art from other regions is to succeed quickly and unproblematically within such a system, it must submit to the imposition of the system's categories. Much more than simply market forces and the economic disparities between East and West are at play here. Compared with the West, the level of institutionalization of modern and contemporary art in Eastern Europe is low, and we may not expect this state of affairs to change significantly in the near future. Still, large state institutions with extensive collections can play a key role in the collection and dissemination of local histories of art and in the promotion of contemporary works abroad.

Judgment of a domestic art scene's significance based on foreign categories can only be forestalled by the thorough study of the fragmentary history of that domestic art scene. It is not only that numerous important figures of Czech art have not had monographs devoted to them and their work has not been presented in retrospectives; in addition, there have been almost no exhibitions in recent years with historical themes that juxtapose Czech art and art from other countries and thereby make it possible to discern any divergences and incongruities.

[1] Jindřich Chalupecký, *Na hranicích umění* [On the Frontiers of Art], Prague, Prostor–Arkýř 1990, p. 123.
[2] Hans Belting, *Art History after Modernism*, Chicago–London, University of Chicago Press 2003, pp. 54, 57–58.
[3] For example, Ekaterina Degot, *Russkoe iskusstvo XX-go veka* [Russian Art of the 20th Century], Moscow, Trilistnik 2000; *Art from Poland 1945–1996*, ed. Anda Rottenberg, Warsaw, Galeria Sztuki Współczesnej Zachęta 1997; Piotr Piotrowski, *Avantgarda w cieniu Jalty. Sztuka w Europie Srodkovo-Wschodniej w latach 1945–1989* [The Avant-Garde in the Shadow of Jalta: Art in Central and Eastern Europe in the Years 1945–1989], Poznań, Rebis 2005; and the underappreciated projects of the Slovenian collective IRWIN, including *New Moment Magazine—East Art Map: A (Re)Construction of the History of Art in Eastern Europe*, Ljubljana, New Moment 2002. *New Moment Magazine* attempted to create an independent system of Eastern European art, an alternative history that appropriated the graphic design of the cover of prestigious American art magazine *Artforum* as its graphic branding. The project is available at www.eastartmap.org.
[4] See Stanislav Kolíbal, *Kresby, sochy, komentáře* [Drawings, Sculptures, Commentaries], Prague–Český Krumlov, Arbor vitae—Egon Schiele Art Centrum 2004, p. 68.
[5] Stanislav Kolíbal, p. 111.
[6] Marie Klimešová, “Forma—koncept, hmota—dotek, positive—negativ. Dílo Evy Kmentové” [Form—concept, substance—touch, positive—negative: The Work of Eva Kmentová], in *Eva Kmentová*, Litoměřice, Severočeská galerie výtvarného umění [North-Bohemian Fine Arts Gallery] 2003, p. 9.
[7] Jindřich Chalupecký, *Nové umění v Čechách* [New Art in the Czech Republic], Jinočany, H+H 1994, p. 112.
[8] Despite the lyrical impression these works might make, they all contain in various forms the additive principle, which is one of the basic characteristics of minimalism. It appears that what Kmentová found most interesting in the form of *Sloup* [Column] was the precise and yet gentle fraying of the surface, arising from the roughly cut pieces of round paper stacked on top of one another.
[9] See Lisa Phillips, *The American Century: Art and Culture, 1950–2000*, New York, Whitney Museum of American Art–W.W. Norton 1999, p. 190.
[10] Cindy Nemser, “An Interview with Eva Hesse,” in *Artforum*, 1970, vol. 7, no. 9, May, p. 60.
[11] Note from 2017: As Karel Císař has pointed out, Jiří Kovanda was familiar with the works and theoretical concepts of the American minimalists. At the time he created *Sugar Tower*, Kovanda translated an interview with Carl Andre for *Minimal, Earth, Concept Art*, an anthology of theoretical texts published in Czechoslovakia by the semiofficial organization Jazzová sekce [Jazz Section]. See Karel Císař, “Dějiny současného umění v zúženém poli” [History of Contemporary Art in a Narrowed Field], in Karel Císař, *Abeceda věcí; Poznámky k modernímu a současnému umění* [An Alphabet of Things: Notes on Modern and Contemporary Art], Academy of Arts, Architecture, and Design in Prague, Prague 2014, pp. 125–127.

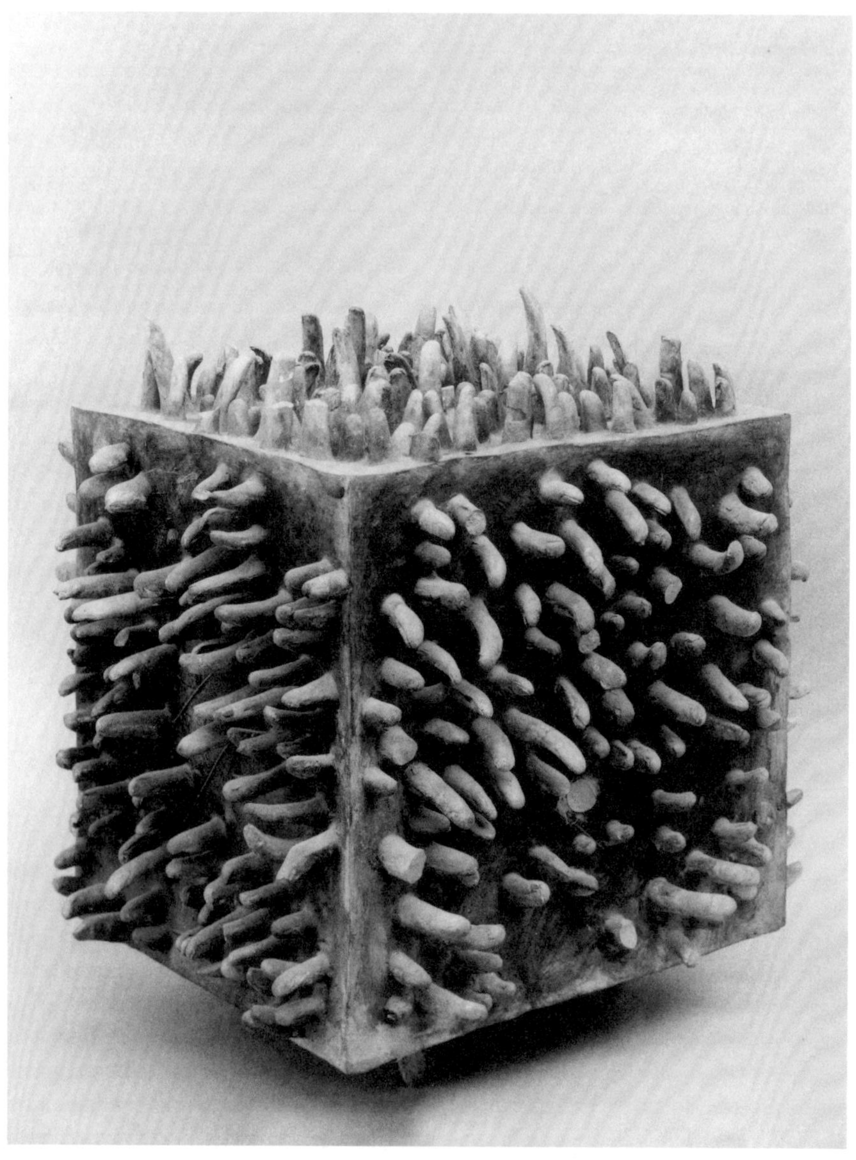

[ill. 2] Eva Kmentová, *Agresivní krychle* [Aggressive Cube], 1970
Colored plaster, 52 × 52 × 52 cm
Courtesy of the Olomouc Museum of Art

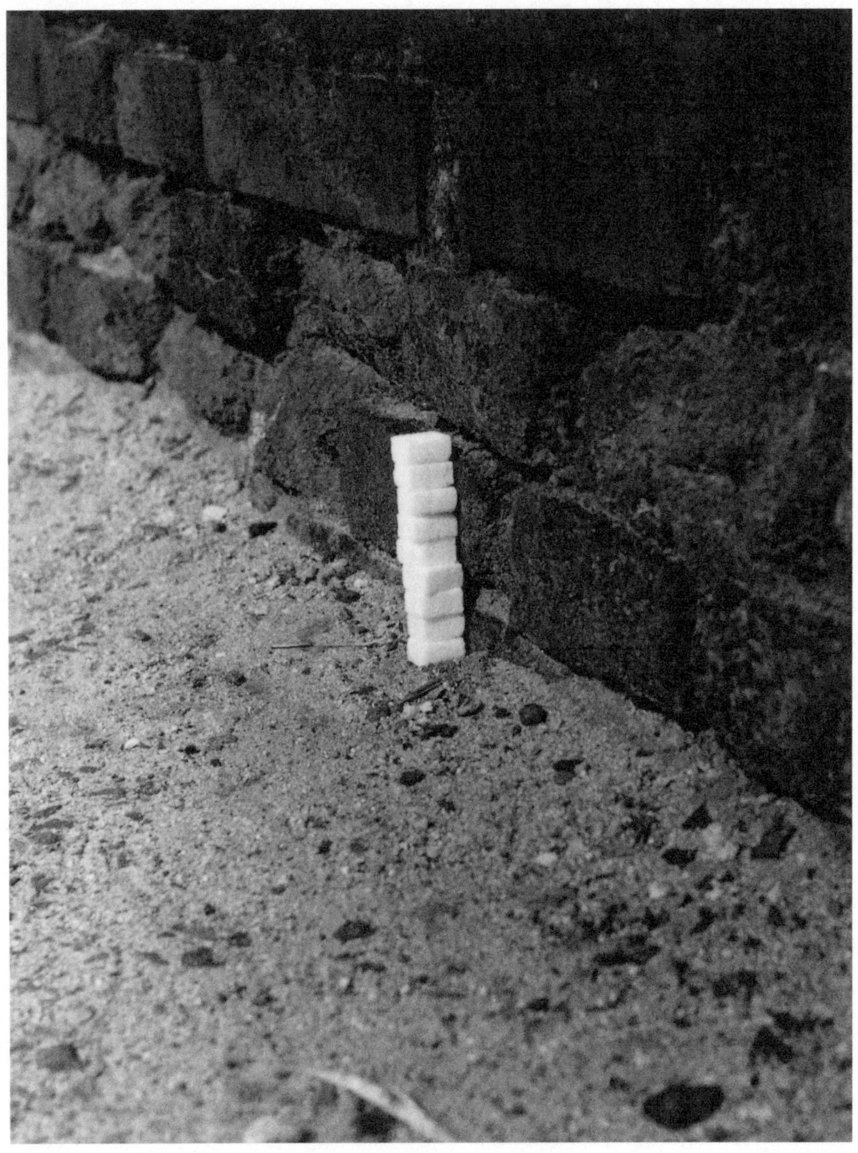

[ill. 3] Jiří Kovanda, *Věž z cukru* [Sugar Tower], spring 1981
Ephemeral installation in a public space, Vyšehrad, Prague
Documentary photograph
Courtesy of the artist

A Collage between Generations: Jiří Kolář as Witness to Modernity and His Contemporary Successors

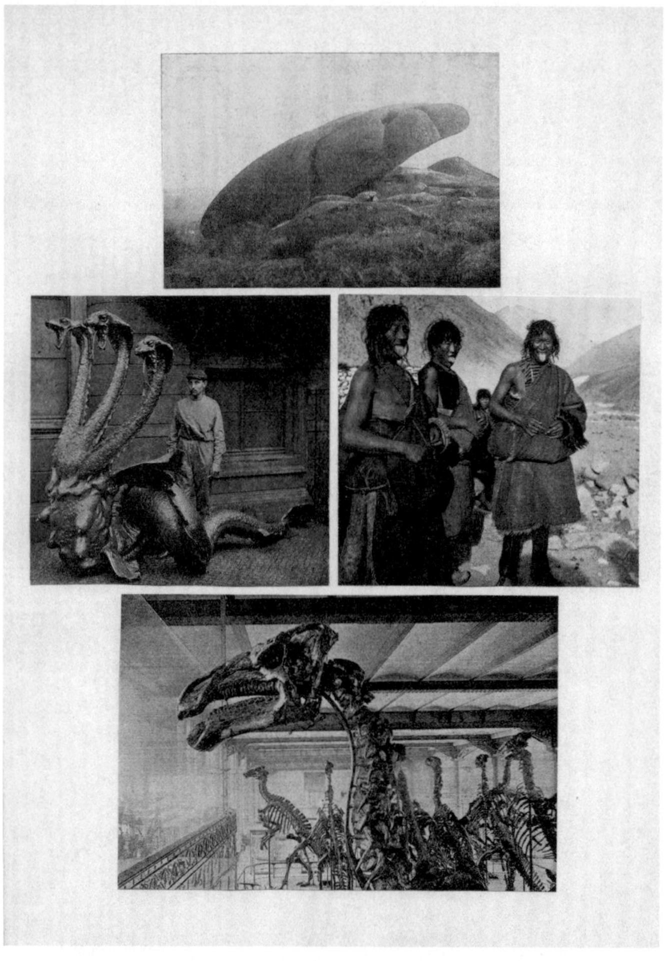

[ill. 1] Jiří Kolář, *Untitled*, early 1950s
Collage, 30 × 21 cm
Courtesy of the Estate of Jiří Kolář

I.

Since 2007, young artists in the Czech Republic have awarded an annual prize that is a counterweight—or rather a complement—to the Jindřich Chalupecký Award. Artists over 35 are nominated for the honor. The prize is meant as way to acknowledge influential figures whom young people consider to be their role models and whose work inspires them in different ways. The prize was established spontaneously; it came out of a community effort with no institutional backing. The thought of continuity, of passing along inspiration—a little like an artistic relay race—is emphasized in the name of the prize—every year it changes, based on the previous winner. If Vladimír Skrepl won the Jiří Kovanda Prize in 2007, Adriena Šimotová received the Vladimír Skrepl Prize in 2008. A year later the duo Lukáš Jasanský and Martin Polák won the Adriena Šimotová

Prize. In this way, the community of young artists highlights the importance of intergenerational relationships, creative continuity, and the indispensable role of the personal genealogies that make up the fabric of the artistic community.[1]

A component of the prize in its first years was the announcement of the best solo and group exhibitions of the previous year. In 2010 the group exhibition winner was, rather surprisingly, *Roky ve dnech, české umění, 1945–1957* [Years in Days: Czech Art, 1945–1957].[2] Never before or since had this competition category included a historical exhibition dealing with materials over half a century old by artists with whom young artists could not have been in personal contact. The organizers of the prize that year, who, for example, included Dominik Lang, said that they were led to such a choice by the sense that the field of contemporary art had never seen an exhibition so inspiring.

The curator of *Years in Days*, Marie Klimešová, had gathered works from a period during which both Czech modern visual arts and the society as a whole found themselves in a difficult crisis. Nazi totalitarianism had swiftly been replaced by Communist totalitarianism, and it was easy to yield to the opinion that modern art had failed in much the same way that the ideals of prewar democracy had failed. The utopian ethos of prewar art seemed completely exhausted, incapable of reflecting the new times, and it was necessary to begin anew somehow, to make a fresh start. A considerable number of the works included had originated as the private efforts of stubborn individuals trying to find not new forms but, rather, a renewed inner meaning for art. How could such works find a similarly strong reception among a new generation of artists in 2010? Art today, which may seem to be undergoing a crisis, finds itself in a completely different situation.

Among the least known yet most striking works in *Years in Days* is an extensive collection of collages by Libor Fára, Zbyněk Sekal, and Jiří Kolář. Libor Fára's collages are part of the Surrealist tradition, although the use of colorful pictorial backgrounds from *Life* magazine recalls the socially critical, proto-pop-art works of the avant-garde in the West. However, the works of Kolář and Sekal differ significantly in character from Surrealist collages: in their mostly straightforward compositions, they are more reminiscent of items from a clipping service or a pictorial archive. The aim of Kolář's collages was not to create a unified pictorial composition out of each clipping; instead, the pictorial materials laid side by side constituted a syntax through which the artist found expression. We find a similar approach in the work of Sekal. Nonetheless, we can only speculate as to the functions and aims of Sekal's collages, which did not steer clear of allusions to the politics of the day. They were being exhibited for the first time ever, and interpretations were fraught with uncertainty.[3]

Among the explanations that suggest themselves for the attractiveness of these historical materials was a renewed interest in collage. Around 2010 we find them in the work of young Czech artists like Daniel Pitín, Eva Koťátková, Dominik Lang, Vasil Artamonov, Alexey Klyukov, Vladimír Houdek, and many others. These contemporary artists often stress work with authentic pictorial materials, images from old magazines, intaglio book illustrations, and private photographs. Such old-fashioned techniques of paper collage were apparently revived for reasons other than simple visual appeal or nostalgia for bygone times. During the past decade, both Czech and foreign artists have been increasingly turning to the past, interesting themselves in the works of their predecessors or even physically locating, exhibiting, and reinterpreting them.[4] There is talk of a historiographic turn in contemporary art.[5] Czech art in recent years has also become attracted to "modernology"—research into relationships between modern art and the present.[6] Artists are turning to modernism, a closed chapter of European culture, as a space in which to explore issues important to the present day. An interest in collage, one of the key expressive resources of modern times, accords with such a mind-set.[7]

II.

In the Czech cultural consciousness, Jiří Kolář (1914–2002) is remembered as a poet who renounced literature in 1960, when he began making collages, and eventually found worldwide fame as a visual artist. Understandably, this narrative is an oversimplification. In Kolář's work, literature and the visual arts represent two strands that intertwine and influence each other.[8] Kolář had created collages influenced by Surrealism before World War II and devoted himself to writing literary texts after 1960. He freely combined literary and artistic methods, and for this reason many of his works, though interconnected, are impossible to categorize. The dichotomous developmental model that may be characterized as "first a poet, then a visual artist" has roots in the local tradition of clearly distinguished artistic disciplines. The blending of multiple expressive resources and intermediality, so important for the development of artistic approaches in the 1960s, existed naturally in the Czech art world but, in many cases, was not perceived by experts or the public.[9]

The pictorial works Kolář made before 1953—that is, until the several months he was imprisoned in connection with his poetry collection titled *Prométheova játra* [Prometheus's Liver]—constitute a clearly identifiable ensemble. From their lack of discipline, their "unartistic" quality, and, at the same time, their straightforward, striking character, they may come across as unfinished experiments. In contrast with later collages, brimming with aesthetic refinement and formal ideas, those made before 1953, though seemingly simple, look like works in progress, not quite finished works. They often involve a simple juxtaposition of a few magazine photographs whose form or contents create interrelationships, for example, or freestanding photographs set against a white background. In the context of the Czech art of the day, such works did not overtly display some of the key traits artworks were supposed to have—namely, elements of originality, personality, or individuality. Kolář merely collected and juxtaposed already existing images. It was as if they were not yet the final products but were materials being assembled for other works. Here the creator receded into the background; his role was ostensibly that of a mediator, not an artist. How then are we to understand Kolář's pictorial work from 1949 to 1952? To which traditions can his collages from the period be critically linked?

Collages were not—and are not—merely a format of artistic expression for avant-garde artists, Cubists, Dadaists, and Surrealists, they also represent a phenomenon inextricably associated with modern culture. Ever since the 19th century, the experience of modern life has been closely tied to the mass media, with ideas of rapid movement and discontinuity. The phenomenon of combined images and writing emerged not only in the pages of newspapers and magazines but in public spaces as well. Inhabitants of the modern world are confronted with such a flood of information of all sorts that it all begins to mix together into a jumble. The genesis of collage as a creative method and a specific artistic format cannot here be traced and described in detail. We find collages on amusing postcards and humor magazines before the onset of the 20th century, when avant-garde artists started to make use of similar techniques. As art historian Jindřich Toman has shown, the Czech sphere was no exception in this regard. Before 1900 there were already jocular postcards in the region, incorporating several different photographic elements, and periodicals like *Svět zvířat* [Animal World] regularly printed intentionally misleading photomontages before World War I.[10]

Collages attracted avant-garde artists for several reasons. In Cubism, the technique effectively countered the illusion of a unified three-dimensional space and emphasized the flatness and constructed nature of an image. The variegated character of the materials used—drawings, newspaper clippings, wallpaper, colored paper, etc.—enriched and complicated the semantic reading of the resulting work. Just a few years after the Cubists, Dadaists began using photo collages as a tool for political subversion and the negation of the values of traditional art. In the Soviet Union, photomontages were used for mass political propaganda purposes. As Benjamin Buchloh has noted, it is evidently no accident that the new possibilities offered by photographic depiction resonated among artists at a time when it appeared that mimetic depiction in art had been abandoned for good.[11]

The principle behind photo collage and photomontage is the assembly of different photographic images into one, with a new image arising out of the composite of the component ones. Creators take advantage of the fact that individual photographic images have the ability to mediate the time and place where they were taken with indexical authority—they are records of real events. Through the techniques of photo collage and photomontage, however, the image in a photograph can be commented on and intensified; alternatively, its original meaning can be modified. The invention of the photo collage in the circle of German Dadaists is captured in a legendary account that demonstrates the multivalent capacity and expressive resources of the medium well. During World War I, George Grosz and John Heartfield sent postcards to Wieland Herzfeld, who was at the front. Patriotic images were combined with other photographs to transmit a provocative anti-war message. It was, they thought, a way to bypass censorship—by creating a montage of officially published photographs, which could thus not be prohibited, they conveyed a message diametrically opposed to that contained in each element used.[12] John Heartfield later developed the method further in his famous interwar photomontages. None of the original postcards Heartfield and Grosz sent to the front have survived. From this period and the years following, we have only a few examples of Heartfield's collage works. In his collage *This Is What the Death of a Hero Looks Like* (1917), two photographs of war victims are juxtaposed, along with the handwritten title. The words, which may recall the patriotic pathos of contemporary propaganda, contrast all the more starkly with the portrayal of the horrific reality at the front. In the 1924 yearbook of the Malik Publishing House we find Heartfield's *The Worker's Place*, which employs a similar strategy. It is a simple photographic juxtaposition of the pompous funeral of a Prussian general and a mass grave for foot soldiers, assembled to create a unified whole. Added to the pictures are two captions: "Funeral of general who died in the rear" and "Disposal of proletariat massacred on the front." With this juxtaposition, Heartfield wanted to show what war really looked like and thus undermine the voice of state propaganda.

The photomontages of John Heartfield are a substantially different type of artwork than Cubist and Surrealist collages. They were meant to be printed and distributed on a mass scale. The composition of the photographic images and the texts that sometimes accompanied them did not acquire meaning until they were brought together: "They are not primarily aesthetic objects, but images for reading."[13] Heartfield's goal was to expose the truth of photographic images that had been distorted or completely covered up by the language of popular culture and political propaganda.

His compositions called the reliability of the photographic medium into doubt; paradoxically, they added meaning to the photographs by conspicuously manipulating them in a grotesque manner. "Yet this most modern and realist of pictorial media (along with film) [i.e., photography] consistently proved inadequate to its seemingly self-evident task of representing the actual […] In short, photography had lost its social mission and now did little to engage Heartfield or his larger audience with the day's pressing reality. Heartfield's fevered response forced the medium to convey the reality to which it was photochemically linked but which it inadequately represented."[14] Rosalind E. Krauss associates a similar ambition to reveal the truth of photographic images with the use of photomontage by the avant-garde of the 1920s: "Throughout the avant-garde in the 1920s, photomontage was understood as a means of infiltrating the mere picture of reality with its meaning. This was achieved through juxtaposition: of image with image, or image with drawing, or image with text."[15]

Alongside Heartfield's politically motivated photomontages, we find other artworks in the mid-20th century that recall his juxtapositional method, not in the use of photographs with intense subject matter but in the ways they work with pictorial materials. Regardless of their content, the photomontages seem to express feelings about the world of mass media. We may assume that they are reactions to the development of pictorial periodicals and the growing influence of photojournalism.[16]

The availability of photographs and reproductions of artworks also influenced the manner in which artists built their studio archives. It was possible to mediate the history of visual arts with the help of photographic images that served as sources of inspiration or confrontational foundations for their own work. The pictorial archive of Czech painter Emil Filla may serve as an example here. Beginning in the 1920s, he assembled reproductions of both historical and contemporary artworks and affixed them to a uniform background. Filla did not conceive of the result as a standalone artwork. However, as early as the interwar years, certain artists, such as Josef Albers and Hannah Höch, turned the combination of archive-based approaches and collage into a means of self-expression. In 1933 Höch created *Album* (which survives to this day) by pasting photographs—ornaments composed from the bodies of athletes, photographic dance studies, ethnographic pictures, unusual natural phenomena, bird's-eye images of urban sprawl, and works of industrial architecture reminiscent of modern sculptures—over and over again onto the pages of the magazine *Die Dame* [The Lady]. The album appears to have served as a sort of analogue sketchbook. She interconnected the pictures associatively, based on the principles of visual analogy and content-based parallels. George Grosz did similar work from 1941 to 1958. He gradually covered over a copy of *The New Yorker* with a layer of pasted-in photographs, predominantly from the field of advertising. Because both of them used an existing magazine as a foundation, their work represents a clear appropriation and development of the aesthetics of the pictorial magazine by means of a literal entry into the medium of magazine meta collage, through which the unrelated is related into a unified whole within the framework of the individual pages of a magazine—and the magazine in its entirety.

The reaction to the world of modern magazines was logical. Even before the war, both photographic news reports and photomontages had become a commonplace component of the language of modern book and magazine design, and this was true in the Czech sphere as well. In popular magazines with traditions dating back to the 19th century, such as *Světozor* [Seeing the World] and *Zlatá Praha* [Golden Prague], the significance of pictorial materials grew, and specialized rubrics devoted to photographic images emerged. These periodicals "had already become a solid part of the middle-class culture of reading in the 19th century and had created a certain type of public space in which the middle class could not only read up on the world, but could also become acquainted with new forms through which it was visualized."[17] Titles like *Pestrý týden* [Colorful Week], *Letem světem* [Flying across the World] and other newly conceived pictorial magazines added to the ranks of such traditional magazines during the time of interwar Czechoslovakia. They came to include photo-feuilletons, amusing photographs, or various "sensation bazaars"—rubrics devoted to curious, exotic, or humorous photographs with brief captions. A "photo-saturated page" filled entirely with photographs became a staple of magazine layouts.[18] Particularly noteworthy were interwar film magazines, which constructed full-page montages of stills from popular films, and even leftist political periodicals, which were inspired aesthetically by progressive Soviet magazine design. In addition, the specific genre of photo-poetry, which combined photography and poetry, began to appear in popular magazines.

Space limitations in this text require us to draw attention solely to the symbolic importance played by the collage in Surrealism. The significance of the technique lay in that it was one of the central ways an artist's subconscious could be activated. From the Surrealist perspective, it went straight to the essence of the surrounding world in an uncommonly effective and yet subversive manner. From the artistic perspective, Surrealist photo collages represented a technique for constructing a surreal world. Combinations of cuttings—and thus of motifs, perspectives, and evaluative criteria—made it possible to create the illusion of an alternative existence within the framework of a single composition. The Surrealists recast Freudian free association into a creative method for diving into otherwise-inaccessible levels of experience. Collages pervaded Surrealism as a whole: we find them not only in Surrealist visual art and literature but also in the ways Surrealists thought and behaved. They made it possible to realize Lautréamont's conception of unexpected associations and to accomplish convincing metamorphoses of banal realities.

III.

In the *Years in Days* exhibition catalogue, Marie Klimešová examines the collages of Jiří Kolář from 1946 to 1952, casting light on their genesis and attempting to situate them in an international context. In view of the space limitations of a group exhibition catalogue, as well as the importance of the material under consideration, I believe that it is but the beginning of a discussion devoted to Kolář's early collages. Several hundred similar works have been preserved in the artist's estate and in other collections; thus, we have at our disposal a remarkable and rich sampling of the artist's activities at the time. Until 1953 Kolář's pictorial works were created using several original methods, some of which will be discussed in detail below. Anti-anatomy, rapportage, confrontage, works from the *Urban Folklore* cycle, or authentic or found collages have, in addition to their own defining traits, several common features. In contrast to Surrealist collages or prewar photomontages, Kolář did not combine the photographic images he selected into a single whole, dominated by a single perspective, but attached them alongside one another to white sheets of paper. He was often content to use no more than two to three images. It might seem that Kolář was implementing Breton's *Surrealist Manifesto* to the letter, juxtaposing two greatly dissimilar realities to produce new images.[19] Nonetheless, the aesthetics of prewar Surrealist collages are not like those of these sober works. [ill. 1]

Kolář does not cut elements out of pictures but leaves them whole; he neither fragments nor disfigures them. He leaves the cuttings in their original form and simply juxtaposes them. Instead of being individual works that might hang on a gallery wall, for example, his works at this time represent extensive collections that call to mind a literary work or an archival collection that must be scanned and interpreted. The pictorial composition acquires the character of a textual communication whose form and content we become aware of only after "reading" the whole.[20]

Kolář's early collages don't seem to have been intended for display in a vertical position on a wall. Instead, it seems they were meant to be horizontal; we are to read them, like a book or a text. They are not meant to create the illusion of a window onto an imaginary world; they are images that already exist that have been cut up and assembled, a composition of symbols spread out in space, intended to be read and not "looked at." A collage is not an expression of the artist's subjectivity in the way that a painting or drawing is; in lieu of his or her own signature, the artist is only working with the conceptual arrangement of the work. He or she does not create images but places already existing ones in the same context. Hence the shift from the vertical to the horizontal and from the iconic to the indexical, as Rosalind E. Krauss mentions.[21]

Photography is causally connected to things in the world, yet it is capable of lying. In it, truth is encrypted; it arises solely out of a knowledge of the context. By comparing different tableaux in the spirit of John Heartfield, Kolář calls the truthfulness of photography into doubt, transforming it or completely flipping original meanings. Kolář is also able to create a similar effect—the transformation of a photograph's meaning—simply by taking a photo out of its original place in the magazine. Instead of occupying its place in the magazine, the picture finds itself in a carefully selected location on a white paper background. The photograph no longer illustrates a text or falls under a specific section of the magazine; it is presented, decontextualized, to the viewer for a detailed analysis. In principle, Kolář's collages before 1953 did not require knowledge of a craft or any skills then associated with the visual arts: he made do with selecting, cutting, and pasting images. Close examination reveals painstaking compositional work. We discover as we read each one that the cuttings are realities unto themselves. It is in the mind of the viewer that they are ultimately joined together. The artist manipulates perspective by means of the arrangement of the cuttings, determining the way we connect the individual fragments. He or she produces a sequential composition through which the images are given meaning and then interpreted. We read what the artist is communicating "in-between the images," because it is not strictly present in the images themselves nor could it have been prefigured beforehand. Kolář was evidently aware of the analogical expressive possibilities: "In a particular grouping, each thing responds to the message transmitted by the other things, no matter how different, so clearly and intently that a non-different whole is created."[22]

Kolář worked with copious pictorial sources in his collages before 1953. At the time, he was already working with reproductions of art from all across the world, which was characteristic of his later work. The materials that most captivated him, however, were photographs from magazines devoted to entertainment. His selection of materials from the field of popular culture must have been conscious, particularly following the debates on kitsch in the 1940s.[23] Kolář had British, French, and German periodicals, mostly from the interwar years, at his disposal, though he had some contemporary ones as well.[24] A significant number of the cuttings came from domestic pictorial magazines, many from the 1920s and 1930s, particularly those from *Pestrý týden*.

Among Kolář's pictorial sources we also commonly find clippings from old Austro-Hungarian magazines.[25] Nonetheless, contemporary Czech magazines are conspicuously lacking among his image sources. Kolář cut up not only pictures but also the attendant captions. In a snapshot of Filippo Tommaso Marinetti, Kolář was apparently also interested in the accompanying words, "Marinetti, der Führer der italienischen Futuristen" [Marinetti, the leader of the Italian Futurists]. He especially sought out materials that could be seen as photographic gags or even as photojournalistic kitsch. Kolář was interested in photographs from sections devoted to pictorial curiosities that were themselves collages of sorts, drawing unusual connections: a sports team's canine mascot in a rugby helmet, a man drinking whiskey from a bottle shaped like a revolver, trained pigs on a seesaw, or a group of carnival visitors dressed up as mushrooms. Kolář's attention was captured by the French Church of Saint Christopher (the patron of motoring and sports), whose Gothic-style stained-glass windows depicted automobiles and locomotives. Photographs that play with scale and make viewers unsure of what they are actually looking at seemed to be particularly appealing to him: children with a kite shaped like a large bird, architectural mock-ups, a dwarf with a barbell, a miniature stagecoach, and an archivist leafing through the *Codex Gigas.*

A number of Kolář's collages from the early 1950s are doubtless completed works: they are fixed to a ground and are sometimes dated or inscribed with their titles and the techniques used.[26] Other sets are probably only archival materials Kolář was planning to work with. Under the label "Collector's Cycles" in Kolář's estate, we find several titled folders with thematically organized free cuttings.[27] Separate folders with similar source materials, this time limited to scenes from art history, are suggestive of schemes for a series of book projects in preparation, and Kolář explains the idea of each in concise typescript annotations: "MUSIC—A relatively large number of publications were devoted to this cycle in the artistic literature. But all collections settled for samples typical of a particular artistic period, like the Renaissance, the Baroque or the Rococo. So a comprehensive survey—one which portrays the fact that the theme is woven through the history of art quite on a par with other themes—is altogether missing. Most of all, a perspective that might encompass the whole spectrum of works by modern artists who deal with the theme is missing."[28] Certain cycles make us question the state of completion we find them in. For example, a folder titled "Two" contains a series of sheets of paper with cuttings capturing a wide variety of doubles—Adam and Eve from a Renaissance breviary, a portrait of Guillaume Apollinaire and Marie Laurencin by Henri Rousseau, contemporary athletes in competition, and reproductions of many types of historical art. A set like this could be extended at will. Here Kolář acts as the curator of an "imaginary museum" of the type proposed by André Malraux during the same period. According to Malraux, the possibilities offered by reproduction enabled art to rid itself of its dependence on time, place, and limiting art-historical categories.

Jiří Kolář probably approached some of his cuttings, predominantly those presented individually on a paper background, as he did his ready-made pictures. In them, photography captures something we may today term an art object, an unintentional assemblage or situation that comes close to being a performance—military equipment or natural items reminiscent of sculptures, patterns consisting of the bodies of gymnasts, a woman with a braid several meters long, and Lionel, a hirsute Russian who had become a cabaret sensation in Prague before World War I. The basis for Kolář's interest in certain images only becomes clear when they are compared with others on the page. Four reproductions of historical art are connected by the motif of pointing fingers, which we only discover upon inspecting them. Certain combinations of images display no obvious relationship or connection, aside from the fact that the things depicted look like something other than what they really are. Kolář merges the abstract meanings into something like a visual version of a musical chord—a house with a cubist facade and realistic relief, a woman cooking under the open sky on a tin stove, a child wearing boxing gloves.

Among Kolář's early collages, we find at least two well-represented thematic fields: first, the motif of the double or the relationship between the real and the artificial. Kolář cut up photographs of famous actors or models with painted portraits of them and arranged them to mimic famous artworks and historical figures. He cut up a photomontage combining the faces of Greta Garbo and Marlene Dietrich, a 1909 photo of the robot Barbarossa in an embrace with its creator, Adolph Whitman, or a woman preparing a figure for exhibition in a wax museum. A similar field of interest is represented by a photo of a carnival costume, half-bride, half-groom, set against a half-restored painting of the emperor Ferdinand II. A similar motif brings us to the second theme, which we might call an interest in forms of representation and the deconstruction of display techniques. Kolář was interested in photographs taken in the process of making a film in which the off-set reality of a shot was revealed; he was attracted to photographs of museum exhibits and inventive arrangements of display cases. One of his collages incorporated a photo reportage of the rolling up of the gigantic painted panorama *Bitva u Lipan* [The Battle of Lipany] by Luděk Marold or reproductions of photographs Marold had had made in order to paint his figural tableaux. He was also interested in photographs documenting the emergence of public art in Prague. He immediately used several photographs taken at the workshop of Josef Václav Myslbek that included bronze casts of his *Saint Wenceslas* and captured workers fabricating enormous fragments of the equestrian statue. Other similar photographs include one of a silhouette in outline of the Jan Hus Memorial at one end of Old Town Square, used to make sure that the sculpture was scaled properly, to the as-yet-empty but already-staked-out area for the Mácha Memorial in Prague's Petřín Park.

Kolář's early collages are surprisingly poor in contemporary subject matter and explicit political themes.[29] One might relate a photograph of film viewers wearing dark-tinted glasses to the Czechoslovak context at the time. Dark glasses, due to the presence of film reflectors, were also worn by attendees at political trials during the Stalinist period. And a photograph of a sealed door is certainly linked to the period of social terror that began in February 1948, the door symbolizing the state apparatus moving against the enemies of the new regime. The significance of this image is underlined by the fact that it is Kolář's smallest cutting, which has been positioned quite independently on a white sheet.

Jiří Kolář also reacted to the globalized world of consumption and advertising. He cut out British and Dutch magazine advertisements showing carefully arranged products from small shops, snapshots of enormous billboards in the countryside, and photographs in which elegant models posed amid ruins. I think the attempt to come to terms with the war and the political state of affairs was the hidden common denominator of the entire ensemble of Kolář's early collages. Kolář goes through photographs from old magazines and finds in them meanings that resonate with contemporary issues. It is as if the artist's own articulation of war-related and political themes or his use of contemporary photographs might have undermined the authenticity of his account. The activities of Group 42 had been marked by difficulties in communicating life experiences that had taken place against the background of war. The war was like an invisible influence, impossible to name or depict, a phenomenon that had directly impacted the lives of all. One solution was a return to realism through the use of citations, the technique of the collage, and a new understanding of what constituted authorship on the part of the artist.

IV.

Jiří Kolář's visual art arose in parallel with his poetry and was intimately bound up with it. Kolář's collections of poetry from the late 1940s, such as *Roky ve dnech* [Years in Days] (1946–1947) or *Očitý svědek* [Eyewitness] (1949), were marked by a retreat from lyrical language and a movement toward journal entries, citations, and descriptions of daily life. The first cycle in the collection *Prométheova játra* [Prometheus's Liver] (1950), titled *Rod Genorův* [The Genor Dynasty], takes the form of a literary collage: in it, the author juxtaposed an overheard pub conversation, an interpretation of a text by Ladislav Klíma titled *Skutečná událost zběhnuvší se v Postmortalii* [A Real Occurrence that Happened in Postmortalia], and "By the Railway Track," a short story by Zofia Nałkowska (with a printing of the original story). The meaning in the words emerges not from the words themselves but from their juxtaposition. Kolář clarified his method in the afterword, which he incorporated directly into the text of the collection. Such self-interpretation has the character of an allusion. Of profound significance for Kolář during this period was T.S. Eliot's *The Waste Land* (1922), a modernist textual collage that drew from a variety of sources, quoting and paraphrasing Ovid, Shakespeare, and Baudelaire and borrowing from the Bible, Sir James Frazer's *The Golden Bough*, Celtic mythology, Buddhist verses, and popular songs of the day. Along with the poem, Eliot provided extensive notes, which enumerated the dozens of literary sources he employed. Among the members of Group 42, *The Waste Land* had the status of a cult work of modern literature, with Jindřich Chalupecký, Jiřina Hauková, and Jiří Kotalík referencing it in their work alongside Jiří Kolář, in partial or complete translation.[30]

It wasn't only in *Prometheus's Liver* that Kolář worked with the methods of citation, interpretation, and collage; they run through his entire oeuvre, beginning in the early 1950s. In his poems we find transcripts of chance conversations, snippets of newspaper articles, descriptions of dreams, copies of official speeches and administrative records, the overheard utterances of children, and public notices. In his poetry, Kolář does not assume the role of the traditional creator of texts but is rather a transcriber, carrying out a variety of appropriations and interpretations. He is no longer the creator of a new world but primarily a witness to the one that already exists. From different perspectives and angles, he creates records that are as faithful as possible and presents them to the reader for evaluation. We also find a turn toward reality, the use of citations, and the method of the collage among other authors of the unofficial Czech literary scene at the time, including figures such as Egon Bondy, Ivo Vodseďálek, Vladimír Boudník, and Bohumil Hrabal. The approaches of Bondy and Vodseďálek were of a grotesque, politically subversive character: "We discovered the possibility of turning the pseudoaesthetics of Stalinist mythology back against itself and put the discovery to work. We did not fall back on irony or antipropaganda, for that matter; for example, we took advantage of the phraseology of slogans so as to appropriate them aesthetically, much as Duchamp had done with his ready-mades."[31] With regard to literary collages, Bohumil Hrabal recalled the importance of the model represented by T.S. Eliot, whom Jiří Kolář had introduced him to, and called attention to the ability of citations to bring literary tradition and the past into the present: "Both Eliot and Joyce are full of citations of thoughts voiced in long-bygone times—a thousand years ago—that suddenly come to life in the present and thus become contemporary."[32]

In addition to writing literary work, Jiří Kolář was making collages during the same period. In 1949 he tried to make a visual interpretation of "A kamení začalo oživovat" [And the Stones Began to Revive], one of his own poems from the collection *Days in Years.* But it would probably not be appropriate to use this attempt as a kind of Rosetta Stone to interpret Kolář's later collages. Kolář "illustrated" each part of the poem with magazine photographs, which shifted the meaning of the text, taking it into new spheres. He continued making similar efforts for a short time.[33] From then on, Kolář concentrated on purely visual work. "Perhaps—the vacuum—I'm haunted by the desire to own a book of photographs that might enact some story, to simply have a photographed poem, story, novel; not just a literary analogy of a poem, story, or novel, but a cycle including the world and the life of the photographer himself."[34]

Marie Klimešová places the creation of Kolář's surviving collages in the years 1951 and 1952. "In keeping with the moderation of the poetic conception of *Days in Years* or *Prometheus's Liver*, a marked structural simplification established itself in his pictorial work of the early 1950s, based on the regular arrangement of found cuttings."[35] From the late 1940s to the mid-1950s, the whole group of artists around Jiří Kolář kept a journal, which members would discuss in periodic meetings. In addition to Kolář, the group included Zdeněk Urbánek, Jan Hanč, Kamil Lhoták, Jan Rychlík, and Vladimír Fuka. In his memoir *Ztracená země* [Lost Land], Urbánek recalls how this originally literary practice spilled over effortlessly into the creation of pictorial artifacts:

> The title [Reportage] is the same as the title of my invention from the beginning period of the group journal. When sometime around 1950 from one Thursday (the day of the journal meetings) to the next I hadn't been able to write or translate anything up to scratch, on Wednesday evening I took a pile of foreign and domestic illustrated magazines, some scissors, glue, and paper, and I started combining couples or larger numbers of images into what I'd

> give a name to, right then or later […] First came "confrontages," striking comparisons of two different moral/social perspectives on the same thing. Reportages came into being as a natural and more complicated offshoot: in a woodcut from an old copy of *Illustrated London News* some ladies and girls wave enthusiastically from a balcony; using the same technique a war-devastated street is pasted along their line of sight.[36]

Dramatic effects were achieved not through refined composition but simply by presenting different realities and the relationships between them. "Reality was more accessible to us [Kolář, Urbánek, and friends]. It was mostly a matter of materializing a short connection. We had an advantage: we weren't artists; we didn't want to imitate but to do something without the intervention of scissors and scalpels."[37] The group's cuttings also played a role in their collective games in the spirit of the Surrealist *cadavre exquis*.[38] In Kolář's estate there is a collage dated April 23, 1952, and signed U.F.K. (Urbánek, Fuka, Kolář). Other similar works are to be found in private collections.

From the group around Kolář, Vladimír Fuka soon turned toward the pictorial journal as well. His drawings capture everything the artist encountered or could have encountered at the time—pictorial propaganda in the street, in queues, or in parades; social changes brought about by the Communist coup; concentration camps. But Fuka also drew over news photographs, including pictures from the Korean War, atomic mushroom clouds, or world metropolises he was only able to visit in magazines and postcards. He made collages out of cuttings from daily newspapers. In photographs of a Nazi demonstration, he replaced the symbol of the swastika with a hammer and sickle or placed celebratory propagandistic articles alongside drawings depicting reality. A dozen full-page collages from the second half of May 1950 could have easily been interchanged with works by Jiří Kolář from the same period if Kolář had used contemporary pictorial materials. Fuka set a photograph of Stalin, a trained bear on a motorcycle, and a photo of telegraph poles against drawn-in hanging victims. He juxtaposed reproductions of historical art, photo reportages, and film stills. We find similar juxtapositions in the collages of Zbyněk Sekal, as well as in Bertolt Brecht's book *Kriegsfibel* [War Primer], for example. As an immigrant in Stockholm and the United States, Brecht cut out war-related photographs from Swedish periodicals and *Life* magazine and added short commentaries in the form of poems. (Nonetheless, a magazine photograph of a "sexy carrot" reminiscent of a woman's legs came to light among the horrors of war.) The book first appeared in 1955, and it is noteworthy that both Brecht and Sekal used the same photograph of the ruins of Nuremberg in their collages. Sekal comments on it by means of other photographs, whereas Brecht does so by means of a quatrain. It is as if they themselves could not believe the explicit photographic evidence of the horrors of war .[39]

The mistrust of printed words and images felt by Kolář and his whole generation was based on extensive experience. Not only during World War II, but starting again in the late 1940s, officially published magazine and newspaper illustrations lost their credibility with regard to capturing reality. Understandably, in the Nazi-controlled Protectorate of Bohemia and Moravia, the war was mediated chiefly by the mass media in a way that manipulated reality propagandistically. No one believed what was written and displayed in Protectorate newspapers. At best, the news influenced by the state apparatus might be read attentively; people would read between the lines to extract information that might reveal that the Wehrmacht was not doing as well as official journalism was proclaiming. The situation during the Stalinist period was identical in this regard. Newspapers filled with empty phrases did not reflect the reality of everyday life; at best, they might serve as a yardstick for readers to understand the struggles among Communists, for example, by noting who was or was not mentioned in type. I believe the general aim of Jiří Kolář's early collages was to understand how images work, how it was possible to find expression through them, and also to document the manner in which both photography and words might be abused: "For what lies about the real state of reality more than today's photography, film, radio, gramophone records, or newspapers?"[40] It is no coincidence that Jiří Cieslar characterizes Kolář's journal entries as "private news articles" filling the need to create an alternative to the existing and misleading information channels of modern times.[41]

Moreover, we cannot doubt the political character of Kolář's collages dating from 1953, even though the artist avoided openly political assertions. Much as in *Prometheus's Liver*, Kolář's formal experimentation was a part of an artistic intention intended to critically evaluate the present. Even though his collages lack the explicit nature of certain passages of *Prometheus's Liver*, their pictorial and poetic content are doubtless related.[42] Nevertheless, it appears that no politically objectionable collages were confiscated in 1953.[43]

V.

In his book *Symboly obludností* [Symbols of Monstrosity],[44] Josef Vojvodík asks to what extent we can consider the activities of the Czech Surrealists after 1945 to be a direct continuation of the interwar avant-garde, or whether this designation would represent a neo-avant-garde in the Western sense. Here Vojvodík makes reference to the understanding of the term in the spirit of Peter Bürger. He asserts that the neo-avant-garde movement—including the contemporary circle of "unofficial" artists of the time—has become an institutionalized part of the culture industry, even though it uses a similar language as the avant-garde had in the period leading up to World War II. The products of the neo-avant-garde, however formally provocative, are accepted as art; social subversion by means of art is no longer possible. Vojvodík's theory of the uninterrupted continuity and permanent subversion of the Czech avant-garde is supported by the fact that the institutionalization of any artists independent of the state, not just the Surrealists, was unthinkable after 1948. The heirs of the avant-garde—whether direct, or simply because they came afterward—did their work outside institutions, bereft of contact with other centers of art and unknown to the wider public.

How can we assess the connection between the work of Jiří Kolář and the avant-garde or the neo-avant-garde at the turn of the 1950s? Such an evaluation of Kolář's work is important to potential comparisons with analogous expressions of Western European art, as well as for determining its relationship to contemporary art. Kolář's work sprang directly from prewar avant-garde influences. According to Jindřich Chalupecký, his encounter at the age of 16 with Marinetti's *Words in Freedom* in the Kladno library was pivotal for him.[45] It provided the impetus that put him on the artist's path. From the perspective of the collage, the Devětsil group and the activities of the Surrealists represented a strong tradition in Czechoslovakia that could either be championed or rejected. However, differences with regard to the prewar state of affairs derived not only from the different political situation following 1948 but also from the differing artistic ambitions of postwar artists. Whereas Devětsil's photomontages and Marinetti's *Words in Freedom* were examples of "“art in print” aimed at mass distribution, Jiří Kolář seemed to take the opposite approach: he cut images out of magazines, taking them out of circulation, and put them on display, for private handling and, eventually, individual viewing. Nevertheless, we find a similar shift from the public to the private sphere in the case of Surrealist collages. In addition, we may also consider Kolář's fascination with old pictorial materials from the turn of the 20th century to stem from Surrealism. Whereas the Surrealists (in Czechoslovakia, that meant not only Karel Teige but also Libor Fára, who was closer generationally to Kolář) uncovered the mysteries of the psychological subconscious by means of photo collages, Kolář's postwar endeavors pointed in a different direction, toward a critical reading of images in public spaces in order to understand their mode of manipulation. All of Kolář's work is a quest for truth, for authentic ways to reflect reality.

The barrier separating Kolář from the prewar avant-garde is the experience of World War II and an inability to convey that experience. He has a deep-seated need to understand how the meaning and significance of images are constituted. Based on a similar type of understanding, he wants to invent a new artistic language and find a new vantage point for artists themselves. In his essay "Snad nic, snad něco" [Probably Nothing, Probably Something], Kolář mentions the fundamental impact a visit to the Auschwitz concentration camp had on him: "And my visit to the Auschwitz Museum showed me the way to the idea of assemblages. It was one of the most profound shocks I'd ever experienced in my life: enormous glassed-in rooms full of hair, shoes, luggage, clothing, prostheses, tableware, glasses, children's toys, etc. Everything imprinted with a horrendous fate, imprinted with something art could not hope to capture or would probably never manage to capture."[46] Confronted with the monstrous dimensions of the "death factory," in the presence of piled remnants of lost lives, Kolář comes to a conclusion similar to the oft-misconstrued thought attributed to Theodor Adorno, that to write poetry after Auschwitz is barbaric.[47] Art must be invented anew and differently. Kolář's visit to Auschwitz impelled him to think beyond the frontiers of his previous perceptions of art: his poems became journal entries or speech transcripts and his once-Surrealist collages were replaced by simply collecting and presenting individual images.

The manner in which Jiří Kolář works with images in his collages from the turn of the 1950s was not unusual at the time. In contrast to Surrealist collages, with their complicated compositions emphasizing patterns of images, other postwar artists also made do with the simple assembly and mediation of existing materials. The artist stresses his or her role not as author but as viewer. We find parallels in various movements of avant-garde art around the world in the 1950s and 1960s. Arman, Piero Manzoni, and Yves Klein did not create sculptures but worked with found objects. In addition to painting, reproductions and collages assert themselves; the motif of the direct print gains importance. It is as if both the political and artistic crises of the postwar years required a return to the world in its "real" form and provoked a wave of a specific type of new realism.

I am convinced that Kolář's work bears the marks of neo-avant-garde art in the sense of the potential for direct comparisons with pop art, Fluxus, or Situationism, albeit perhaps against the artist's own convictions. Kolář felt no kinship with French *Nouveau réalisme*; he considered his endeavors to be diametrically opposed to it. Nonetheless, it is precisely there—chiefly at the level of intellectual ambitions—that we might find clear parallels with his own approaches. The strategy of the *affichistes* and many other postwar collagists—whether in the fields of art, literature, or film—is parallel to the Situationist method of *détournement*, or variation on a previous work. The Situationists would forfeit their own voices and work exclusively with existing artifacts. They certainly did not, however, forswear the creation of meaning. They would rework existing images, texts, or film in a way that subversively altered and critically transformed their original meanings. "*Détournement* operated according to the logic of the negation of the negation; I mean to say that here we are still witness to the conviction that the only way out of the paralysis and anomie of the present was through mining and mimicking the lowest depths of nothingness, randomness, abjection, dispersal, insignificance—in the hope that out of the utter detritus of the 'modern' would come something charged and whole."[48] In Czechoslovakia, Egon Bondy and Ivo Voseďálek also trawled through similar cultural detritus originating in the alienating language of consumer society and political propaganda. Photographs and articles from newspapers back then ostensibly represented reality; in actuality, however, they were entirely mendacious. The images and words did not mirror the surrounding world but were mere carriers or containers of meanings which the propaganda machine filled in as needed. Such linguistic alienation and abuse might be shocking to those who were aware of it; nonetheless, artists were looking to elicit a similar reaction. Egon Bondy debased language—emptied it of content—in order to show subversively how the process worked. Along with its other layers, he sought possibilities for new contents that might undergird a story diametrically opposed to the dreck published in newspapers. Similarly, Kolář made use of kitschy images from popular magazines to speak of the fate of modern people and the ability of art to reflect it.

As an example of the change in Kolář's literary work after the war, we may put forward his later poem *Sun Tzu on the Art of Poetry* (1957). Several years after his release from prison and his forced exile from the cultural sphere of socialist Czechoslovakia, Kolář appropriated the ancient Chinese text on war strategy as a vehicle for his own ideas, substituting the reflections on military matters with his own on the character of poetry.[49] As Petr Šrámek wrote, "it was as if Kolář was not the author, or only in part—perhaps as translator, for example."[50] Nonetheless, Jiří Kolář was not translating from a foreign language but "translating from one poetics into another, from one context into another."[51] The same may be said of Kolář's collages: he used images from magazines of dubious quality that fell within the sphere of mass culture or even kitsch, but through them he told the story of the avant-garde.

Marie Klimešová compares Kolář's early works chiefly to those—sometimes remarkably similar from a visual perspective—of British artists Eduardo Paolozzi and Richard Hamilton of the Independent Group, the founders of "British pop art." Klimešová claims that one of the determining phenomena of postwar art globally was the new relationship between art and popular culture that would eventually produce pop art. Considering the extent to which Kolář used historical images, it appears that he pursued his interest in popular culture on a more general level than did his British counterparts. He was not interested in postwar developments involving the expanding complex of mass media, culture, and the market—he had no opportunities to familiarize himself with them anyway. He was attracted by the language of images; 50-year-old photographs would serve to demonstrate its systematic nature. At the same time, Kolář articulates a visual syntax with much greater precision; in his works from the *Bunk* series, Paolozzi intuitively heaps up images that capture his attention.

However, relating Kolář's early collages to British pop art is not the only contemporary international parallel we can draw. For example, in the 1950s the loose gathering of artists and literary figures known as the Wiener Gruppe moved about in territory similar to that explored by Kolář. Members Gerhard Rühm and Oswald Wiener created text-and-picture collages from magazine and newspaper clippings. A careful selection of works from *Kind und Welt* [Child and World] (1958), a series that set photographs from social and political magazine rubrics against medical photographs of disabled children, would be hard to distinguish from Kolář's collages. If we take into consideration Kolář's collages until 1953 as a whole, there is no doubt they share much with postwar neo-avant-garde tendencies and demonstrate an interest in work with archives. For example, German painter Gerhard Richter began assembling magazine cuttings and other visual materials less than a decade after Kolář. Although the first dozens of panels of his monumental *Atlas*, dating from the early 1960s on, have a different compositional structure, they evoke Kolář's collages nonetheless: once again we observe something like a clipping service established with multiple purposes in mind. Richter's *Atlas* was originally conceived as a source of inspiration for his painting and did not become its own artwork until later. Art historian John J. Curley interprets Richter's fascination with photographic images and his need to modify them in different ways as the result of a cultural phenomenon he calls "Cold War visuality."[52] After World War II, the socialist and capitalist worlds clashed ideologically. Photography became an important tool of propaganda. In connection with the context it was used in, one and the same photo could have different meanings; the medium of photography lost its trustworthiness. Indeed, it became a means of conveying disinformation and concealing truth. "Lying" or manipulable photography became the basis for artistic projects.

The degree to which Kolář's approach in his early collages may be considered conceptual art, or as prefiguring it, is an open question. As a visual artist, he is aiming to transcend traditional verbal poetry or, more generally, to go from text to image—in other words, to move against the current of most conceptual art, in which the importance of textual information grows. However, as a collagist, Kolář reduces his basic means of expression—the image—to a linguistic principle and works with it as one might work with language. In addition to the other characteristics of his work, this should be taken as one of the main constitutive elements of a conceptual understanding of art. If we consider the collages Kolář made before 1953, the most progressive of Kolář's oeuvre, then the way the artist himself saw them is confusing. As far as I know, at the time they were made, he showed them to his friends. Nevertheless, later, when conditions allowed, he never tried to exhibit these collages on their own and apparently considered them, in comparison with his later artwork, to be insufficiently representative. Instead, he saw them as a historically important phase. To a large extent, Kolář remained indifferent to questions regarding the nature of art itself. He thought of art as a tool for revealing the world. Kolář always emphasized the unique quality of works of visual art to make a forceful impression.

The question arises: to what extent does Jiří Kolář's oeuvre as a whole—despite his rhetoric involving a "dictionary of methods" and his constant formal experiments—say anything at all about his need to explore the character of his chosen artistic medium and its expressive capabilities? Kolář's unflagging variations on the possibilities of poetry and collage served him, first and foremost, to speak in a unique manner about what people were going through at the time. The question also arises: to what extent did Kolář really systematically break down the meanings of words, decomposing images into their prime elements in an analytic spirit, and to what extent did he simply like the way the results of the process looked?

VI.

The ways contemporary Czech artists have worked with collages since the forays of Jiří Kolář, over half a century old, are understandably varied. We can see a commonality in the initial process of creation—a prolonged examination of existing images and the need, by means of the manipulation collages make possible, to uncover their inner meanings. Nonetheless, current artists are doing their work in a different historical context—one in which images themselves have a different status than in the mid-20th century. In connection with the rise of the Internet, images became even more omnipresent beginning in the 1990s. Copying artifacts of cultural history and making use of that history are simple operations today. Artists no longer have to spend ages paging through faded magazines; smart searches in the universe of digital images are enough. The ease with which artists engage in collage work is influenced by their experience with digital technologies. TV surfing, playing computer games, browsing the Web, experience with remixing music and creating software all take forms we might compare to making collages today.[53]

Nevertheless, artists like Dominik Lang and Eva Koťátková do not use the Internet as a source for their images. For them, working with original paper materials is important. They think of images as authentic bearers of history that function as materialized memories helping to evoke an otherwise-inaccessible past. Most of the active

Czech artists making collages today are not interested in analyzing images spread by the media or in conceptually exploring their visual syntax. They return to the historical compositional form of the collage as a method for constructing a unified pictorial space. Often, in openly nostalgic works, the collage functions chiefly to strike up a dialogue with the past, whether on a personal or a more general level, with the historical forms of modernist thought and its legacy. Through collages, the legacy of aesthetic universalism and the heroic times of the artistic avant-garde may be read in a new way. An example of such an understanding is provided by a cycle of small paintings incorporating pasted cuttings created in 2012 by Vladimír Houdek. It is directly related to modernist art. Among the cuttings—in addition to photographs of different body parts alluding to the prewar period and its pictorial aesthetics—we may recognize famous figures of the world avant-garde at the turn of the 1920s (e.g., Emma Hennings, Mary Wigman, and Tristan Tzara) and references to iconic works such as *Abeceda* [Alphabet] by Vítězslav Nezval, Karel Teige, and Milča Mayerová. The artist juxtaposes photographs from the period with contemporary painterly interpretations employing modernist visual language; the result is a sort of homage or staking of a claim to a similar historical legacy.

Nonetheless, most of the time, contemporary reflections on the modernist past do not possess the kind of celebratory character we find in Houdek's works. The impressions they make are usually far less unambiguous. They are opportunities for relating subjectively and, at the same time, critically to a historical notion of modern society and its hopes. For this reason, such approaches play an important role in countries that were subjected to 20th-century socialist experiments associated with both modernization and totalitarianism. Paulina Olowska, an artist of world renown in this respect, was fascinated with Polish modernist visual culture from the 1930s to the 1970s. She and similar artists were no longer satisfied with a superficial rejection of the past; they were interested in the possibilities for evoking everyday life in the socialist era and bringing it into the present.

The dynamic of past and present in the Czech art scene is illustrated by *Spící město* [Sleeping City], a project by Dominik Lang from 2010 and 2011.[54] Exploring old photographs of his father, Jiří Lang, a sculptor active mainly in the 1960s and 1970s, enabled him to better understand not only his work but the time he lived in. This dialogue took the form of collages Lang created using photographs from the family album. In this way, his father's sculptures, which rarely left the confines of his studio, were displayed in a contemporary public space. The collages were a means to come up with a form of public presentation. Lang pasted them into nonexistent exhibitions, presenting them before an imaginary public, and placing them before contemporary architectural structures. Though in reality he would not have known how to deal with the sculptures' conceptual references or the logistics of their placement, at least in collages he could place them on drawn-in shelves or boxes. In addition, he juxtaposed them on paper with his own artworks. Similar experiments became the basis for subsequent sculptural assemblages that interconnected the work of Jiří and Dominik Lang in reality. For Dominik Lang, the collages and drawings associated with *Sleeping City* were not mere preparatory works. Nor does Lang's arranged photo in his father's studio in the project catalogue serve merely as an illustration of the final sculptural project. All of these components are equivalent parts of a whole that cannot be reduced to simply a sculptural installation in the Czechoslovak pavilion at the 2011 Venice Biennale.

Dominik Lang's use of authentic private pictorial materials takes the form of a subjective reflection on the past. However, I am convinced that it also has a political dimension related to the present day. Lang's *Sleeping City* introduces into the present a forgotten and suppressed past and forces us to take a stand on it. The displacement mechanism is demonstrated here through the specific example of his father. Nonetheless, after witnessing his investigation, it is hard for the viewer to escape the thought that the mechanism also functions more generally in relation to our own recent history.

In this respect, the work of Eva Koťátková, whose central theme is the ways in which individuals are formed (or deformed, to be more precise) in the environment of modern society, is even more explicit. In her case, the body of work we have is certainly not a private meditation or a historical project. Her collages involve images from textbooks and medical manuals, often combined with official expressions of socialist public life. In addition to images of children, her collages incorporate floor plans, clippings from anatomical atlases, and photographs of aboriginal peoples and animals. She uses authentic, time-worn photographs taken in the mid-20th century that evoke the period. She focuses her attention on phenomena having to do with modern education, hygiene, prefabricated architecture, correctional facilities, and collective exercises. She cuts up photographs and combines the pieces, often complementing them with drawings. Her works also transcend the collage form, often delving into spatial installations and performances.

Koťátková is interested in the regulation of interpersonal relationships and the instruments of social control, especially as represented in the school system. In the name of general welfare, education participates in the constitution of a comprehensive system of social surveillance in the Foucauldian sense. The visual forms its methods take can evoke not only medical practice but also imprisonment. Teaching, exercises, and games are interpreted by Koťátková as means to form flattened-out personalities in the name of social engineering. Thus, her collages enable her to expose the repressiveness of rationally justifiable and science-based pedagogical practices by juxtaposing them with similar systems of repression. During the educational process, children are comparable to animals being tamed and studied. Education aims to break the "savage" or the "animal" in each child.[55] In her collages and drawings, children are confined in cages or cramped spaces, which allow them to move only in predetermined trajectories. A less corporeal but no less physically limiting element in Koťátková's collages is modern architecture, whose utilitarian character brings to mind correctional facilities or animal paddocks.[56] Motifs often found in her artworks include blindfolded eyes and effects involving perspective. The mechanics of children's movements are insinuated by means of drawn-in skeletons. Just as it is possible to repair a broken bone using splints or crutches, an unformed or broken mind can be corrected through simple restrictive techniques. The result is an outwardly imposed geometrization of both corporeality and social structures. [ill. 2]

On a substantive level, we could perhaps draw a parallel between Jiří Kolář, Dominik Lang, and Eva Koťátková based on their need to deal with personal or social issues or even traumas by means of their art and the media they select. Their use of authentic photographic images has the character of a symbolic represention of real situations for therapeutic ends. War debris and the wreckage of modernism, a lost faith in the truthfulness of images and an effort to find truth in them again, finding and revealing the hidden facets of seemingly straightforward statements—all this speaks of the status of human beings and the social environment they create for themselves. There might seem to be something paradoxical in the comparison of the artists: Jiří Kolář worked mainly with pictures from the turn of the 20th century, but a dialogue with premodern history was not important to him; he was mainly concerned with his time and its future development. Both Lang and Koťátková deal with the mid-20th century, but their interest in the past does not represent a turning away from the present. On the contrary—it represents a way of coming to a new understanding. Václav Magid expressed the importance to contemporary artists of the relationship between past and present in a text devoted to the works of Vasil Artamonov and Alexey Klyuykov, two other artists who also devoted considerable time to collage work: "The intention of reconstructing a project for the future acquires personal dimension: we are creating our own history."[57] The collage is thus not only a way to look upon the past but also a means of interpreting it—or perhaps even of proposing alternative ways to articulate it.

At one time, collages had helped uncover how the visual world of modernity functioned, to facilitate a better understanding of the ways in which modernity had simultaneously both defined and deformed images. During the intellectual crises of the mid-20th century, creating collages functioned as a way to examine the present and demonstrate to what extent the mass media and the new visual languages of the time were relativizing images and their meanings. Today, standing in a time set apart from modernity by its ostensible stability and its relative lack of domestic sociopolitical conflict, Czech artists take up collage as a tool to return to modernity. Nonetheless, they are not interested in a programmatic anachronicity or in resigning themselves to a postmodern present. Like Kolář, they address a crisis of meaning in art, even though theirs may not be as dramatic as the crisis of about 60 years earlier. They embarked on an exploration of the historical context and the foundations on which the present rests as well, which is evidence of the changing thought processes of contemporary artists and the chronological expansion of their fields of interest, expressed in their selection of expressive resources.

For most of the 20th century, dramatic discontinuities caused by historical circumstances have characterized the Czech cultural scene. Not surprisingly, we see an intense, though sometimes primarily rhetorical, desire for continuity. Since entire layers of cultural heritage were forcibly eliminated several times during the 20th century, artists felt, and feel, a need to lay claim to them publicly and pick up where others had left off. Again and again, both artists and art historians confronted the task of envisaging a local cultural history capable of being integrated with the present. Similar perceptions arose out of historical circumstances, whether they represented a specific reaction to the workings of totalitarian political systems, or the idea of cultural history as a single given and unchanging hierarchy of creative achievements. Dominik Lang and Eva Koťátková build on this tradition, albeit in a new way. Today we see the past as much more dynamic than it was thought to be even a few decades ago—it changes substantially depending on who is considering it and when. Nonetheless, the urgency of Lang and Koťátková's present-day efforts finds expression in a poem by Jiří Kolář: "We are eyewitnesses to how the disintegration of our cultural heritage is becoming something worse than when that heritage stops dead and stagnates."[58]

[1] For more information on the prizes and recipients in particular years, see http://www.laureat.cz/ (accessed April 10, 2014).

[2] *Roky ve dnech, české umění 1945–1957* [Years in Days: Czech Art 1945–1957], Prague City Gallery, May 28–September 19, 2010; exhibition curator, Marie Klimešová.

[3] As Marie Klimešová writes: "these collages represented a veritable *privatissimum*, a form of therapy and an artistically conceived inner dialogue." See Marie Klimešová, *Roky ve dnech* [Years in Days], Arbor vitae, Prague 2010, p. 315.

[4] In the Czech sphere, we must mention Barbora Klímová, whose *Replaced* is the subject of the chapter "The Politics of Intimacy: Czechoslovak Performance Art in the 1970s and Its Remakes" in the present volume (p. 206). In addition, in 2013 Klímová published *Navzájem, umělci a společenství na Moravě 70. a 80. let 20. století* [Mutually: Artists and Society in Moravia in the 1970s and 1980s], a book that is basically an art-historical study of the life and works of a certain segment of the artistic community of Moravia. Other authors dealing with historical artists and their works who deserve mention are Zbyněk Baladrán, Václav Magid, and Jiří Thýn.

[5] In the Czech sphere, this way of thinking has come to be represented by theorist Karel Císař, curator of the exhibitions *Vzpomínky na budoucnost* [Memories of the Future] (2009) and *Obrazy a předobrazy* [Images and Prototypes] (2013). The same year, the first Czech publication on the subject was published—see Jan Zálešák, *Minulá budoucnost* [Past Future], VUT in Brno, Faculty of Visual Arts, and tranzit.cz, Brno and Prague 2013.

[6] The term *modernology* was first used by artist Florian Pumhösl in the context of the project he presented at *Documenta 12* in 2007. One of the slogans of the showcase was the provocative question: Is modernity our antiquity?

[7] According to Jan Zálešák, collage is a key tendency in the art of the historiographic turn. See Zálešák, *Minulá budoucnost* [Past Future], p. 50.

[8] "I was interested from the beginning in finding an area of friction between art and literature." Jiří Kolář, *Odpovědi* [Answers], Index, Cologne 1984, p. 8.

[9] See, for example, Miroslav Lamač, "Koláž v současném českém umění" [The Collage in Contemporary Czech Art], *Výtvarné umění* [Visual Arts], 1966, no. 6/7, p. 356.

[10] See Jindřich Toman, *Moderní česká kniha, Foto/montáž tiskem* [The Modern Czech Book: Photo/Montage in Print], Kant, Prague 2009, p. 70, and others. This history was even known to Jiří Kolář: "An interest in urban folklore revealed to me that one of the first collages was made by Jaroslav Hašek for *Svět zvířat* [Animal World] and also taught me to see many things in unusual contexts." Jiří Kolář, *Slovník metod* [A Dictionary of Methods], Gallery, Prague 1999, p. 114.

[11] See Benjamin Buchloh, "From Faktura to Factography," *October*, vol. 30 (Autumn 1984), p. 96.

[12] On the genesis of the photomontage and the beginnings of John Heartfield's art, see Andrés Mario Zervigón, *John Heartfield and the Agitated Image*, University of Chicago Press, Chicago and London 2012, pp. 39–64.

[13] See Peter Bürger, *Theory of the Avant-Garde*, University of Minnesota Press, Minneapolis 1994, p. 75.

[14] See Zervigón, *John Heartfield and the Agitated Image*, p. 7.

[15] Rosalind E. Krauss, "The Photographic Conditions of Surrealism," *October*, vol. 19 (Winter 1981), p. 19.

[16] Beginning in 1936, the model for such publications was to be a new incarnation of the weekly *Life*. At the time, there was a marked restriction of text; each number was largely filled with photographs and captions. Numerous other magazines around the world began to copy the format.

[17] Toman, *Moderní česká kniha* [The Modern Czech Book], p. 252.

[18] Jindřich Toman describes the effects of such graphic strategies as follows: "Here, graphic design is part of the magazine's own substance—simultaneity, kaleidoscopic abundance and surprise. In this way, a specific matrix is created that leads the reader to expect the specific view that is typical for each genre." See Toman, *Moderní česká kniha* [The Modern Czech Book], p. 254.

[19] "The image is a pure creation of the mind. It cannot be born from a comparison but from a juxtaposition of two more or less distant realities." André Breton, *Manifestoes of Surrealism*, trans. Richard Seaver and Helen R. Lane, Ann Arbor Paperbacks, 1972, p. 20. In this passage, Breton cites an idea of Pierre Reverdy.

[20] According to Jindřich Chalupecký, this work represents "the pictorial analogy of a poem." See Chalupecký, "Příběh Jiřího Koláře" [The Story of Jiří Kolář], in Jindřich Chalupecký, *Na hranicích umění* [On the Frontiers of Art], Prostor a Arkýř, Prague 1990, p. 57. Other interpreters of Kolář's work arrive at similar conclusions: "For Kolář, the world of the image is only in secondarily a world of artistic forms. He understands it mainly as a world interpreted literarily, as a world of poetic metaphors and metamorphoses." See Miroslav Lamač, *Kolářovy nové metamorfózy* [Kolář's New Metamorphoses], in *Jiří Kolář*, Odeon, Prague 1993, p. 129.

[21] Krauss, "The Photographic Conditions of Surrealism."

[22] Kolář, *Slovník metod* [A Dictionary of Methods], p. 170.

[23] In the late 1930s, both avant-garde theorists and contemporary journalists discovered the phenomenon of kitsch, which they tried to analyze and eliminate from cultural life in a variety of ways. On the Czech context, see Milan Pech, *Umění a kýč* [Art and Kitsch], in Hana Rousová (ed.), *Konec Avantgardy? Od Mnichovské dohody ke komunistickému převratu* [End of the Avant-Garde? From the Munich Agreement to the Communist Coup], Arbor vitae, Řevnice 2011, pp. 317–330.

[24] He might have obtained mainly current issues during his trips to Paris and Great Britain in 1947 or 1948.

[25] We may identify, for example, an issue of the magazine *Český svět* [Czech World] from 1908 or a photograph related to events of 1911 or 1916.

[26] In this respect, it is noteworthy that Kolář never attempted to exhibit them in large quantities during his lifetime.

[27] Categories include not only "Music," "Food–Drink," "Documents," and "Photographs," but also "Fatefulness."

[28] Citation based on a document in the estate of Jiří Kolář.

[29] In view of Jiří Kolář's biography, this need not have been by accident. The collages at issue here were created up until Kolář's politically motivated imprisonment in 1953. However, the first police interrogations had already taken place two months before he was detained, and his home was searched. As a person who had no illusions regarding the character of the regime, he had enough time to dispose of any materials that could have been compromising. This might constitute a practical explanation of the absence of contemporary pictorial materials in Kolář's collages: he got rid of them by way of prevention. For more details on Kolář's persecution, see text in the magazine *Česká literatura* [Czech Literature], vol. 61, no. 4, September 2013, pp. 546–592.

[30] Jiřina Hauková and Jindřich Chalupecký translated *The Waste Land* in its entirety; it was published in 1947 by the B. Stýblo publishing house. Kolář and Kotalík only translated into Czech a fragment that was published in the magazine *Život* [Life], no. 6, April 1947. Both translations were reprinted—see Thomas Stearns Eliot, *Pustá země* [The Waste Land], Protis, Prague 1996.

[31] Egon Bondy, *Kořeny českého literárního undergroundu v letech 1949–1953*, Hanťa Press, no. 8, Prague 1990, pp. 5–9. As cited

in Miloslava Slavíčková, *Hrabalova literární koláže* [Hrabal's Literary Collages], Akropolis, Prague 2004, pp. 59–60.

[32] Bohumil Hrabal, as cited in Slavíčková, *Hrabalova literární koláže* [Hrabal's Literary Collages], p. 153.

[33] Similarly, in 1949 he interpreted "Podzim [Autumn]," a poem by František Halas known today only through secondhand accounts. See Kolář, *Slovník metod* [A Dictionary of Methods], p. 90.

[34] Jiří Kolář, *1. července—pátek, Očitý svědek* [July 1—Friday: Eyewitness]. As cited in Kolář, *Dílo Jiřího Koláře* [The Work of Jiří Kolář], vol. 2, Odeon and Mladá fronta, Prague 1997, p. 188.

[35] Klimešová, *Roky ve dnech* [Years in Days], p. 306.

[36] Zdeněk Urbánek, *Ztracená země* [Lost World], Franz Kafka Publishing House, Prague 1992, pp. 481–482.

[37] Kolář, *Odpovědi* [Answers], p. 38.

[38] A Surrealist game during which participants collectively create a drawing or text. Individuals take turns, with the next participant seeing only an insignificant part of the previous participant's work.

[39] Roland Barthes also concerned himself with the character of newspaper photography in the postwar period. His 1961 essay "Photographic Report" analyzes how photographic images work in printed periodicals. He concludes that newspaper and magazine photographs apparently shows only what they are presenting. In reality, however, they contain other meanings. So photography conceals a paradox within itself: it encompasses two messages. The first can be found on the level of the photographic image itself, as mediated by a perfect analogy with the reality depicted. The second message is inserted into photographs by the manner in which the photographic image is produced and presented; moreover, it mediates between society and a given reality.

[40] Jiří Kolář, *16. prosinec—pátek, Očitý svědek* [December 16—Friday: Eyewitness]. As cited in Kolář, *Dílo Jiřího Koláře* [The Work of Jiří Kolář], p. 284.

[41] Jiří Cieslar, *Kolářovy dávné otázky (Nad Jiřím Kolářem, hlavně deníkovým)* [Kolář's Long-Standing Questions (On Jiří Kolář, Chiefly as Diarist)], in Jiří Cieslar, *Hlas deníku* [The Diary's Voice], Torst, Prague 2002, p. 264.

[42] Paradoxically, the politically faulty passages for which Kolář was imprisoned for nine months in 1953, escaping further punishment thanks to an amnesty, did not become available to readers until 2013—over half a century after they were written. In them, he openly criticizes the political system, Stalin, Gottwald, and the leading representatives of Czech society and cultural life. See *Česká literatura* [Czech Literature], vol. 61, no. 4, September 2013, pp. 546–592.

[43] See the home search report dated February 9, 1953, in the archives of the Institute for the Study of Totalitarian Regimes (ÚSTR).

[44] Marie Langerová, Josef Vojvodník, Anja Tippnerová, and Josef Hrdlička, *Symboly obludnosti* [Symbols of Monstrosity], Malvern, Prague 2010.

[45] Chalupecký, "Příběh Jiřího Koláře" [The Story of Jiří Kolář], p. 43.

[46] Jiří Kolář, *Snad nic, snad něco* [Probably Nothing, Probably Something], in *Slovo, písmo, akce, hlas* [Word, Script, Action, Voice], Československý spisovatel, Prague 1967, p. 182.

[47] Theodor W. Adorno, "Cultural Criticism and Society," in Theodor W. Adorno, *Prisms*, MIT Press, Cambridge 1995, p. 34.

[48] Tom McDonough, "The Beautiful Language of My Century," in *Reinventing the Language of Contestation in Postwar France, 1945–1968*, MIT Press, Cambridge and London 2007, p. 6.

[49] Guy Debord would use the same strategy ten years later in numerous passages of his book *The Society of the Spectacle*. Without citing his sources, he quotes long passages from works by Marx and others.

[50] Petr Šrámek, "Abordáž aneb O zajímavém proslovení o zbraních a umění" [*Abordage* or On an Interesting Speech on Weapons and Art], in Oldřich Král and Jiří Kolář, *Mistr Sun o válečném umění / Mistr Sun o básnickém umění* [Master Sun on the Art of War / Master Sun on the Art of Poetry], Dokořán, Prague 2008, p. 213.

[51] Ibid., p. 213.

[52] John J. Curley, *A Conspiracy of Images: Andy Warhol, Gerhard Richter, and the Art of the Cold War*, Yale University Press, New Haven and London, 2013.

[53] Charlie White, "Cut and Paste: On the Collage Impulse Today," *Artforum*, March 2009, pp. 210–215.

[54] See Dominik Lang, *Spící město* [Sleeping City], tranzit, Prague 2011.

[55] Her work with animal motifs or photographs of primitive tribes recalls the techniques developed in the 1930s by Hannah Höch.

[56] In 2008 architecture was a frequent element in the collages of Daniel Pitín. He was interested in the social dimensions of the spaces architecture creates.

[57] Václav Magid, "Budoucnost je naším jediným cílem" [The Future is Our Only Objective], in Vasil Artamonov and Alexey Klyuykov, *Budoucnost je naším jediným cílem* [The Future is Our Only Objective], SVIT, Prague 2011, p. 29.

[58] Jiří Kolář, *30. leden—neděle, Očitý svědek* [30 January—Sunday: Eyewitness]. As cited in Kolář, *Dílo Jiřího Koláře* [The Work of Jiří Kolář], p. 129.

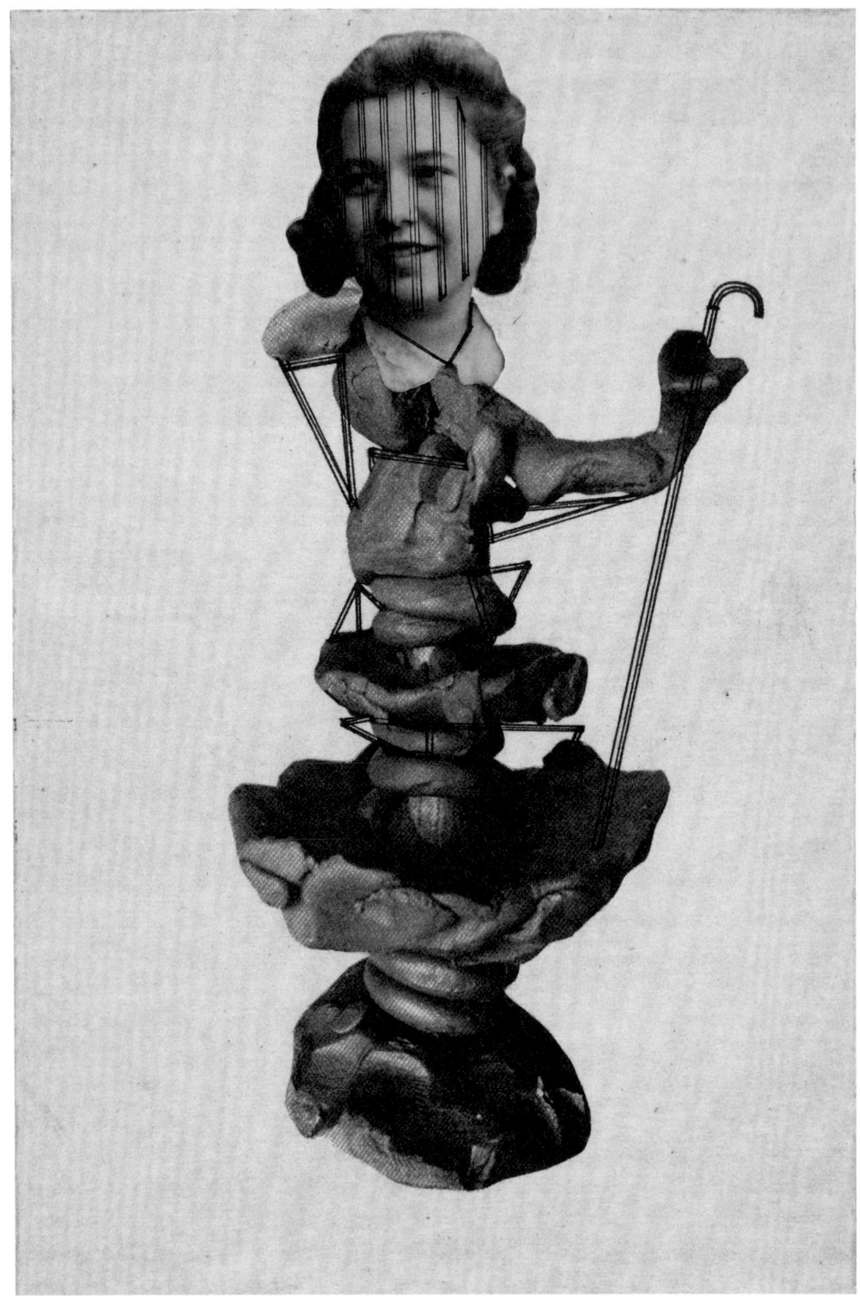

[ill. 2] Eva Kořátková, from the *Převýchovný stroj* [Re-Educational Machine] series, 2011
Collage, 21 × 30 cm
Courtesy of the artist

Fluxus in the Czech Lands and Czechs in Flux: Communication Networks, Information Services, and the Art World Hierarchy

I.

Communication between the global and local art contexts was limited in Communist Czechoslovakia during the 1950s and 1960s. Still, information on new cultural trends would make it across the Iron Curtain. It was possible to peruse out-of-date publications—and some recent ones—on contemporary art at the library of the Museum of Decorative Arts in Prague. During the political thaw in the late 1950s, reports on Western art began to penetrate into the official art periodicals as well. We find the first serious mention of contemporary abstract art in 1957 in "Umění nezobrazující a neobjektivní, jeho současný stav" [Non-Depicting and Non-Objective Art: Its State Today], a famous article by Jiří Padrta that appeared in the journal *Umění* [Art] in 1957.[1] However, any awareness of global trends among Czech artists was based mainly on the ability of individuals to obtain foreign magazines or catalogues and on contacts with other artists: particularly important were individual trips abroad. For example, a series of organized trips to Expo 58, the world exhibition in Brussels, played an important educational role, as did the formation of communities of friends that shared information about contemporary trends in art.

In circles of Czech artists, loans of otherwise-inaccessible materials, translations, group viewings, and debates were contemporary rituals. There is remarkable evidence of this, for example, in *Let let* [The Flight of Years], a memoir by poets and cultural organizers Bohumila Grögerová and Josef Hiršal. In a report from December 1958, we read:

> This time things were particularly exciting at the Medeks'. As soon as we sat down, an upset Mikuláš showed us a catalogue of pop art, a new art movement whose first works had already been exhibited in London and New York last year, apparently, and asked what we thought about it. We were seeing it for the first time and couldn't get over our amazement. That Santa Claus on the cover, for starters! […] And Kolář adds: in New York recently an artist named Allan Kaprow organized the first so-called happening. Nobody can quite imagine what it's all about, actually, but we're guessing it's related to pop art somehow.[2]

This short excerpt gives a good idea of the mechanisms of information transfer and their reach. Members of the cultural elites who had access to information from the West would share it with their friends. With some exceptions, they generally did not have immediate experience of the artworks themselves but through catalogues, magazines, and books that brought news from the rest of the world, which the close-knit Czech community did not have much access to. In one excited, admiring, but also charmingly puzzled passage, the memoir combines pop art and happenings—two positions that in reality represented quite distinct artistic phenomena that were also unconnected in time.

We must call into question Grögerová's and Hiršal's dating of the reminiscences to 1958, for they probably took place subsequently. Although *This Is Tomorrow*, the exhibition that defined British pop art, was held in London in 1956, there was no Santa Claus on the catalogue's cover. Moreover, the term "pop art" had not yet been used in connection with the exhibition. It was first used at the end of 1958 by the critic Lawrence Alloway—who, moreover, was not naming a new art movement but using it in a different sense. The same is true of the use of the term "happening" and the mention of Allan Kaprow. If we take the dating at face value, it would have been a remarkably speedy instance of information transfer. Aside from a single occurrence in a university magazine in February 1958, Allan Kaprow did not use the word "happening" until the October 1958 issue of *ARTnews* magazine, in a famous essay titled "The Legacy of Jackson Pollock."[3] The work *Eighteen Happenings in Six Parts*, considered the first of its kind, was performed by Kaprow in New York in October 1959. Unless the whole encounter at the Medek apartment is meant as literary hyperbole, it probably took place sometime after 1960. For the standards of Czechoslovakia at the time, the intellectual salon comprising—in addition to the Medeks—Kolář, Grögerová, and Hiršal, and later Jindřich Chalupecký and Vladimir Burda was lively and well informed.

The word "happening" soon took hold in the American and world press, even though the new art form was perceived mainly as involving outlandish stunts. By the early 1960s, happenings had already become synonymous in the tabloid press with wild parties or unusual and provocative behavior. Even in the official Czechoslovak press there were reports, perhaps distorted, of this new form of avant-garde expression. One such source was *Současná hudba na Západě* [Contemporary Music in the West] (1963) by musician Jaromír Podešva.[4] In his travelogue, Podešva describes his experience in the music world of Western Europe and the United States in 1960 and 1961. Though the book, which had a print run of 6,500 copies, is grounded in the ideology of its time, it still provides information about various avant-garde musical currents. The book includes two *Tragikomické přílohy aneb Malé seznamy neodadaismu, případně neosurrealismů* [Tragicomical Appendices or Small Neo-Dadaist or Perhaps Neosurrealist Lists].[5] In them, Podešva describes three dozen artworks, more than half of which are by John Cage. For his readers in Czechoslovakia, Podešva describes prepared musical instruments, compositions for radio receivers, and scripts for stage performances, including details of the artist's instructions for how the piece should be executed. Although Cage's work seemed decadent and amusing to him, he gave an altogether impartial account of it. In other places Podešva describes pieces by Stockhausen in which the sound of a motorcycle is imitated and explains the principles of aleatoric music. However, we can hardly consider such a book a rigorous introduction to the above art practices on the Czech scene.[6]

In 1965 writer Jiří Mucha published a book titled *Černý a bílý New York* [Black and White New York], about the American cultural capital. The first edition had a print run of 12,000 copies, and in 1966 there was a 20,000-copy reprint.[7] In the book, Mucha provided comprehensive information about current art movements, pop art, op art, and happenings. We even find a 14-line quotation from Kaprow's "The Legacy of Jackson Pollock." Compared to Podešva, Mucha is not ironic; he tries to situate happenings for the general reader in the broader context of 20th-century art. Information about the new art form penetrated into the Czechoslovak popular press as well. In February 1966, an article taken from the German magazine *Stern* was published in the magazine *100 + 1 zahraniční zajímavost* [100 + 1 Interesting Things Abroad].[8] With some exaggeration, but in essence accurately, it described the history of happenings in America and Europe, named the first artists who organized them, and even offered readers a glossary of basic terms related to the new art form.

We read of many other articles, whether in the specialized or popular press, in Pavlína Morganová's study titled *České akční umění šedesátých let v dobovém tisku* [Czech Action Art of the 1960s in the Contemporary Press].[9] This creates the impression that Czech newspapers and magazines were full of reports on happenings and avant-garde art. Even the popular weekly magazine *Mladý svět* [Young World] and the tabloid newspaper *Večerní Praha* [Evening Prague] printed stories on the Prague Fluxus festival in spring 1966. However, they interpreted the event as an eccentric student prank. Nonetheless, information was available in periodicals with circulations in the hundreds of thousands. George Maciunas, founder and coordinator of the Fluxus movement, could only dream of such coverage in the United States. May we therefore regard the Czech public as especially well informed about the world of avant-garde art? Certainly not.

In 1960 John Cage appeared live on *I've Got a Secret*, a humorous panel game show on the American TV network CBS, with his live rendition of "Water Walk." The show was watched by millions of viewers, but such events evidently had little influence on the reception of avant-garde music. We can find simplistic, sensational, or directly misleading articles about unusual artistic expressions at the time all over the world, most often in contexts devoted to entertaining curiosities—with the difference that in Paris or New York, for example, those who were seriously interested could get information not only from *Newsweek* or *Paris Match* but also from specialized journals, lectures, or even the galleries and museums where such art was presented. In other words, these new modes of artistic expression were being debated on many different levels. The quality of art in the 20th century is less obvious in the artwork itself; instead, it derives mainly from context, from the place the work occupies in the debate about art as a whole.

It is necessary to distinguish between awareness and understanding, which for postwar art are two completely different ways of perceiving works of art. Apart from a few exceptions, the information to be had in the Czech lands during the 1960s was predominantly superficial. The meanings of words and terms associated with the avant-garde in art were unclear, and because there was no sufficiently broad specialized deliberation, they were easy to misconstrue in journalistic practice. In 1969, for example, the term "happening" appeared in *Muž v zástěře* [Man in an Apron], a fictionalized cookbook by humorist Achille Gregor. In a chapter titled "What to Do with a Bear," we find a description of a variety show featuring trained bears. One of them has gotten out of control and destroyed the articles in its cage: "It did something with a container of water in its cage that people later started calling a 'happening' and later 'pop art' and which to this day you can see in the display window of a cultural stand on Národní třída [National Avenue, in central Prague]. It wasn't very involved, as it had so few materials. But it tried. And if it had persevered, it might even have outdone Salvator [sic] Dalí."[10]

Even though the author confused pop art and happenings and got Dalí's first name wrong, we must deduce from the quotation that the procedures of action art were even familiar, at least in a simplified and deformed form, to Czech readers of entertaining cookbooks. Moreover, from the comments regarding Národní třída, the reaction to Jindřich Chalupecký's program for the exhibition taking place at the time in the Václav Špála Gallery is evident. Curiously, the close journalistic connection between pop art and happenings brings us back to the introductory citation from *The Flight of Years*, with its excited confusion of terms and the exotic, cabaret-like image of the avant-garde based on a mistaken reading of simplistic journalistic texts.

One of the dominant trends in Czech writing on art in the 1960s was "reports on trends in Western art." The authors of such texts—Jindřich Chalupecký being among the best of them—were inspired by a sincere effort to acquaint the Czech public with world events, which almost always led to facile and sometimes comical generalizations. A text by Miloslav Topinka published in the journal *Sešity pro mladou literaturu* [Notebooks for Young Literature] in November 1968 may serve as an example. Based on an article in *Newsweek*, Topinka provided a succinct review of current events in the US art world. If we examine the text in detail, we must ask what benefits such writing—published without any reproductions—could have brought. Topinka's text, for instance, acquainted Czechs with the work of Bruce Nauman: "Bruce Nauman photographs mounds of flour being poured on the floor. His book *CLEARSKY* presents just ten photographs of a perfectly clear cloudless blue sky which is different each time."[11] Both Chalupecký and Topinka adopt, each in his own way, the manner of the personal exchange of information on new trends among friends, which, beginning in the late 1960s, began to take place in the pages of Czechoslovak cultural magazines.

Personal contacts played a significant role in the penetration of information about developments in international avant-garde art into Czechoslovakia. Contact that had taken place between artists in Western capitals and in Czechoslovakia prior to 1948 was largely suspended in the 1950s, though in the late 1950s, some of it resumed. For example, Jan Kotík was able to travel to Europe several times at that point. Not only did he know artists from the former COBRA group, he also kept in touch with a circle of artists around the nascent Situationist International. Kotík met with its members repeatedly in the years 1956–1964. However, the frequency of Kotík's trips abroad was quite exceptional for the time. Those artists who managed to get permission to go on short-term foreign trips mostly had enough trouble coming to terms with their direct experience of different social systems.[12] For understanding the evolution of art across the world, for networking, or for organizing joint international activities, the best medium proved to be correspondence with or visits by foreign artists.

In the postwar period, certain types of artistic expression arose that proved particularly suitable for international exchange. One of the model cases in the 1950s and 1960s was concrete poetry. A lively intercontinental community of like-minded artists arose within the framework of this literary movement (which was, however, strongly associated with the visual arts and music). Sometimes they did without translations and communicated at a distance through letters, magazines, and other publications. One such publication was an international anthology of concrete poetry put together by American poet Emmett Williams for Something Else Press in 1967.[13] It contained several contributions from Czechoslovakia, and in scope it was reminiscent of the *Experimentální poezie* [Experimental Poetry], a variation published by editors Bohumila Grögerová and Josef Hiršal the same year. Emmett Williams had lived in Western Europe for nearly two decades and was well acquainted with the community of artists doing concrete poetry there. Moreover, he was in contact with certain artists from Czechoslovakia. His own work was translated into Czech by Karel Burda. Alongside works by pioneers of the movement, such as Eugen Gomringer and Helmut Heißenbüttel, Williams's anthology included poems by Jiří Kolář, Ladislav Novák, Bohumila Grögerová, Josef Hiršal, and Václav Havel. Williams saw them as manifestations of the second generation of concrete poetry, which nonetheless did not lessen their importance. Still, it is worth noting that Williams took some of the Czech contributions from Brazilian publications, which calls into question the idea of an unproblematic artistic exchange.

Something Else Press was owned by Fluxus artist Dick Higgins. Fluxus itself became an example of a global art initiative that, at the height of the Cold War, tried to transcend the geographical and political boundaries of the world. When Higgins and another Fluxus member, Ken Friedman, attempted to reformulate its foundational ideas in the 1980s, this internationalism took pride of place. It is well known that figures from the early 1960s associated with George Maciunas were engaged in a wide range of activities; among such figures we find poets, artists, and musicians. At the same time, Fluxus members came from an equally diverse range of countries. Ways of maintaining and facilitating communication became one of Fluxus's leitmotifs. Maciunas's network of correspondents and Nam June Paik's vision of global telecommunication bridges were based not only on utopian ideas about the democratization of human existence but also on the practical needs of a movement that refused to acknowledge the existing world borders. Artists connected with Fluxus visited Czechoslovakia several times in the 1960s: in 1966 there were two Fluxus festivals in Prague, and there was a relatively lively correspondence between members of the Fluxus movement and Czechoslovak artists and critics. Nonetheless, Fluxus and its ideas did not—with some exceptions—set root in Czechoslovakia. The difficult relations between the movement as it existed locally and abroad are evident in the following three case studies, which explore the history of the correspondence between certain artists associated with Fluxus and some artists from Czechoslovakia. At the same time, these specific examples also showcase the progress and nature of the relationships between artists on both sides of the Iron Curtain.

II.

Many sources as well as readily available publications indicate a direct link betwen Jiří Kolář and the Fluxus movement. For example, in a 2001 interview with Kolář, Marie Bergmanová discovered that "according to his recollection, Fluxus named Kolář an honorary member, even though on many points their views on the meaning of their activities diverged."[14] Evidence of the special relationship between Kolář and Fluxus can also be found on the side of the Fluxus movement. George Maciunas, the inspirer and coordinator of the movement in the mid-1960s, created dozens of logos of names of Fluxus members, including one for Kolář. Maciunas designed them for artists from the Fluxus movement, though he was not exhaustively systematic. In numerous other lists, directories, and other materials in which George Maciunas carefully identifies the core members of Fluxus and its sympathizers, Kolář—unlike Milan Knížák—is never mentioned. How are such inconsistencies to be explained? And how do they influence an evaluation of Kolář's work in the context of the international neo-avant-garde?

The exhibition *Fluxus East* and the accompanying publication help reconstruct the relations between Fluxus, Eastern Europe, and Czechoslovakia. In particular, a study by art historian Petra Stegmann and a memoir by Eric Andersen deal with the Czechoslovak context at the time.[15] The latter, along with Tony Andersen, visited Czechoslovakia in September 1964 and again in February 1965. The purpose of their trips was to establish contacts, organize Fluxus activities, and exchange printed materials. Not all of the information contained in the texts of *Fluxus East* can be considered corroborated and complete. Petra Stegmann probably did not have access to all the relevant archival materials and individuals—the Jiří Kolář Archive at the Museum of Czech Literature, for example, has not yet been studied thoroughly, and several of the individuals with direct memories of events are no longer alive. Moreover, Eric Andersen's memory may have developed lacunae in the course of half a century.

The first-ever Fluxus soirée thrown by Eric and Tony Andersen for Prague's art community in September 1964 did not take place in the apartment of Herberta Masaryková, as Stegmann claims. Such a large group of people would hardly have fit into its tiny rooms. Masaryková's daughter, Charlotta Kotíková, who was present that evening, recalls that it took place in Mikuláš Medek's riverside apartment on Janáčkovo nábřeží, which was one of Prague's cultural salons.[16] Kotíková, to her surprise, is even mentioned explicitly in *Fluxus East* as a participant in the first Fluxus performance in Czechoslovakia.[17] After many years, Kotíková remembers that Andersen asked her for a very inconspicuous intervention, perhaps consisting in a special way of making coffee. As she recalls, the reason for the embarrassed reactions—if there were any at all—was that the performance was neither a visual artwork nor any other sort of artistic performance but an event that was hard to classify.

A very diverse group would meet at the Medeks' in the 1960s, including not only artists but also personalities from the fields of literature and music. Particularly important for the penetration of Fluxus into Eastern Europe were contacts from the area of new music, which carved out a space of relative freedom for itself in the countries of Eastern Europe, as it was perceived to be obscure, specialized, and essentially apolitical. Musicians—in the field of electronic music, for example—vindicated the importance of their field by pointing to the scientific and technological progress so favored by the regime. Censorship and bans originated more in the musical community than in the state apparatus.[18] Eric Andersen recalls that the main figure for brokering contacts in Czechoslovakia was the head of the Polish Radio Experimental Studio, Józef Patkowski, a promoter of contemporary music and co-organizer of the Warsaw Autumn Festival. Jiří Kolář went to the festival at least three times in 1958–1961, and Patkowski held him in high regard as a prominent representative of Czech culture.[19] Petra Stegmann asserts, without any details, that before the Andersens' visit to Prague, Patkowski had sent Kolář a set of Fluxus materials dispatched by Maciunas.[20] Patkowski also knew Herberta Masaryková, Mikuláš Medek, and other Czech figures.[21] Beginning in 1962, when they first met at the International Summer Courses for New Music in Darmstadt, Patkowski maintained contacts with George Maciunas as well. Since Herberta Masaryková spoke English, unlike Kolář or Medek, Patkowski entrusted her with the coordination of Eric and Tony Andersen's Prague visit. The Andersens had started their Eastern European tour in Warsaw, where they planned the subsequent trip to Prague.[22] It seems that in Czechoslovakia, the Danish artists were primarily looked after by Kolář, whom they saw on their own as well as at group gatherings.[23]

This is evidenced by the fact that as early as 1965, Eric Andersen arranged for a low-cost edition of Kolář's book

Poem R in Copenhagen. Fifty copies out of a hundred remained in Denmark; the rest went to the Netherlands, into the hands of Willem de Ridder, head of the European distribution network of Fluxus publications and multiples.[24] As a result, *Poem R* became very popular among Fluxus artists and supporters worldwide. Eric Andersen also gave Kolář's address to George Maciunas in New York, who sent Kolář a packet of Fluxus materials that he received by the middle of April 1965.[25] Kolář thanked Andersen for these contacts and for the materials from New York in a letter dated April 23, 1965: "I know it was you who made all the arrangements for the books to be sent to me, and I'm grateful. I sent a few poems to the Fluxus address ('Báseň pro slepce' [Poem for a Blind Man], 'Transparentní báseň' [Transparent Poem], 'Uzlová báseň' [Knotted Poem], and others) and please send my thanks to your friends and also tell them how happy they made me. What you saw when you were here shows how close my work is related to the work of your friends."[26]

The friends in New York meant primarily George Maciunas, whose efforts to establish relationships with artists in Eastern Europe dated back at least to 1962. Due to his lack of actual contacts and his preconceptions about this part of the world, his idealistic efforts were mostly unsuccessful. Maciunas's calls for participation in Fluxus activities were directed mainly at people involved in classical music at the time. For Fluxus, he wanted to win over Krzysztof Penderecki and had plans involving 60-year-old Soviet pianist Maria Yudina and Czech composer Václav Kašlík. For a while, he managed to establish a collaboration with Hungarian composer György Ligeti. Maciunas's utopianism regarding the real world of socialism was made plain in his legendary letters to Nikita Khrushchev and the idea that Fluxus might find an ideal place for its activities in the Soviet Union. In 1965 he sent packages not only to Kolář but to Milan Knížák and Josef Hiršal as well.[27]

The relationship between Kolář and Maciunas is evident in two letters from Kolář's estate.[28] The first was sent from New York on June 22, 1965. In the introduction Maciunas explains how he had discovered Kolář: "I heard about your work first through Jozef Patkowski and then through Eric Andersen. In the hope of making contact with you, I have already sent several Fluxus publications I have edited. Later, I got some very interesting pieces from you."[29] In the letter, Maciunas asked for permission to reprint his work in Fluxus publications and include them in the next *Fluxus Yearbook*. He also invited him to coordinate a concert/performance evening that, according to his instructions, would transpire in New York. At the same time, he informed Kolář of his plan to travel to Czechoslovakia in spring 1966 and asked him for help organizing a festival to take place during his visit. The other surviving letter from Maciunas to Kolář dates from August 24, 1965. In it, the writer gave thanks for a new shipment, sent more materials and films himself, and inquired about the possibility of collaborating to organize concerts, theatrical performances, and publications.

Although no letters from Jiří Kolář have survived in the estate of George Maciunas, we can still find several traces of Kolář there,[30] namely, a folder with several dozen photocopies of Kolář's collages from the 1960s and an original of the 1965 collection *Evidentní poezie* [Evident Poetry].[31] In the archives of the Czechoslovak secret police, a list has survived of persons abroad to whom Kolář sent his anthology *Básně ticha* [Poems of Silence], published privately in late 1965 by the Umělecká beseda [Art Society]. Among the recipients were George Maciunas and Fluxus artist Mieko (Chieko) Shiomi, but we do not know whether the parcels arrived at their destinations, considering the interest of the police.[32] Maciunas also reportedly owned a personal printing of *Poem R*.[33]

However, it seems that the relationship between Kolář and Maciunas did not develop after the mid-1960s. This may partly have been because of problems of a technical nature. Even though Kolář made a partial living in the 1950s and 1960s as a translator of English poetry, he himself was not fluent in English. He had to have Maciunas's letters translated, and his English-language correspondence was mediated both linguistically and logistically by Herberta Masaryková.[34] The absence of translations of Kolář's poetry, his difficulties corresponding, and perhaps even a lack of interest on Kolář's part led to the gradual waning of their written exchanges.[35] Kolář felt no need to organize evenings of performances or festivals dedicated to unusual art forms. Although in 1965 Andersen wrote of the "close connection" between his work and the written expressions of the Fluxus movement, it was probably a misunderstanding. A skeptical and crotchety individualist, Kolář was doubtless not impressed by the utopian, strongly leftist political and social dimension of the Fluxus movement—which, however, was inseparable from their work. Although Kolář was in contact with Mieko Shiomi and participated in some of her mail-art projects from the *Spatial Poems* cycle, doing so required no inordinate investment of time or energy.

III.

George Maciunas met with a completely different level of interest and understanding in Milan Knížák. Maciunas began corresponding with Knížák in 1965, and from the outset he invited him to the United States to participate in Fluxus activities.[36] The oldest surviving letter from Maciunas to Knížák dates from January 1966; in it, he discusses the details of a trip.[37] Both figures saw eye to eye, chiefly based on the similar way each understood their efforts. Although Knížák remained critical of many of the manifestations of Fluxus—whether in connection with the presentation of certain artists from his circle in April 1966 at the Prague jazz club Reduta or, later on, with regard to his stay in New York—his disapproval was grounded in the same, or at least related, positions. Knížák's criticism was based on the belief that Fluxus was still too focused on art. At the time, he was putting special emphasis on the transformation of life itself. The fact that in the mid-1960s Knížák began corresponding with other artists from the Fluxus movement is further evidence of the kinship of positions. Their correspondence was not just a matter of greetings among artists from around the world. For a long time, Knížák and Ken Friedman tried to coordinate joint art projects. Moreover, a letter to Dick Higgins dated June 10, 1966, and another to Alison Knowles dated June 1, 1967, demonstrate the correspondents' interest in Knížák's theoretical thinking, which elicited numerous comments and polemics.[38] The idea of the union of art and life, a sense of playfulness, intermediality, and other elements were shared by both Fluxus and Knížák. But it would be hard to find them—except in a much more mediated form—in the work of Jiří Kolář. Kolář may have been directly inspired by Fluxus before Knížák was; Kolář's experimentation, however, took place in other dimensions.

To shed light on the relationships among Maciunas, Kolář, and Knížák, it is instructive to mention two authority-related conflicts that flared up around an issue of *V TRE*, a Fluxus newspaper, and the preparations for Fluxfest in Prague in the autumn of 1966. George Maciunas had long considered producing a special issue of *V TRE* that would be wholly dedicated to Czech artists. Like so many other of Maciunas's plans, this one was never carried out. A dispute triggered by an undated letter from Knížák to Kolář burdened preparations for the issue: "I learned by chance of your telling Maciunas that you are the representative of the Fluxus in Czechoslovakia. You and a certain 'Vl. Burda.' This despite the fact that if Fluxus is very traditional and conservative and Dadaist, then as far as convention and tradition go, you're a thousand meters deeper. In reality it's like this: if the real avant-garde is the son and Fluxus is its uncle, then you are the great-great-great-great-grandfather of that uncle's neighbor."[39] Knížák's ill-tempered letter angered Kolář, who—as we may read in a text by Jindřich Chalupecký—did not hesitate to complain to friends. Chalupecký tried to recapitulate to Kolář the circumstances under which Knížák's letter was written:

> 1. I received a letter from Maciunas (with whom I am in contact), which defines his position. In conclusion, he notes that many Fluxus publications and numbers are in the possession of Jiří Kolář, who he says "is some sort of representative of Fluxus in Czechoslovakia," and that he wants to publish an issue of the Fluxus newspaper with contributions by Jiří Kolář, Ladislav Novák, Vladimír Burda, etc. At the same time, he asks Knížák for materials. 2. I showed this letter to Knížák. He expressed the view (with which I agree) that the poetics of Fluxus and your own poetics are two different things. 3. Upon which Knížák wrote you a letter—but from that point on, the matter concerns just the two of you, and I really don't understand why you phoned me about it, going on at such length and so excitedly.[40]

George Maciunas had a great need not only to communicate with artists from around the world but also to organize international festivals and soirées with live performances of works by artists from the Fluxus movement. Most of his letters contained requests for the exchange of written materials, followed immediately by proposals for the organization of such performances. This was the way he addressed Kolář, Chalupecký, and Knížák in the Czech sphere. Kolář did not respond to the proposals. But it happened that both Chalupecký and Knížák began organizing Fluxus performances in parallel in the summer of 1966. Maciunas asked Knížák to organize a Fluxus concert in a letter dated August 15, 1966. At the same time, he asked if Jindřich Chalupecký or Herberta Masaryková might not assist in the endeavor. The following September he sent Knížák a detailed (and highly unrealistic) program schedule and a list of items he would need for the festival.

Knížák complained in a letter to Maciunas about the lack of coordination around preparations. Jindřich Chalupecký was, according to Knížák, too closely tied up with official artistic life and was thus unsuited to the task of organizing such a festival. On September 23, 1966, Maciunas responded with this statement: "Chalupecký recently wrote me that he was organizing a solo concert for Dick Higgins and a Fluxus concert in a space that you originally procured. I immediately wrote back that you're a member of Fluxus and represent it, that you organize and coordinate all Fluxus projects in Prague, and therefore he [Chalupecký] must contact you and see if you need any help."[41] Maciunas believed the root of the confusion was Dick Higgins, whom he was in a dispute with, and his attempts to harm Fluxus. The personal quarrels concerning Fluxus performances in the autumn of 1966 were well noted by Knížák, as shown in a 1966 text called *Fluxus in Prague*: "Concerts. Jealousy. Letters beforehand. Higgins vs. Maciunas."[42]

We can probably interpret both "affairs" as follows: Maciunas initially thought Jiří Kolář was the person to help him establish contacts in Czechoslovakia, but Kolář showed no interest in closer cooperation. When Maciunas found out about Knížák and his work, he naturally reoriented himself toward Knížák, became enthusiastic about him, and appointed him director of Fluxus East. Knížák defended his position as the official representative of Fluxus with a great deal of youthful impudence, as evidenced by the letter to Kolář quoted above. In principle, however, he was right. The difference between Kolář and Knížák was not just generational but lay chiefly in their understandings of how art is produced. Maciunas, a graphic designer and an expert in the field, was impressed mainly by the formal aspect of Kolář's poems. The familiarity of Fluxus artists with the phenomenon of Czech visual poetry is apparent in this remembrance of Milan Knížák: "Larry Friefeld is a bad poet, but he has a Czech book of concrete poetry and is all gaga over it. But Jackson Mac Low said it's got the same graphic design Maciunas used in their 1962 anthology and that therefore Hlavsa probably ripped it off."[43]

Despite its experimental character, Kolář's literary work was still strongly anchored in the realm of poetry. The poems of Kolář's that made their way to Maciunas were printed on individual index cards due to the lack of proper book publishing in Czechoslovakia. As a result, they might easily have created the impression of being artifacts of their own or cards on which scripts for performances were distributed. Nonetheless, Kolář's work at the time had no such interdisciplinary compass. Here we may recall a key observation from a text by Pavlína Morganová comparing Kolář's work to that of artists from the Fluxus circle: "The noteworthy intersection of the work of Jiří Kolář and the experiments of the New York neo-avant-garde is to be found beyond any direct influences or information that penetrated through the Iron Curtain. Jiří Kolář […] made inroads into the sphere of 'expanded poetry,' not that of 'expanded music,' as did members of Fluxus."[44] However, we may not automatically draw similar conclusions regarding other Czechoslovak artists Maciunas was in contact with in the mid-1960s—e.g., Ladislav Novák and Vladimír Burda.[45]

IV.

Milan Knížák and Ken Friedman—men that Maciunas had at one point appointed the directors of Fluxus East and Fluxus West—had an unstinting intercontinental relationship. Knížák lived in socialist Czechoslovakia, Friedman in California. They were separated not only by the Atlantic

Ocean and North America, but by the Iron Curtain as well. They came from different backgrounds and spoke different languages but almost immediately found a common vocabulary. Nevertheless, the dialogue between Knížák and Friedman was far from a utopian example of seamless global communication.

Beginning in the mid-1960s, Milan Knížák's work abandoned the field of traditional art and set off in a new direction defined by social undertakings. It aimed to reform existing ways of living life. In 1964 Knížák founded the Aktual association, and a broad community of nonconformists coalesced around him. Sometime in late 1965 or early 1966, Knížák began corresponding with George Maciunas and later with other artists from the Fluxus movement. In 1965 the American Ken Friedman, who was then only 16 years old, also came into contact with both Fluxus and George Maciunas and quickly found his place among Fluxus artists. In his years of intensive collaboration with Knížák, Friedman was studying at San Francisco State University or living with his parents in San Diego; beyond that, however, he was furthering his own artistic activities.

As indicated by the titles Maciunas gave them as Fluxus directors, despite their efforts to achieve global reach for the Fluxus movement, Knížák and Friedman operated on the peripheries. This was due not only to their physical locations but also to the nature of their activities. Although they became steadfast members of the movement, Fluxus accounted for but one of the many directions the efforts of Friedman—and Knížák in particular—were turned toward. Aside from his involvements with Fluxus events and contacts, Friedman developed his own projects, whose goals could be described by Knížák's motto "to live otherwise." Both were more interested in social engagement, in attempts to build new types of human togetherness, than in art.[46]

Even before coming into contact with Fluxus and Friedman, Milan Knížák was obsessed with communicating by correspondence. It represented for him the ideal way to reach the public. By 1965 he was sending a large number of unsolicited letters on behalf of Aktual, sometimes choosing addresses at random. Some of them resembled rhetorical chain letters whose aim was to create virtual communities of letter writers.

The letters were meant to promote the feeling that those involved were not alone in the world but constituted a community. Even before he met Friedman, Knížák had developed the concept of a Keeping Together Manifestation. He wanted to promote global interpersonal togetherness through written correspondence and by organizing synchronized events and celebrations all over the world.

Knížák is often viewed in a global context as little more than an Eastern European member of Fluxus, which, in view of the wide range of his activities, is decidedly misleading. For him, in the isolated environment of Czechoslovakia, Fluxus meant a validation of the path he had taken and of many friendships. However, far more important for him were the activities related to his own organization, Aktual, which, though actually quite marginal, took on a significant international dimension in the person of Ken Friedman.[47] To a certain extent Aktual reflected the loosely structured way Fluxus operated—but with the figure of Knížák as main organizer and the movement's intellectual leader. Sometimes, in correspondence with Friedman, he was even jokingly referred to as the bishop of the Aktual religion.

The exchange of letters between Ken Friedman and Milan Knížák began sometime in late 1966 or early 1967.[48] This correspondence was different from the letters Knížák exchanged with George Maciunas and Dick Higgins. They, too, convey the euphoria of kindred souls who had independently arrived at similar ways of thinking. But the correspondence between Knížák and Friedman was more intense, more crazed and visually wild, even when it came to practical matters such as coordinating joint events. The cadence and tone of the letters from the spring of 1967 are comparable to those of impetuous lovers. Their eagerness to communicate was frustrated by the speed of the postal service at the time. Both lost track of what the other had written or sent. Besides greetings, the same questions are repeated: "Did you get my letter?" "Why is it taking you so long to respond?" It should be mentioned that at the time of the feverish exchange, Knížák was 27 and Friedman not yet 18.

The letters that Friedman received from exotic Prague were from a world that was distant yet in many ways familiar. It was not Milan Knížák alone who wrote to him from Czechoslovakia. For example, 21-year-old Aktual member Soňa Švecová introduced herself in a letter as someone for whom life was more important than art. Although she would sometimes send anonymous letters and packages and would stage performance pieces in trams, she did not document them, because it was the experience itself that was essential for her. She pasted playful photographs onto her letter to Friedman and closed with the irresistible appeal, "Tell us something about yourself!" They even developed a curious form of correspondence-based physical contact: in an envelope, Knížák or Švecová would include a sheet of paper with an outlined outstretched hand. Then Friedman would trace the outline of his own hand over theirs; in this way, the friends could touch each other over a distance of thousands of miles.

Friedman's remote identification with Aktual, its ideas, and its representatives was strong. In one of his first letters to Knížák, he wrote that as soon as he had received the materials about Aktual, he realized that his Instant Theatre had qualified him as a member long ago. Without delay, Friedman founded a Californian—or, more precisely, an American—branch of Aktual. In March 1967 Knížák wrote back enthusiastically: "Dear Ken, I love you for your activity. We must keep together more places on the globe! To want to live—otherwise. To live otherwise. I'm shaking with your hands for basing of Aktual USA. Right idea!"[49]

In the early years of the correspondence it was Knížák who initiated most of their collaborative activities and emphasized the need for reciprocity between the Czechoslovak and American branches of Aktual. This was supposed to happen mainly through the organization of "Keeping Together Manifestations," or KTMs. Knížák sent Friedman a mock-up of a multi-page publication on KTMs, which he hoped might be published in the United States. He even composed a song in English meant to be a sort of KTM anthem: "Shake my hand, shake my heart. World is nice, world is love." The slogan "Keep Together" appeared in English on the cover of the third issue of *Aktual*, which was published in samizdat form in Czechoslovakia. And in the form of a full-page ad for *Aktual* USA, he printed Ken Friedman's address.

The planning and coordinating of KTMs account for a considerable portion of the correspondence between Friedman and Knížák. The inaugural World Keeping Together Day was to take place during the whole of March 1967. Each year thereafter, the occasion was to be celebrated on the Sunday following the first day of spring. KTMs could include a variety of events and activities; the important thing was the knowledge that others, perhaps halfway around the world, were participating in something similar at the same time. Thanks to their simplicity, Knížák's proposals for KTM togetherness events could easily be carried out anywhere. In the spring of 1967 Knížák conceived of a KTM, later titled *Difficult Ceremony* and performed two years later, in which participants spent 24 hours without eating, drinking, smoking, sleeping, or communicating. The 1968 proposal was less demanding: "Put a table in front of your house and take a lunch. Invite passers-by." Knížák asked Friedman to hold this event in the United States and to promote its widespread organization by others.[50] To this end, he even mimeographed English-language posters, produced in his characteristic handwriting design. Surprisingly, the Czechoslovak post sent the unusual package at the reduced rate for printed matter.

Ken Friedman was far from having the means to fulfill all of Knížák's plans. He even declared performances that were not directly related to the idea of human togetherness to be KTMs.[51] Moreover, he organized many activities that were unrelated to the ideas coming from Czechoslovakia. As early as March 1967, he printed his own posters promoting *Aktual* USA and KTMs that aligned with Central European ideas about the late-1960s Californian lifestyle: "Aktual is holding hands, making love, being people, keeping together. Aktual is now—is you." Friedman did not shy away from forays into fiction when he described the success of the Aktual movement: "*Aktual* USA reached 10,000 people in public instant events in its first week of operation. If you wish to be Aktual, let us know, and we can bring Instant Theatre toward liberation, satori, truth, fun, and games in your neighborhood soon." The actual reach of Aktual appears to have been somewhat more modest.

In Czechoslovakia, Keeping Together Day was celebrated in a more markedly public way on March 24, 1968.

Surviving photographs show several members and supporters of Aktual with handmade posters on Prague's Národní třída. The posters, designed in the style of psychedelic art from San Francisco made famous in posters of rock bands, exhorted people to organize communal public lunches.

One specific element that Knížák brought to KTMs was the motif of anti-war activism. Within the framework of the 1967 Keeping Together Manifestation, Knížák planned to send (or perhaps even sent) hundreds of letters to foreign embassies and various army officers, asking them—in the name of the global movement for peace, freedom, and nonviolence—to carry out personal demilitarizations. The culmination of these efforts was an anonymous mimeographed flyer urging people to "Assassinate All Those Who Wage War." This flyer was conceived by Aktual member Robert Wittmann, working closely with Knížák in those years. For decades, propaganda efforts had thoroughly discredited the struggle for peace in what was then the Eastern Bloc. For this reason, despite the trendiness of pacifism and nonviolence associated with the hippie movement, few seriously intended art projects east of the Iron Curtain took up the cause of world peace.[52] Readers were schocked by militant, almost absurdist rhetoric calling on people to kill in the name of nonviolence.

Knížák and Wittmann developed not only the Keeping Together Manifestation but also the Aktual Atentát [Assassination] Project before they came into contact with Ken Friedman. Their message, however, was not clear to foreign readers and did not gain the broad support abroad that his calls for togetherness did. This is highlighted in a letter from Dick Higgins dated February 25, 1967:

> Dear Milan, we are 100% with you, and we will keep together with you all. I'll send you some info about how we keep together here. We'll get 500 people to keep together in New York and another 500 in San Francisco. Here is some info on how they are doing it there. Your letter ends with the words: Commit "atentát" on each man which is preparing warm! Although the mechanics of language are terribly boring, they do exist. Just mechanically—I can't quite figure out what it means. The word "atentát" doesn't

> exist in English, nor does the phrase "preparing warm." Does your sentence mean "Kill all those who are preparing war?" If yes, then I agree. Venceremos!!![53]

Aktual planned to hold International Atentát Day on Sunday April 9, 1967. To promote it, Knížák sent Friedman miniature brochures that were typewritten and copied using carbon paper. We do not know, however, how widely they were distributed.

Knížák and Friedman first met face to face in the spring of 1969. During his stay in America in 1968–1970, Knížák had been invited to California for a lecture: "Friedman was waiting for me. He looks like a younger version of the Czech artist Franta Sedlák. But K. F. is a conceptual artist and is 19, although he doesn't like to say so about himself, and his parents have a beautiful house in San Diego with a terrace and a pool where I even went for a swim."[54] Knížák's stay in California was not one of sustained artistic activity; it was more of an excursion, a practical fulfilment of the motto "live otherwise," filled with long discussions about the future.

Knížák's almost two-year stay in the United States did not entail a flourishing of the Aktual movement but a waning of its activities. It is clear from Knížák's travel journals that he had little interest in the New York art scene or the interactions within its art community. He was repelled by the degree of institutionalization, for example, of galleries, museums, or the nascent field of conceptual art. He did not use his time in the United States to intensively build new and lasting relationships within the art community. Before arriving in the United States, he had already exchanged letters with the circle of people he considered to be key figures. During his stay in America, Knížák's need for universal rapprochement appeared to decline. Paradoxically, the modest Aktual movement, which was more virtual than anything else, had been better off when its leaders lived in different countries, in spite of the fact that, for political reasons, people from the "Second World" were at the time not allowed to move about freely. The free movement we know today did not exist then. With rare exceptions, long-term stays abroad meant exile with the prospect of no return.

When Knížák's permit to reside outside Czechoslovakia expired in April 1970, he decided to return home. His correspondence with his Californian friend continued after his return, with Friedman wanting to continue pursuing their shared experiences and plans: "We believe in the same truth, love the same love, work for the same goal." Knížák turned to him with the kinds of requests that are common among good friends: he was looking for a book on the history of communes and regularly reminded Friedman to send him the records he received free from a famous music critic. The need to coordinate joint social art projects weakened. Czechoslovakia in 1970 was different from what it had been in 1968; the repression following the Communist regime's consolidation of power was in full swing. Knížák could not stage public activities and was dealing with serious problems in his everyday life. Aktual had been hit by a wave of emigration and was reduced to just a few of his closest friends. At home, Knížák was isolated from both the public and the broader community of artists. After returning from the United States, he found it even harder to find people who shared his ways of thinking. As an artist, he was more highly valued abroad than in his own country. After 1970 almost all of his exhibitions, collectors, and supporters were located abroad. Knížák moved from Prague to the countryside, but he found himself under police surveillance and apparently did not even consider organizing more World Togetherness Days. Friedman kept the KTM celebrations going at a time when they could no longer be held on a large scale in Czechoslovakia. At the sixth annual KTM in 1972, Friedman began corresponding with artists from Canada and throughout the United States. Friedman also sought to help Knížák, who was arrested for several months in 1972 and 1973 when some of his artworks were confiscated at the Czechoslovak border. The Communists had judged them pornographic and harmful to the image of socialist Czechoslovakia. In February 1973 he was given a two-year prison sentence.

In their time, Keeping Together Manifestations had represented a utopian attempt to create a global network of togetherness. However, it took another letter-driven project—this one led by an effort to protect Knížák from judicial prosecution—to really mobilize the international community. Various individuals or groups associated with

Fluxus helped distribute a petition for his release. Knížák, who was aware of the power of international public opinion and letter campaigns, helped initiate protests. In a letter to German collector Wolfgang Feelisch dated February 19, 1973, he wrote, "Please ask the people around the world, all the people you know, to write protest letters to the Czech government against it [his conviction], to publish protests, reports, and news items about it in all the newspapers and magazines around the world […] Please do all you can because I […] can do very little myself, please tell everyone in the world what has happened because if I go to jail, all Czech art will go with me, all artistic freedom will be jailed along with me."[55] Feelisch put together and distributed a special brochure that contained detailed information about Knížák's case. In it we find reprinted facsimiles of Knížák's letters and statements written in his support by various figures of the international art world.[56] The international petition was probably one of the reasons that the Communist justice system commuted Knížák's sentence to probation. However, in practice this meant a drastic reduction of his public activities. He was not allowed to exhibit in Czechoslovakia, to work in public spaces, or even to organize private group activities. Knížák, along with other Eastern European artists, illustrates an interesting paradox: the international art world, accessible through the mail, became one of the few ways he could present his work to a wider public. Knížák would have to wait until 1979, when the Czechoslovak authorities again allowed him to travel abroad, to come into direct contact with the international art world once more.

V.

If we were to look for parallels to Milan Knížák's projects in the 1960s, it appears we could not fail to mention certain of the projects Kateřina Šedá has carried out over the last ten years. We would be struck more by the differences than by the similarities, however. The common denominator of the work of both artists is a desire to work with social relationships, to build new communities by means of acts of togetherness, and to promote qualitatively better models of interpersonal coexistence so as to combat alienated lifestyles. They want, at least at a rhetorical level, to distance themselves from "art" and yearn, for the most part idealistically, to effect enduring change in people's lives. A strategy both Knížák and Šedá often used to achieve these goals is the restoration of damaged relationships or the building of nonexistent ones within the framework of group activities. In Knížák's *Událost pro poštu, Veřejnou bezpečnost, obyvatele domu č. 26 A, pro jejich sousedy, příbuzné přátele* [Event for Postal Service, Public Security, and the Residents of House no. 26A, their Neighbors, Relatives, and Friends] and Šedá's *Každej pes jiná ves* [For Every Dog a Different Master], both artists made similar use of anonymous letters or parcels as a pretext for establishing relationships. With some of the recipients, in both cases, the uninvited invasion of people's privacy provoked misunderstanding and panic. While in 1966 Knížák was investigated by the police in connection with his activities, however, Šedá's project involving the residents of the Líšeň housing estate was exhibited at the Moravian Gallery in Brno and showcased at documenta 12.

Knížák wanted to set himself apart from the art world and saw the significance of his activities in the establishment of small but long-term communities of people who "lived otherwise." Knížák's influence in the late 1960s was likely limited and focused more on utopian calls for the creation of new communities than on actually rectifying existing interpersonal relationships. Šedá, in contrast, always enters into an open dialogue with existing communities. She does not try to rouse them with confrontational manifestos or anonymous calls to action but talks with them in person, convincing them to participate. The shared schedule for a day in Ponětovice for *Nic tam není* [There's Nothing There], the group trips to Berlin and London for *Furt dokola* [Over and Over] and *Od nevidím do nevidím* [From Morning till Night] can in essence be seen as togetherness manifestations made possible thanks to Šedá's painstaking fieldwork. In Šedá's wake are real communities that have undergone therapeutic group experiences and exhibit at least some traces of social rehabilitation or changes in mind-set. "Living otherwise" here need not mean a radical transformation but simply a small shift in a positive direction. Šedá's projects are presented in an acknowledged artistic format—they are enacted in the midst of events occurring in the art world—and thus elicit responses from people beyond those directly involved. When exhibited as installations of documentary materials, they are offered as models. In just a few years, Šedá's projects had established her in the global art world. The value of Šedá's work in this sphere is to be found not in any specific changes in Ponětovice or Líšeň but, rather, within the genre of socially engaged art.

They say the world has never been smaller than it is today. And art has never achieved a similar level of global interconnectedness. According to philosopher Peter Osborne, three circumstances are responsible for the transnationalization of contemporary art: first, there is a strong art market that does not recognize any borders. Second, large-scale biennale-type international exhibitions are currently seen to be the most important mediators of contemporary art. And, last but not least, artists are migrating, and global art scenes are concentrating in a few centers.[57] Let us now try to generalize these individual cases of communication between the former Czechoslovakia and the rest of the world in the context of these claims, particularly in relation to the present day. Information crossing the Iron Curtain and contact flourishing between the Fluxus movement and artists in Czechoslovakia can in retrospect be perceived as remarkably successful examples of the exchange of ideas across political and geographic world borders during the Cold War. At the same time, however, they showcase the many distortions and misperceptions that burdened communications at the time. Although news of the neo-avant-garde abroad spread like wildfire in Czechoslovakia, it was unsystematic and superficial; thus, with a few exceptions, neo-avant-garde principles did not set root. It was common for Czech artists to enter into dialogues with other artists abroad, but the significance of the interchanges lay more in individuals successfully circumventing the information blockade than in the establishment of real, working, and sustainable connections between art scenes. Visual poetry may be considered a notable exception. Since it was possible to disseminate this work entirely by mail, artists from Czechoslovakia were able during liberalization to become part of the global movement and present it—including its theoretical background—at home.

In the 1960s, especially in the case of the Fluxus movement, information and art flowed across borders without the aid of official institutions such as galleries or museums. Today, doubtless due to the commercialization of art, such a free flow would be hard to imagine. As the first years of Fluxus make clear, the artistic exchange was originally a matter of the community of artists organizing itself. It was able to produce a working communication network, albeit one with a minimal range, seen from today's perspective: several artists viewed as marginal exchanged letters and parcels and invited one another to modest art festivals. The fact that they established and operated international art associations on their own may be seen as an expression of resistance against the existing social order. The Fluxus movement, whose ostensible aim was to change lives, was driven by similar motives. Unlike political revolutionaries, however, Fluxus remained a community linked mainly by kindred views on art. This was evident in the movement's variable public reception. Some described Fluxus as a unique attempt to establish art unions, others as a grouping that functioned essentially as an industrial trademark.[58] Nevertheless, Fluxus was characterized—as are many other similar associations—by a strong tendency toward excessive bureaucracy. It is difficult to determine the extent to which this tendency was tongue-in-cheek or meant sincerely. The creation of official names, flags, slogans, stamps, greetings, and rituals can be seen both as an expression of independence and as an acerbic commentary on social rules. This is also true not only of the titles of the directors of Fluxus East and West but also of the letters, flyers, and magazines produced by Aktual. They are not devoid of hyperbole or a sense of humor, but they are still primarily gestures made by people who wanted to set themselves apart from their surroundings. If we look at the way the art world operates today against the backdrop of Fluxus, the degree to which the contemporary art world has become institutionalized and professionalized (retroactively, even) over the last half-century becomes clear.

Over the years Fluxus has become a subject of interest not only to artists and art historians but also to gallery owners and collectors. The performances of the Fluxus artists, who had been so skeptical of art institutions, the commercialization of art, and even its possibilities, have by now become just more art. Galleries and museums often produce art themselves. The friendly letters once exchanged by Fluxus participants are housed today in the archives of large institutions and in some cases have even become works of art themselves. In the 1980s, the New York Museum of Modern Art acquired some of the correspondence between Ken Friedman and Milan Knížák. The museum recently moved a selection of the materials from the archives to a curatorial department. Such upgrading—taking something that originally had a different role and making an artifact for its collection—is not exceptional. To Fluxus members—and even more so to Knížák, who in the 1960s was trying to break out of the art world—this sort of transformation of what were originally calls for a change in lifestyle must seem like a disappointment. Their manifestos, leaflets, and proclamations brought few real changes to people's lives; instead, they ended up becoming successful art.

The world has often been described in the past decades as being increasingly globalized. Traditional borders have become less important; people, goods, and information flow far more freely than in the past. The dawn of a qualitatively new interconnected world is usually dated to the period after the collapse of the imperial system, which began in the late 1940s and reached a pinnacle in the 1960s. It was doubtless also associated with technological advances: telephone rates dropped, and transatlantic air travel proliferated. Multinational mass media concerns expanded their reach, and television broadcasting saw enormous growth. The 1960s were also characterized by social transformations. Outspoken opposition to the authorities emerged among the young. Powerful movements that fought for social, racial, and ethnic equality sprang up. From today's vantage, Knížák's trip to the United States must have seemed like a journey to another world. After 1970, unlike the countries west of the Iron Curtain, Czechoslovakia experienced restrictions on freedom, travel, and communication with the outside world. Censorship was introduced. The struggle for free artistic expression in the 1970s was a major focal point of dissident activities. During the political chill that fell across Eastern Europe and the Soviet Union, people tried to create independent art communities. Although in part arising from a need to set themselves apart, such efforts were primarily defensive: the options for communication outside the scope of those communities were restricted.

In contrast, in the 1960s there had been noticeable efforts to decentralize and build networks in the Euro-American art world. For conceptual artists at the turn of the 1970s, establishing international connections and communities, particularly between the United States and Western Europe, became the norm.[59] In recent years historians of art have analyzed these communication networks.[60] The relationships created in the sphere of Western art were not built solely on friendships and artistic interests, as was most often the case in the East, but also on business interests. Such communities included not only artists, art historians, and critics but also curators, gallery owners, and collectors. The international art trade grew. In 1967 the first Art Cologne art fair took place in Germany, attracting over 15,000 visitors. The next year that number doubled and, apart from a few short-term drops, the numbers have continued to grow. A few hundred kilometers to the East, however, a contemporary art market was virtually nonexistent.

If today's theorists agree on a common feature of contemporary art, it is its global dimension. Biennales and major international contemporary art fairs are taken as the chief manifestations of the globalization of the art world. In the 1990s biennales were perceived as spaces for bringing together the art from different regions, as expressions of the overcoming of political, economic, and geographic barriers and as evidence of the opening up of various previously overlooked parts of the world. It seemed that biennales, where artists from Great Britain, Senegal, Russia, China, and Argentina exhibited alongside one another, were calling into question the division of the world into center and periphery. However, after 2000 such exhibitions have routinely been criticized on the grounds that they consistently reinforce the importance of the same region of the international art spectrum. In reality, biennales do not reveal the pluralism of the world but produce a new uniformity. Their formulaic character and their dependence on commercial interests confirm that the hierarchical structure of the art world is alive and well. The political changes since 1989, as well as new technologies, have undoubtedly played an important role in the increasingly interconnected world. Since the 1990s, processing an almost limitless volume of digital information has become a dominant part of our lives, and the computer has become the most important tool of both communication and the spread of culture. The transformation, primarily a quantitative one, has made the opportunities we have to work with information incomparably greater than those that people had in the 1960s. By using search tools on the Internet today, we can go through and sort an incredible amount of data without ever having to read anything.[61] In theory, with the help of computers or mobile telephones, we can be exquisitely well informed about almost anything and talk to anyone in the world. Thanks to technology we are now experiencing something like a gigantic Keeping Together Manifestation—without anyone feeling closer to anyone else, however. What is at issue here is not an unintentionally perverse shift in the original meaning of the term. Knížák's Keeping Together Manifestations were utopias of shared awareness and informational interconnection—which, however, grew in the spirit of the 1960s out of needs based on nonalienated forms of communication and an emphasis on immediate experience.[62] Though today we have almost limitless technological access to information, we often find that we lack the goals necessary to make a positive use of our resources.

[1] Jiří Padrta, Umění nezobrazující a neobjektivní, jeho současný stav [Non-Depicting and Non-Objective Art: Its State Today], *Výtvarné umění* VII, no. 4, 1957, pp. 214–221.

[2] Josef Hiršal and Bohumila Grögerová, *Let let* [The Flight of Years], Torst, Prague 2007, p. 225.

[3] "The Legacy of Jackson Pollock," in Allan Kaprow, *Essay on the Blurring of Art and Life*, University of California Press, Berkeley 1993, pp. 1–9.

[4] Jaromír Podešva, *Současná hudba na Západě* [Contemporary Music in the West], Prague 1963.

[5] Ibid., pp. 36–41, 161–165.

[6] Evidence of the rapid changes in the Czech cultural scene in the 1960s is the fact that John Cage performed in Prague just one year after the publication of Podešva's book.

[7] Jiří Mucha, *Černý a bílý New York* [Black and White New York], Mladá fronta, Prague 1965.

[8] *100 + 1 zahraniční zajímavost* [100 + 1 Interesting Things Abroad], vol. 3, no. 4, February 25, 1966.

[9] First printed in Vít Havránek (ed.), *Akce slovo pohyb prostor, experimenty v umění šedesátých let* [Action Word Movement Space: Experiments in the Art of the Sixties], Prague City Gallery, Prague 1999, pp. 54–61.

[10] Achille Gregor, *Muž v zástěře* [Man in an Apron], Lidové nakadatelství, Prague 1969, p. 75.

[11] Miloslav Topinka as "mt," "Nové umění, to je cesta ven" [New Art—That's a Way Out], *Sešity* [Notebooks] 25, November 1968, p. 48.

[12] We can get a sense of the hidden dilemmas, including thoughts of emigration, that such trips entailed from the letters Jiří Balcar wrote to Jindřich Chalupecký in 1964. At the time, Balcar had an occasion to spend four months in the United States. His stay brought him much inspiration but was also a destabilizing shock for his complicated psyche. See Marie Klimešová and Jan Rous, *Jiří Balcar*, Arbor Vitae, Galerie výtvarného umění v Chebu [Cheb Fine Arts Gallery], and the Academy of Arts, Architecture, and Design in Prague, Řevnice, Cheb and Prague 2013, pp. 273–275.

[13] *An Anthology of Concrete Poetry*, Something Else Press 1967; reprint of the original 1967 printing, Primary Information, New York 2013.

[14] Marie Bergmanová, *Jiří Kolář, Sběratel/Collector*, Gallery, Prague 2001, p. 28.

[15] Petra Stegmann, *Fluxus East: Fluxus Networks in Central Eastern Europe*, Künstlerhaus Bethanien, Berlin 2007, pp. 5–52. Eric Andersen, "The East Fluxus Tour 1964," in *Fluxus East*, pp. 53–62.

[16] Interview with Charlotta Kotíková by the author, summer 2008.

[17] "She performed with us at a soirée in the hughe [sic] Masarykova apartment," E. Andersen, *The East Fluxus Tour 1964*, p. 56.

[18] See, for example, David Crowley and Daniel Muzyczuk (eds.), *Sounding the Body Electric*, Muzeum Sztuki, Łódź 2012.

[19] The State Security file on Kolář documents his trips to Warsaw during these years.

[20] Stegmann, *Fluxus East*, p. 22.

[21] On the contacts and interconnections among artistic circles in connection with new music, see Rudolf Komorous, Petr Kotík, Ladislav Kupkovič, and Viktor Pantůček, *Začátek nové hudby v Praze 1959–1964* [The Beginnings of New Music in Prague 1959–1964] (transcript of a panel discussion), Ostravské dny (a festival), Ostravské centrum nové hudby [Ostrava Center for New Music], Ostrava 2008.

[22] Herberta Masaryková was later in contact with other artists from the Fluxus circle, mainly regarding their visits to Prague. Several postcards from Dick Higgins have been found in her estate. In 1966 he sent her his condolences for the death of Alice Masaryková; in 1967 he showed interest in the case of Serge Oldenburg when he was detained in Prague; and a year later he wrote to find out if, in connection with the occupation of Czechoslovakia, he needed any help.

[23] In autumn 1964, Eric and Tony Andersen also visited Brno and Bratislava. However, we know nothing of these trips to this day.

[24] Details are contained in an undated letter from Birgit Giedekier found in the Jiří Kolář estate at the literary archives of the Museum of Czech Literature in Prague. Many thanks to the Museum for providing access to the Kolář archive, which had not yet been subject to scholarly scrutiny.

[25] Interesting in this regard is a letter from Jindřich Chalupecký dated April 5, 1965, in which he addressed the "European Fluxus headquarters," in the figure of Willem de Ridder, with a request that he send Fluxus materials. In the letter, Chalupecký observes that he found out about the Fluxus movement from a Leningrad (today St. Petersburg) friend named "Gurvich," though Czech art historians have not been able to ascertain his first name or even to confirm his existence. At any rate, Chalupecký found out about Fluxus independently of Kolář, who at the time had known about the movement for more than half a year and had just received a package with materials from New York, or for some reason he does not mention his existing contacts with Andersen and Maciunas. A year later, however, Chalupecký presents an informed account of Fluxus in his book *Umění dnes* [Art Today], NČSVU [Czechoslovak Artists Publishing House], Prague 1966).

[26] Literary Archives of the Museum of Czech Literature (hereafter LA MCL), Jiří Kolář Archive.

[27] Entry from May 1965, Hiršal and Grögerová, *Let let*, p. 554.

[28] Literary Archives of the Museum of Czech Literature, Jiří Kolář Archive.

[29] Ibid.

[30] The George Maciunas Archive is part of the Gilbert and Lila Silverman Fluxus Collection Archives, which is housed in New York's Museum of Modern Art (MoMA).

[31] The collection, essentially a set of independently printed typographical poems, was published by Kolář in a private printing.

[32] Until he left for France in 1979, Jiří Kolář was more or less constantly monitored. In the 1960s, the State Security even believed he was the head of an antigovernment group. A manuscript version of the poetry collection titled *Prométheova játra* [Prometheus's Liver] from 1950 is preserved in his police file—the only surviving copy without any traces of censorship. It was not discovered until 2012. For more details, see "Prameny," *Česká literatura* [Czech Literature], vol. 61, no. 4, September 2013, pp. 546–592.

[33] I am grateful to Jon Hendricks for providing me with this information in January 2014.

[34] See the abstract of a translation of Maciunas's first letter or a mention in a letter from Eric Andersen in the Jiří Kolář estate, which is housed in the Literary Archives of the Museum of Czech Literature.

[35] Evidence of the enduring, albeit sporadic, contacts on George Maciunas's side is the multiple *Spell Your Name with These Objects* from the 1970s, housed in the Jiří Kolář collection.

[36] Milan Knížák lists the year 1965 in a 1990s memoir. See Milan Knížák, "Konec pilota Jonese" [The End of Pilot Jones], in *Fluxus je stále luxus* [Fluxus Is Still a Luxury], Czech Museum of Fine Arts, Prague 1995, p. 4.

[37] The Gilbert and Lila Silverman Fluxus Collection Archives, MoMA, New York.

[38] Transcriptions of the letters George Maciunas, Dick Higgins, and Alison Knowles wrote to Knížák in the 1960s were the heart of the samizdat publication *koresp fluxu* [Fluxus Correspondence], which was prepared in the late 1970s by Petr Rezek. There is an original in the archive at the Academic Research Center of the Academy of Fine Arts, Prague.

[39] The Jiří Kolář Archive in the Literary Archive at the Museum of Czech Literature. The letter was part of a retrospective of the artist's work at the National Gallery, Prague, 1999.

[40] Literary Archives of the Museum of Czech Literature, Jiří Kolář Archive.

[41] The Gilbert and Lila Silverman Fluxus Collection Archives, MoMA, New York.

[42] *fluxus*, a samizdat publication prepared by Petr Rezek after 1979, p. 34; as cited in an original at the Academic Research Center of the Academy of Fine Arts, Prague.

[43] Milan Knížák, *Cestopisy* [Travelogues], Post, Prague 1990, p. 14.

[44] Pavlína Morganová, "Smysl slova spočívá v jeho použití. Jiří Kolář, Yoko Ono" [The Meaning of the Word Is in its Usage: Jiří Kolář, Yoko Ono], in *Sešit pro umění, teorii a příbuzné zóny* [Notebook for Art, Theory, and Related Zones], 2013, no. 15, p. 55.

[45] Hiršal and Grögerová, in *Let let* [The Flight of Years], speak of Burda as a student of English who "is relatively well informed regarding the work and aesthetics of the American group Fluxus." Unfortunately, only a fraction of his estate was preserved after his untimely death.

[46] Friedman emphasized this basic idea in later years as well. For example, the *San Diego Daily Aztec*, an independent student newspaper, published a story in 1971 on the Keeping Together Manifestation organized by Friedman, which they described as a disorganized bacchanalia of building, giving, and receiving. According to Friedman, who is cited in the article, the KTM was an instrument for changing social behavior. Geoffrey Anderson, "Aktual Art Is Just Part of the KTM," *San Diego Daily Aztec*, April 16, 1971.

[47] At one time, Friedman and apparently Knížák, too, considered Dick Higgins and Branko Dimitrijević from Belgrade to be members of Aktual as well, though without any particularly strong response from either artist.

[48] In a 1974 letter, Ken Friedman remarked that he had known Knížák for eight years. In his *A Brief History of Fluxus West*, Friedman dates the onset of the correspondence mediated by Dick Higgins to March 1967. Mariane Mazzone claims the written relationship began in 1967. See Mazzone, "Keeping Together Prague and San Francisco: Networking in 1960s Art," *Technoetic Arts: A Journal of Speculative Research*, vol. 7, 2009, no. 3, p. 285.

[49] Letter in the Ken Friedman Collection postmarked March 14, 1967, Box 2, Folder 6, Mandeville Special Collections Library, University of California, San Diego, as cited in Mazzone, "Keeping Together Prague and San Francisco: Networking in 1960s Art," p. 286.

[50] Note from 2017: Artistic activities aimed at establishing or strengthening of human togetherness occur frequently in the history of postwar art. In addition to Knížák and Friedman's Keeping Together Manifestations, we find many parallel attempts to reform what were seen as modern civilization's perverted and inequitable social relationships. The conditions were right for dining together to become a tool for reform. In 1968 Milan Knížák made an appeal to this effect in Czechoslovakia; at the same time the potential of food as a cohesive element was discovered by his friend Alison Knowles in the United States. Knížák's appeal to "set a table in front of your house and eat outdoors" was repeated in a remarkably similar form—albeit by chance—a decade later by Slovak artist and activist Ján Budaj and his Dočasná spoločnosť intenzivního prožívání [Temporary Intense Experience Society]. In *Oběd II* [Lunch II], an event organized in 1978, friends of his at a Bratislava housing estate set dining tables and chairs in front of their buildings and had lunch under the gazes of the passers by. The work had a marked political tone: it was an attempt to turn the closed-mindedness and passivity of socialist society inside out, exposing its untouchable and hidden private plane.

[51] For example, within the framework of the 1967 Togetherness Festival, Friedman performed *Telephone for You*. Participants take a common phone into a car, stop a random passer-by and hand over the receiver, saying, "It's for you ... "

[52] One of the few similar examples from the Eastern Bloc was *Indigo Peace Call*, an antinuclear manifesto published by Hungarian artists in 1983.

[53] As cited in the samizdat publication *koresp fluxu*, edited by Petr Rezek in the late 1970s. The original is housed at the Academic Research Center of the Academy of Fine Arts, Prague.

[54] Knížák, *Cestopisy* [Travelogues], p. 16.

[55] As cited in *Action on Behalf of Milan Knížák*. Press release distributed by the Beau Geste Press association, March 1973.

[56] Such as Allan Kaprow and Harald Szeemann.

[57] Peter Osborne, *Anywhere or Not at All: Philosophy of Contemporary Art*, Verso, London and New York 2013, p. 163.

[58] Chris Gilbert, *Art & Language and the Institutional Form*, in Blake Stimson and Gregory Sholette (eds.), *Collectivism after Modernism: The Art of Social Imagination after 1945*, University of Minnesota Press, Minneapolis and London 2007, p. 78.

[59] See Sophie Richard, *Unconcealed: The International Network of Conceptual Artists 1967–1977: Dealers, Exhibitions and Public Collections*, Ridinghouse, London 2009, esp. pp. 55–62.

[60] An example of a similar project is MoMA's 2009 exhibition and publication *In & Out of Amsterdam: Travels in Conceptual Art, 1960–1976*, which explores Amsterdam as a center of artistic activity involving a wide spectrum of international artists.

[61] See Lev Manovich, "Introduction to Info-Aesthetics," in Terry Smith, Okwui Enwezor, and Nancy Condee (eds.), *Antinomies of Art and Culture: Modernity, Postmodernity, Contemporaneity*, Duke University Press, Durham and London 2008, pp. 333–344.

[62] In the 1960s we already see numerous critical commentaries on technological progress in Aktual texts and an emphasis on experiencing the world immediately and directly. See, e.g., Milan Knížák, "O budoucnosti" [On the Future], in *Milan Knížák (názory* [Opinions]*) 1995–1964*, Vetus via, Brno 1996, pp. 451–452, or "Aktual," in: Milan Knížák, *Nový ráj* [A New Paradise], Galerie Mánes and the Museum of Decorative Arts in Prague, Prague 1996, unpaginated.

National Conceptualism: Slovak National Revival Motifs in the Work of Stano Filko and Július Koller

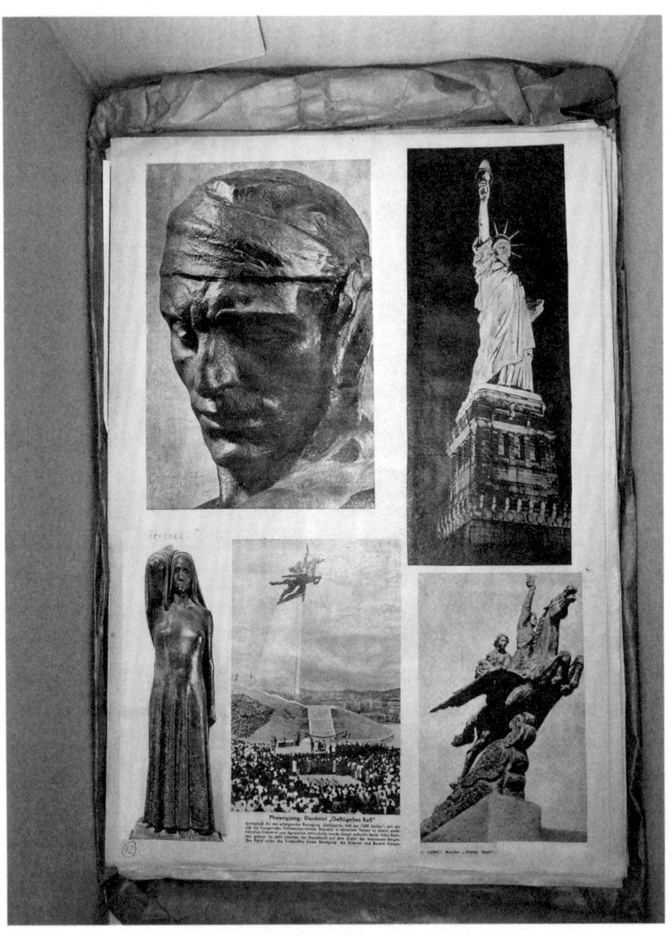

[ill. 1] Július Koller, from the Július Koller pictorial archive, 1970s
Courtesy of the Július Koller Society, Bratislava

I.

In recent years, we have been experiencing a reawakening of interest in Eastern European art of the 1960s and 1970s, particularly in conceptual art. Any advances made in the decades after the fall of the Iron Curtain have been made in this field.[1] Little-explored layers of Eastern European cultural history that were laid down in relative isolation parallel the global canon of conceptual art in interesting ways. This canon is in itself a global phenomenon, and its division into west, east, and south is largely absurd. Nonetheless, it grows out of different conditions in different places and takes on different forms. This may be explained most simply by the generality of the definitions of conceptual art, which seem to be easily adapted to a wide variety of variations.[2] The visual and conceptual similarities shared by art from different parts of the world may be the reason we favor the unifying, universalist view dominant in the Western perspective over the critical analysis of individual artifacts.

While in Western Europe and the United States, conceptual art developed in response to the crisis of modernism and the achievements of the postwar neo-avant-garde, Eastern Europe lacked a similar environment. Progressive art there was far more marked by its position at the cultural periphery, which was due to both geographical location and the long-term effects of totalitarian regimes in the region. In Eastern Europe, for a very heterogeneous group of nations—with a few exceptions, including, for example, the former Czechoslovakia and Yugoslavia—there was no stable, continuous tradition of modernism. The occasional appearances and reappearances of modernism after World War II coincided with unpredictable, usually short periods of political liberalism and increased accessibility of current information on the art world. All the Eastern European countries shared the experience of socialist realism or, more generally, the ideological abuse of culture. Most Eastern European avant-garde artists lacked the critical stance (which was a matter of course in the West) toward modernist thinking and modernist positions of power or even institutions (which were almost nonexistent in the region). Eastern European art originated in an environment where there was no art market in the Western sense; as a result, it was shaped all the more markedly by ideological pressure from the state. Conceptual thinking in Eastern Europe generally emerged in the late 1960s—paradoxically, at the moment when the legacy of the modernist avant-garde was being revitalized.

According to Hungarian art historian Edit András, traditional modernism played an important oppositional role in Hungary with regard to official culture and was therefore spared the attacks and criticisms it was subject to in the West: "Modernism worked well for the artists and critics as a field of projection, a kind of dreamland of freedom and equality […] while conceptualism in Western countries played an active role in the critique of modernism, the local Eastern variants were deeply embedded in it; therefore, the critique of modernism has remained unfinished business in Hungary well after the political changes."[3] Jana Geržová attributes the absence of critical conflict between modernism and conceptualism in Slovakia to the weakness of the modernist tradition. "If conceptualism meant revolt in Slovakia, it was paradoxically still a revolt against the lingering socialist art that dominated the 1950s; at the same time, it was also a revolt against the numerous waves of lingering '-isms' that had overwhelmed the domestic arts in Europe for a short period during the liberal sixties."[4] For this reason, conceptual art in Eastern Europe acquired its specific form as a response to totalitarianism and, at the same time, to the seeming senselessness of confusing neo-avant-garde movements, which were embraced uncritically, without debate, and without the necessary experiences.

Artists in Eastern Europe during the 1960s were already working with text and the documentation processes characteristic of conceptual art in Western Europe and the United States at the time. Their work, however, often contained messages that were contradictory at best. Western conceptualism was fascinated by the methods of science and, despite claims to the contrary, objectivity; nonetheless, it gave the appearance of being rational and unemotional. The Eastern European variety of conceptual art "objectivity" did not adhere very closely to objectivity; on the contrary, many artists developed approaches that were highly subjective and openly emotional.[5] The Russian variety of conceptualism, as developed in the work of Ilya Kabakov and others working in the Soviet Union during the 1970s, was labeled as romantic by contemporary critic Boris Groys.[6] The Slovenian art group OHO designated its work as transcendental conceptualism.[7] Much conceptual art from Eastern Europe was invested with playfulness, irony, satire, and political allusions; in this particular way, artists responded to the contexts in which their works were created. We find these elements in the work of the Croatian Gorgona group, the Hungarian artist Tamás Szentjóby, the Pole Tadeusz Kantor, and many others. Some of the artists in Eastern Europe who began experimenting with conceptual art for the first time used elements taken from scientific forms of expression, including various typologies, graphs, sketches, and maps. However, the content of their work was often not related to the verifiable facts of the world around them, as if they inadvertently, but literally, fulfilled the first of

Sol LeWitt's "Sentences on Conceptual Art": "Conceptual artists are mystics rather than rationalists. They leap to conclusions that logic cannot reach."[8]

Conceptual art was almost nonexistent in the Czech lands in the 1960s and 1970s; if it did exist, it did so just outside the main currents of both official and unofficial art at the time. Perhaps this can be explained by the strong standing of modernism. In Czech postwar art, modernism enjoyed status as an underlying tradition; progressive artists did not feel a strong need to distinguish themselves from it but instead wanted to build on it. In contrast, several Slovak figures immediately devoted themselves assiduously to conceptual art. Beginning in the late 1960s, Slovak artists Stano Filko and Július Koller produced noteworthy and rich bodies of work that were undoubtedly conceptual in nature, mostly in private and in relative isolation from the global art community. Young Slovak artists in the late 1990s were instrumental in rediscovering them and bringing them up to date. Inspired by the art world of the time, they were searching for creative figures in their own history they might be able to emulate. They designated Koller and Filko as predecessors, thus outlining a genealogy they themselves could be part of. And they initiated directly intergenerational collaborations and projects that included older artists who had become established figures of the distinctive Slovak strain of conceptual art.[9]

Notwithstanding, the work of Július Koller and Stano Filko contains elements we do not usually associate with conceptual art. In the artistic processes and artworks of both artists, there is an insistence that we can only arrive at new knowledge and experiences by perceiving the world irrationally. Both Filko and Koller, each in his own way, gave their work form using an all-embracing, highly subjective system of ideas. In their extensive oeuvre, we also find numerous references to history or to themes that can be, somewhat surprisingly, characterized from the perspective of the Western artistic canon as nationalistic themes. Koller painted Slovak national flags and coats of arms, drew maps depicting the migrations of Slavic tribes during the migration of peoples, and demonstrated a fascination with Slovak folklore. Filko, too, used the tricolor theme and made reference to figures from the Slovak National Revival;

moreover, in his texts one of the most frequently occurring adjectives is "Slovak." Perhaps we may even speak here of a sort of national conceptualism: both artists anchor their work in a national framework, making copious references to specific traditions that are essentially unrelated to the wider context of contemporary art.

Today the work of Stano Filko and Július Koller is commonly seen and interpreted in connection with their interest in the future: along with other Slovak artists, they were preoccupied with utopian visions of space travel or communication with extraterrestrial civilizations.[10] But their interest in the past has remained somewhat neglected. While the projects of most Western conceptualists were created for the here and now, Koller's and Filko's moved freely through time from prehistory to futuristic reflections on the life of the human race beyond planet Earth. They encompass both extremes with similar ease. Both create systems of thought based not on a sequential evolutionary perception of history but on something like a model of parallel flow that simultaneously includes all the moments of history. In a titanic effort, Filko constructs the past and future of the world. Koller, a skeptic, speculatively carries out his own cultural and futurological operations, producing what is purportedly a new cultural reality and a new social consciousness that might possibly be understood at some point in the future, during a new stage of cosmological humanist culture.

As a Czech writer I am aware of the problem involved in embarking on an analysis of historic and national themes in the work of Slovak artists. There is a danger that his views will be perceived as reductive or frankly Orientalist. The concern is entirely justified. Whenever there was an opportunity, Czechs have conducted themselves toward Slovaks from a position of dominance or even in an unabashedly colonialist manner: Slovakia is often perceived as a primitive, unsophisticated, dark, and emotional region. Czechs, in contrast with this construction, have historically painted themselves as a cultivated, rational nation that brought enlightenment and civilization to Slovakia. Finding irrational or even revivalist themes in the works of Koller and Filko would seem to place me squarely within this paradigm. For this reason, I think it is important to draw attention to the following issues in advance: the purpose of my discussion is not to portray the leading figures of the Slovak neo-avant-garde art as exotic crackpots living in worlds of their own. I perceive their difference as a positive trait, and I believe that a similar eccentricity is to be found in the works of other Eastern European artists. This stems from the peculiar cultural logic of the region; I shall try to illuminate its sources and consequences below. Július Koller and Stano Filko represent clear-cut examples of a distinctive approach in the field of conceptual art that I cannot find in Czech art. This is not a result of the supposed cultural superiority of Czechs but of the fact that conceptual art did not flourish or produce the kinds of results in the Czech lands as it did in Slovakia. Slovak artists, unlike their Czech counterparts, were able to grasp its language in an original way. More important for me than the painted tricolor flags or the bizarre quest for a utopian Slovak Paleolithic was the overarching conception of what art is and how artists operate that Koller and Filko were able to imbue their work with. Their Slovak national conceptualism is a distinctive hybrid whose value lies increasingly—both in the East and in the West—in its being an imaginative alternative to the dominant artistic discourse.

The following pages consider the extensive oeuvres of Július Koller and Stano Filko in an unapologetically selective manner. We find historical and Slovak motifs only in certain of their works—albeit key ones. Their works did not originate in a vacuum or in isolation but were a conscious part of the Slovak, Czechoslovak, and European artistic contexts. In their conceptually oriented work, both artists unfettered themselves from the formal traditions of classical art; at the same time, they distanced themselves from fashionable artistic trends engendered in the West. In the 1960s, at a moment of fracture in the chronicle of modernist art history, each dispensed—in his own way—with easel paintings and traditional sculpture and broke radically with contemporary societal expectations for art. Nonetheless, both artists thought it was important to remain part of the traditions of their country. Yes, they were fascinated by space and the future. At the same time, I maintain that they felt the need to build an absurd, humorous, or downright wacky bridge between the 19th and 20th centuries.

II.

In the late 1960s, Július Koller (1939–2007) had already begun to question both traditional understandings of art and inherited artistic media with ironic humor. He created antipictures, antihappenings, and complex "intermedia" works that often reflected his interests in the mysteries of everyday life, including UFOs and the fate of Atlantis.[11] Július Koller was not a purely programmatic conceptual artist in the spirit of the movement as it took shape in Western Europe and America in the 1960s. Koller's broad scope was rooted in the specific conditions of socialist Czechoslovakia and also in his personality, in which a penetrating analytical intellect, a skeptical bent, and a distinctive sense of humor clashed with an uncritical interest in the irrational. Koller was not only an avant-garde artist; he was also interested in conventional forms of art. For his livelihood and pleasure, he produced traditional paintings for many years, selling them through the state controlled gallery *Dílo* [Work]; his paintings track an independent parallel path alongside his acclaimed conceptual work.[12] Koller organized and taught courses in open-air painting for groups of amateur artists.

Paintings and objects that incorporate Slovak flags and ironic uses of folkloric motifs appear repeatedly in Koller's work. Their meanings varied and were based on the historical context. In 1968 alone he made use of the Czechoslovak flag at least three times: in *Československý znak. Anti-obraz (Farbobraz)* [The Czechoslovak Coat of Arms: Anti-Image (Color Image)], *Československá krajina (Zástava)* [Czechoslovak Landscape (Flag)], and *Československá zástava (s odznakom)* [Czechoslovak Flag (with Coat of Arms)]. In 1969, to celebrate a hockey game between Czechoslovakia and the Soviet Union, he combined the flag motif with the winning score of 2:0 for *Anti-obraz–farbobraz (ČSSR–ZSSR 2:0 hokej)* [Anti-Image–Color-Image (CSSR–USSR 2:0 Hockey)]. The series is based on the wave of nationalist sentiment incited by the occupation of Czechoslovakia in August 1968.[13] Two decades later, Koller created *Znaky Oravy* [Orava Symbols] (1995), a series of paintings with the names of historical tribes that had inhabited Slovakia in the distant past, with emphasis on the Slavs and Slovaks, set in geometrical shapes (*Sondy*

1 and *Sondy 2* [Probes 1 and 2], 2001). During the period of the disintegration of Czechoslovakia and the emergence of an independent Slovakia, he produced a large series of images of waves using the national *S* and a question mark motif. In each case the flag was used as a semantic sign; allusions to its nationalistic significance, doubtless tinged with irony, can be found particularly in *Orava Symbols* and *Probes*.

The most striking evidence of Koller's interest in Slovakia's history, however, is his archive. Throughout his life—unbeknownst to all except his closest friends—Koller assembled an extensive pictorial archive whose contents range from artworks and source materials for his conceptual work to manifestations of the artist's eccentricity. Koller would hoard all available newspapers and magazines.[14] He would then methodically cut them up and thematically sort the images and texts that drew his attention for a variety of reasons. He was interested in cars (though he himself did not have a driving license), film and television stars, particular localities, UFOs, the Bermuda Triangle, archaeological mysteries, architectural photography, art reproductions, unsolved crossword puzzles and brain teasers, maps, cartoons, advertisements, fashion, industrial product wrappers, book covers, photographic nudes, children's illustrations, comic books, science and technology, and pictures of things and situations that for different reasons reminded him of contemporary artworks. Koller devoted himself most energetically to his archival activity in the 1970s and 1980s. Eventually, Koller's Bratislava apartment was filled to overflowing with boxes and packages containing thematically arranged clippings.[15] [ill. 1]

What was the intent of Július Koller's archive, and how are we to interpret it today? The collection before us is notably ambiguous. An archive will always be unfinished, just as its significance will always be relative, as is the case with a substantial number of Koller's other activities—which, perhaps lends them much of their charm. Slovak art historian Petra Hanáková concludes that the classification of Koller's archive is open to debate and adds that, for practical reasons, it is probably most appropriate to consider it a work of art, even though the artist himself did not think of it as such and never sought to present it to the public.[16] The Július Koller archive does not represent a clearly formulated art project, and it is devoid of scholarly ambition. We may think of it as a quixotic attempt to assemble a pictorial history of the world, to construct a sort of utopian paper Internet by interconnecting hundreds of thousands of pictorial materials.[17] However, due to spatial, temporal, and material constraints, the archive became an unnavigable expanse of paper not only for its creator but also for future researchers. Koller left no user's manual, and it is quite possible that, even for him, it was more of an outlet for a compulsive obsession to collect information than a mindfully assembled corpus.

The Július Koller archive is like an oddly transposed illustration of the methods for exploring cultural memory devised by art historian Aby Warburg, particularly his picture atlas titled *Mnemosyne*.[18] Like *Mnemosyne Atlas*, Koller's archive leaves the images open to multiple possible interpretations. Most of Koller's clippings were pasted onto sheets of white paper, either alone or in group compositions. The act of creating neutral backgrounds for each individual clipping isolates it from its original semantic context. Understanding the significance of the images involves not only strict formal comparison but also an intuitive method of studying human culture, both "high" and "low," as a whole. Július Koller enjoyed creating visual montages using images from unrelated arenas, and he collected ones with ambiguous meanings. In his archive we find an almost-imperceptible fluctuation between seriousness and humor that, fortunately, Koller sometimes elucidated with labels and notes. Thanks to them, we know, for example, that he viewed a photo of a block of apartments as the work of a minimalist artist and saw mechanical devices as modernist sculptures. In his collages, he combined images related to astronomical research and pictures of consumer products, newspaper photographs of politicians, and humorous headlines belonging to unrelated articles.

The specific physical configurations that Koller created in his image panels are significant, with the positions of individual scenes relative to one another, their rhythms, and even the spaces between them all engaging in dialogue. The formation of relationships and spaces appears to be the main compositional strategy used in Koller's ensembles of clippings. Such ensembles afford insight into his diagrammatic thinking, which extended beyond individual compositions to span the entire archive. Among the information Koller collected, we find much that is unusual or mysterious or that can be read in different ways. His work is, at first glance, intensely methodical but in essence intuitive and even irrational; it is full of Däniken-type mysticism and a belief in UFOs—he was able (and willing) to find evidence of their existence nearly everywhere.

A seemingly straightforward set of photographs of Slovak, Czech, and foreign cities may serve as evidence of this. In the part of the Koller archive in the possession of the Július Koller Society, postcards and magazine clippings from various locations attractive to tourists have been glued onto several hundred A2 sheets of paper. Apparently, Koller collected his photographs of cities based either on the beauty of the individual localities or on the artistic quality of the photographs. He does not analyze aspects shared by different images; neither is he interested in critical readings of the original contexts. In the end, the abundance of locations seems to function as part of the process of documenting unnamed activities or as evidence of some extraordinary occurrence. It is as if those who took the banal photographs had managed to capture normally invisible clues that illuminate for Koller the lives being led in the places photographed. The print media from which most of the photographs originate can be understood as a principal source for the shaping of modern culture. Whereas for classical art it was antiquity that served as the storehouse of our cultural motifs, today mass-printed newspapers and magazines flooded with images and advertisements play such a role. Koller's archive can thus be seen as an attempt to physically bring together the entire universe of images and texts, which not only describe and document their subject matter but whose very existence and efficient distribution constitute our vision of the world.

Koller's intense and unique relationship to cultural history, particularly that of Eastern Europe and Slovakia, is relevant here. The national motifs in the archive are manifested primarily in extensive sets of clippings and drawings devoted to the history of the Slavs and Slovaks. Koller collected a series of articles describing archaeological finds from the Migration Period. He was interested in the relations between the Slavs and the Celts. He drew maps of prehistoric settlements in Europe and the likely movements of their inhabitants across the Eurasian continent. Apparently he was fascinated by the possibility that the two groups of prehistoric people—the Slavs and the Celts—might have had shared ancestors in the inhabitants of Atlantis. He found arguments for similar lines of reasoning in pseudo-scientific articles on mysterious phenomena or by interpreting otherwise unrelated news and information in a similar vein. In 1976, for example, he noted on a piece of paper a possible link between the Portuguese name "Costa" and the Russian "Kostya," compared magazine pictures of archaeological finds (especially Slavonic settlements), and surmised that a deep connection and continuity may have existed among ancient cultures. The tree of life—a simple symbolic drawing reminiscent of a heraldic emblem or a hieroglyph—was proof of the inner connectedness Koller found in archaic reliefs in Asia Minor, in Slavic folklore, and in the modernist sculptures of Joan Miró.

We may safely assume that Koller did not devote the archive, as a whole, solely to relationships between prehistoric cultures. Though perhaps Koller was not aware of it, cultural history for him was a ongoing and continuous tapestry of themes and motifs. Photographs of prehistoric digs, socialist architecture, space technology, and contemporary art were stored in separate places. However, they represented not unrelated chapters but different sections of a single text. Koller used his archive as a device to generate historical continuity, as a framework enabling him to address and interconnect a wide variety of visual materials from the universe of print media.

Július Koller saw culture not as something predetermined but as a phenomenon continually being shaped both materially and in the realm of ideas. Even from an individual perspective, culture can be understood and dealt with both as matter or as medium. This stance corresponds with the historical period of the birth of Slovak national culture out of a movement of national revival, a process of conscious self-definition—one that took place in other Eastern European cultures as well. From today's perspective, the process involved the creation of a culture that had not heretofore existed, one constructed in binary opposition to the existing dominant culture and dedicated to conceptualizing an ideal, model Slovakia whose cultural traditions and national mythology were still in the making.[19] In a pan-Slavic fervor, Koller collected documentation on official sculpture from the USSR and Eastern Europe as if it constituted a modern folkloric tradition merely awaiting the proper interpretation and classification. As an art project, he built a special gallery for extraterrestrial civilizations on one of the slopes of the High Tatras. Since he did not find contemporary art in Slovak galleries, he interpreted ordinary objects and situations captured in magazine images in the spirit of contemporary art. He worked creatively with his own identity, inventing an alter ego in the form of J.K., a space traveler who was not tied to the reality of normalization in Czechoslovakia but could move about freely—even if only in the space of his own imagination—in various regions of both terrestrial and otherworldly existence. This was not just a personal mythology—according to Koller, we are all space travelers.

Part of Koller's archive is strongly reminiscent of the approaches of the national revivalists who had built linguistically defined national cultures in 19th-century Eastern Europe. Prominent figures in the Slovak revivalist movement, such as Ján Kollár (1793–1852) and Ľudovít Štúr (1815–1856), also began by collecting a wide variety of cultural artifacts, creating card files, and extensively documenting dialects and other elements of linguistic interest. Their first task was to establish a codified national language and a national history to match the languages and histories of already-established nations. The basic method here was to find, and sometimes even to fabricate, analogies between existing cultures and the contemporary culture Slovak revivalists were attempting to generate.[20] However, they did not proceed as objective linguists and historians would; their activities had a notable romantic and artistic bent. The first national revivalists had nothing to build on, so they themselves had to become the creators of the genealogies crucial to shaping the emerging national cultures. The first conceptual artists in Eastern Europe were in a similar situation. They had forsworn modern art and needed to start from scratch. Local cultures had generally not produced artists in whose work they could find inspiration, and contacts with international artists were precluded by the Iron Curtain. How were they to begin anew? Perhaps it is not surprising, therefore, that national revival motifs in Slovak culture survived so late into the second half of the 20th century. Individual works by Július Koller did not try to connect the Slovak nation, language, and culture exclusively with earlier historical cultures, as had the national revivalists of the 19th century; rather, he drew connections with prehistoric cultures, the myth of Atlantis, or visions of alien civilizations.

If Július Koller reframed everyday events in cultural life, he was not simply implementing a Duchampian strategy for transforming reality into art. His references have much deeper roots in the past. For national revivalists, agricultural practices, regional forms of religious ceremonies, or local folk costumes not only exemplified a common rural typology of everyday life but constituted evidence of a distinctive national character and a unique identity. One of Koller's favorite activities, one which could be translated into a cultural context, was sports. He saw sports as a model of interpersonal communication that, unlike the "real" world, was governed by the rules of fair play. But in modern times, what activity is a greater trigger of nationalist sentiment than sports? This is illustrated by Koller's works inspired by a hockey match against the hated USSR.

III.

A viewer's first reaction to the work of Stano Filko (1937–2015) is generally amazement; the scale and ambition of his work take one's breath away. The objects, assemblages, texts, and pictures, all linked by a single coherent thought system, constitute a continuously metamorphosing whole, the likes of which we rarely see in contemporary art. His work knows no small gestures. It is characterized by unusually complex conceptual underpinnings as well as a sincerity that borders on naiveté. The core of Stano Filko's work is his own cosmological system. His objects, paintings, and even his life were based on the same principles. His oeuvre is a monumental conceptual collage arising out of a variety of sources, from books and popular magazine articles to his own experiences and reflections, which Aurel Hrabušický characterizes as "a fanciful vision wedged into the realm of verified knowledge."[21]

The next predictable reaction to Filko's work might be skepticism and doubt. Is such a titanic scope even possible? It is still art? Are we dealing with the work of a genius or a charlatan? Are we to believe all the author's claims, or are they all just part of a big game? Is it just a hoax or an ironic critique of existing art, science, and philosophy? Is Stano Filko a public luminary, or has nature burdened him with a talent that has taken him to the edge of madness?

Although there is no lack of humor in Filko's work, it is definitely not a joke. His aim is, in all earnestness, to discover the fundamental principles of being. He is one of the few artists at the turn of the 21st century giving voice in cynical times to the big questions that neither art nor science has the courage to ask. What is the meaning of human existence? What is the nature of the universe? Where in it is there space for the life of an individual? Filko not only poses these questions but also responds to them exhaustively. He conveys to his public a conception of the origins, orientation, and meaning of the world—perhaps so that he himself might ultimately be able to live in it. Filko teaches us lessons about the essence of nature; he summarizes in just a few pages the structure and evolution of the human soul. His art does not address the current problems of contemporary human society; rather, he directly takes on the entire universe in all its complexity, past and future, in all conceivable dimensions. Mirror environments in the late 1960s, objects and paintings in the colors of the chakras, and especially texts that occur in both newer and older works serve as illustrations or explanatory captions for the whole of his work.

Filko is not attempting to construct an imaginary parallel world, some sort of experimental model or mere utopian vision. Everything is real. It is as if at the very beginning of Filko's creative career—or more precisely, at a few well-defined moments—his artistic worldview formed rapidly and in its entirety. He may over the years have worked through its details, but its founding principle remains unchanged. A substantial number of Filko's works—whether objects, paintings, architecture, texts, happenings, or his own life—reflect this world of ideas. His works are an attempt not only to convey this world to others but also to verify its validity for himself. If an essential dimension of Filko's oeuvre involves an elucidation of his subjective cosmological system, we must perceive it as a kind of self-portrait, a mirror to his mind that expands endlessly, just like the universe.

At the center of this ambitious project stands Stano Filko, who sees world issues through the prism of his own being. However, we are not dealing with the normal manner in which biography forms an artist's life. Few artists are so bound up with their work that one is unimaginable without the other. As Vit Havránek has written, Filko "deals with his life story and his life as if they were legends."[22] The origins of Stano Filko's cosmological system can be traced to two experiences with clinical death that marked his destiny, in 1945 and 1952.[23] In later interpretations of these experiences, they acquired the significance of a brush with the absolute associated not only with death but also with a quasi-religious rebirth. They were the decisive moments that shaped his specific system of understanding. Filko divided his life into several hierarchically arranged reincarnations. Each has its own particular characteristics and corresponds to a precisely defined art form. The physical dimension of the world and the dimension of spiritual growth are one and the same. Stano Filko created an all-encompassing personal cosmology. His autobiography is, by the same token, also a history of the universe.

We might characterize Stano Filko's thinking as a sort of solipsism. The boundary between him and the surrounding world seems vague; everything is subordinated to an extreme subjectivism. When considering the universe, he thinks about himself. Meanwhile, however, his life and work reflect the principles of the world. The seriousness with which he imbues his work attests to a boundless ambition. Without traveling to foreign soil, we can find parallels to the life and work of Stano Filko in the former Czechoslovakia and, earlier, Austro-Hungary—in the figure of the Czech writer Ladislav Klíma. His philosophical system differed from the academic philosophy of the day in a similarly radical way; it was more akin to art and was built upon an extreme subjectivism that bordered on solipsism. Reading Klíma's texts, which were written more for himself than for a public readership, gives the impression that his philosophical system was suggested or revealed to him at a particular moment when he perceived completely the absence of boundaries between his body and the outside world, as he later recounts in detail in his correspondence. But Stano Filko was no writer; he expressed himself through images or texts that had neither traditional literary form nor the conceptual coherence of science. Viewers must interpret them for themselves and, in doing so, run the risk of misreading them.

Critics of Filko's early pieces, like *Happsoc I*, *Happsoc II*, or *Happsoc III*—which incorporated events taking place in city, country, or around the world—speak of works that appropriated the surrounding world. These pieces—the first two resulting from a collaboration with Alex Mlynárčík and Zita Kostrová—had the character of textual declarations. In them, the artists listed items in the area—the city Bratislava, its people, and elements of nature—and declared them, taken together, to be a work of art. Viewers saw them primarily as calls to perceive the world in a new, different way. In *Happsoc III* Filko declared the whole of Czechoslovakia from 1966 on to be his own work of art. This total integration of art and life, according to Daniel Grúň, embodied an update to the myth of the radical avant-garde.[24] Far more than a case of classical appropriation, however, for Filko it was perhaps a demonstrative act in which world and creator were united. Filko did not transfer the surrounding reality into a new context but declared it to be a part of him. In an apparent coincidence, these works resonated with similar artistic ventures in Western Europe at the time. Nonetheless, their form and content arose not as part of a conscious reaction to the Western neo-avant-garde but out of Filko's distinctive spiritual world system. Filko and his collaborators defined *Happsoc* as "reality itself, unstylized"—which must, by definition, combine the artists' minds and those of viewers into an indivisible whole.

Filko connects philosophical and religious elements with science and the technological optimism of the 1960s. He often applies the terminology and methodology of science to his work. What he does is "research," and he uses the term "laboratory" to refer to his studio. He is fascinated by technology and the conquest of space; revels in typologies, reports, and hierarchical systems; and makes use of unorthodox drawings and graphs. The conviction that it is possible to know and explain the world pervades his work. Elements borrowed from scientific imaging made their way into his work in the mid-1960s, when he first began working with maps. Filko would modify them, adding photographs, and organizing them into larger assemblages. He saw maps as offering ways to depict the geopolitical state of the world but also as abstract renderings of physical reality. *Globe of the Earth* and subsequently *Globe of the Universe* thus acquired meaning as symbols of higher ontological truths and of the artist's identification with them.

As with his relationships to philosophy and religion, he was not so much interested in real science as in his own vision of science. Filko cited the theory of relativity, quantum theory, Freudianism, string theory, political science, holistic and alternative medicine, the Kabbalah, the Big Bang theory, and popular knowledge from astrophysics without demonstrating any real understanding of them. He handled scientific terms as if they were mythological. Filko was not concerned with analyzing the world scientifically; instead, he offered an anti-Enlightenment "re-enchantment of the world" that cast it in a subjective, irrational light. Art became a kind of parallel science, a pseudoscientific tool for acquiring knowledge of the world, powered by his own creativity.

In addition to philosophical, religious, and scientific elements, Stano Filko's work also contains elements usually associated with eccentricity or psychological abnormality. He lived in an invisible realm of different dimensions. He predicted the implantation of chips into human brains, was convinced of the existence of Atlantis, and believed that devices enabling teleportation and mind reading would soon be invented. He thought the ghosts of our loved ones observe us and influence our lives, and so on. We find closed-off subjective worlds similar to Filko's flowing from the pens of many compulsive writers and mentally disturbed individuals whose work we come across in the context of art brut. They, too, often use pseudophilosophical or pseudoreligious language or convincingly mimic the methods of scientific research. In particular, some of Filko's textual works find parallels in écrits bruts (raw writings), a term inspired by Jean Dubuffet and developed by Michel Thévoz.

Stano Filko writes not to communicate with others but chiefly to satisfy his own needs. Writing and drawing serve to externalize his mental processes. Filko's texts are therefore not final products but, rather, records, in notation, of ongoing thought processes. Filko returns to them often, with enjoyment, seldom regarding what has been written down as definitive. He adds new slogans and text profusely to earlier works, as if by endlessly rewriting he were entering into a dialogue with himself. He often wrote his treatises by hand, sometimes on graph paper. He spewed them forth at a constant pace, driven by the type of uncontrollable need we might see in people manifesting obsessive-compulsive behavior. The borders between normal and abnormal psychology, particularly in areas where they blend into one another, are—and will remain—subjective. As we explore insanity, we understand humanity better; we become better able to see it from perspectives other than those rationality makes possible. Filko's activities inhabit the borderland between two worlds and allow us to peer into both of them.

Stano Filko's system of artistic expression features not just findings from physics, religion, and personal life; it also contains mythological elements that are both personal and national, which is unusual in Western art. While Filko's texts reject nationalism as a political principle, we cannot overlook how strongly and unreservedly his work is anchored in the atmosphere of his native Slovakia. For Filko, aside from Slovakia, only the cosmos exists. In Slovakia, similar references to national identity were relatively frequent in the 1960s and 1970s.[25] Nevertheless, in Filko's work, both the number and intensity of references to Slovak roots are notable. If Filko's universe had an origin and an epicenter, it was in the region of his upbringing, the area surrounding the Slovak town of Piešťany. He was interested not only in its appearance but also in its collective cultural traditions and history. Filko even included in his personal genealogy a prehistoric human settlement whose remains are located near his native village. In his archive, we find the image of a dinosaur inscribed with the words "Slovak pre-Paleolithic." In his annotated maps, texts, and collages, we find references to Celtic settlements in Slovakia and to Pribina, a mythical Slavic prince. As early as 1960 he had marked the hypothetical "center of the Slavs" on a set of political maps using arrows.

A Paleolithic statuette of Venus discovered in 1938 in the village of Moravany nad Váhom, about five kilometres from Piešťany, had a special significance for Filko (who dated its discovery to 1937, the year of his birth). The statuette is Slovakia's oldest artistic artifact. Though shortly after its discovery it ended up, under murky circumstances, in France, it returned to Slovakia in 1967 to great media interest. Around that time, the *Moravian Venus* became a central locus in Filko's semantic world. He claimed that growing up in the region where Slovak national revivalist Ľudovit Štúr and Communist reformer Alexander Dubček had been born was the work of fate. He included a selection of Štúr's writings titled *Myšlienky, proroctvá, budúcnosť* [Thoughts, Prophecies, the Future] in *Happsoc III*, and a photo of Dubček became a central element in Filko's *Katedrála humanismu* [Humanist Cathedral] (1968).

Let us pause for a moment and consider Štúr more closely. He is primarily known as a revivalist who, in the mid-19th century, codified the Slovak language, which entailed establishing the first standard form of the language on the basis of the central Slovak dialect, as well as through lexical and grammatical borrowings from other languages. Cataloguing the Slovak language was not motivated by a purely academic need; according to Štúr, a single language would be instrumental in bringing Catholic and Protestant Slovaks together and forging a unified Slovak national identity. Efforts to exalt and emancipate national languages played a prominent role in the national revival movements of Eastern Europe.[26] Being a national revivalist involved not only linguistic endeavors but social and political action as well. Štúr promoted the idea of a pan-Slavic union under Russia's leadership, but he was also known for his opposition to political democracy and market economics. Some of his views were quite bizarre, even for his time, and unanchored in any form of reality. Filko is also a conceptual descendant of Štúr's ideological rival, Ján Kollár, who moved about in the field of linguistics with freedom and with an artist's inclination toward speculation. On the basis of similar-sounding words, he extrapolated far-reaching conjectures allegedly showing kinship between the ancient Greeks and the Slovaks. Using pseudolinguistic methods, he tried to demonstrate that Latin was in fact an ancient Slavonic dialect. His "scholarly" works—which even during his lifetime were not received sympathetically—contain absurd assertions about the global importance of Slovaks, who, according to Kollár, were at the heart of all civilization.

Filko, too, has an exalted opinion of Slovaks, especially of some of its emblematic figures. He devoted a whole cycle to the politician and astronomer Milan Rastislav Štefánik, incorporating a symbolic pyramid and the inscriptions "Slovak" and "Cosmos" into a portrait of him. In his texts, he repeatedly trumpets Slovakia as special and unique in comparison to the rest of the world. Among Filko's latest clippings, there is an article on the genetic code of the Slovaks. He sometimes writes "Slovakoczechia" instead of "Czechoslovakia." He interprets his name, "Stano"—Stanislav—as "subject—glory—Slovak—Slaviana—world—freedom." Stano Filko is in essence a revivalist, on whose shoulders rests the weight of the entire universe as he knows it. The importance he attaches to his work does not derive only from his personal megalomania; it also corresponds to the aims of the 19th-century national revivalists.

IV.

The megalomania of Stano Filko and the mystifying collecting activities of Július Koller are far from anomalous among artists in Eastern Europe, where, more often than elsewhere, artists take on the roles of prophets, martyrs, prognosticators of transpersonal truths, interpreters of history, teachers, fighters, or leaders—even in the second half of the 20th century. They often acted as intermediaries between history and their communities, between an impersonal social order and fellowship. Milan Knížák perceived his activities in the 1960s and 1970s in Czechoslovakia as part of a mission to educate and enlighten: he wanted to teach people to live better lives. In his manifesto *Zpráva o III. hudebním obrození* [Report on the 3rd Musical Revival], Czech art historian Ivan Martin Jirous suggested parallels between the independent culture of Czechoslovakia in the 1970s, the National Revival of the 19th century, and the religious visionaries of the Middle Ages. The performances of Jerzy Bereś in Poland took the form of divination ceremonies and theatrical masses during which current political and ethical issues were played out on stage. In Slovenia the OHO Group and later one of its members in particular, Marko Pogačnik, created a cosmology based on invented myths designed to save planet Earth from ecological disaster. In Romania, Ion Grigorescu used his body to spark a dialogue between a subjective pseudo-religion and a critique of culture as a whole. The Slovenian NSK group, along with perhaps dozens of other artists across Eastern Europe, created their own imaginary states, postulating a suprapersonal identity based on a set of invented state symbols. Are not all of these artists linked in some way?

The status of culture and art in postwar Eastern Europe was not determined solely by the ruling Communist ideology and the repression it relied on. It was engendered by more general characteristics of the region that were historically anchored in a cultural center-periphery dynamic. Eastern Europe can be defined as the area between Germany and Russia, between Western Europe and Asia. In the Middle Ages, the politically, nationally, and culturally heterogeneous region fell under the sway of the great regional powers. Several movements of national revival were initiated at the turn of the 19th century in connection with the Enlightenment idea of the nation-state. We see them at various points in time in the Czech lands, Slovakia, Poland, the Baltic states, Romania, Bulgaria, Ukraine, Belarus, and the regions of the former Yugoslavia. The Eastern European national revivals were based on nationally defined cultures, the creation or refinement of a literary language, the mapping out of local cultural genealogies, and attempts at self-definition in relation to the dominant culture, whether that meant Germany, Hungary, Russia, or Turkey. The identities of the Eastern European nations did not emerge out of a long evolutionary process; they were the fruits of rapid change and premeditated strategies inspired by Western philosophy (Johann Gottfried Herder)[27] and the creative interpretation of local cultures. Such processes of cultural coming of age are not specific to Eastern Europe. They happened in Western regions that had not undergone political subordination (e.g., Germany, Italy), and they in turn served as models for the lands to their east. There were similar developments in Latin America and in the case of the self-definition of black culture in the United States.

It cannot be overlooked that the activities of the national revivalists in Eastern Europe bordered on artistic gestures: they created new nations, languages, and worlds. They often mystified, created nonsensical typologies, invented terminology, and concocted history based more on mythology than on historical fact. Eastern European conceptual art, with its tendency to invent cosmologies, indulge in language games, and depict the absurd universes of people living under late socialism, was built on such endeavors. The Slovak art of the 1960s and 1970s, which ran the gamut between art and science in both form and content, had similar concerns.

In some areas of Eastern Europe, including Slovakia, nationality was largely a matter of personal conviction, a construct in which culture and art played key roles. The tradition of Western individualism was lacking. Revivalist artists did not speak for themselves alone but came to embody their national identity, assuming roles as spokespeople for their nations. They were not responsible for themselves alone; they formulated and shaped the basic values of their community. Their role was to create local history—often, quite literally, out of nothing—and expound on it either to the nation or to the outside world by means of art.[28] The internationalism and individualism of the avant-garde during the interwar years of the 20th century only partially overshadowed this role. The specific role of the artist in Eastern Europe underwent a remarkable mutation. For Eastern European artists, agendas were nothing new; this time they were to become apostles not of national ideals but of the artistic practices or even the life philosophies associated with the international avant-garde. Beginning in the late 1930s, in connection with the emergence of various nationalistically oriented governments, and later, during the Stalinist 1950s, Eastern Europe underwent a renaissance of interest in national revivals. Popular art and folklore became fundamental cultural touchstones. The works and views of 19th-century national revivalists were still being used for nationalist propaganda purposes a century later, which extended the reach and impact of their ideas.

Artists usually perceive the way their culture constructs its own history as inevitable, not as something artificial or unnatural. The strategies used are visible only from a distance, from the outside. The last two decades have brought many opportunities to probe into the foundations of Slovak and Eastern European identity. After 1989, state ideologies changed throughout the region, which brought on a wave of conscious reevaluation of the past. The year 1993 saw the establishment of an independent Slovak state that addressed the need to newly articulate its standing in the world and in history. Naturally, there were artists among the witnesses to this process. Thus, in Slovakia we find a number of contemporary artists—including, for example, Tomáš Džadoň, Michal Moravčík, Dalibor Bača, and Martin Piaček—whose work deals with history, Slovak collective memory, national stereotypes, and even national myths. The objects of their explorations were often folklore, public art, and the creation of national symbols—all within a time frame beginning in the 19th century, spanning the period of socialist culture, and lasting until the present day. References to revivalist and, at the same time, socialist culture might be motivated by different factors. Objectively, the two cultural stages share much both visually and conceptually. By emphasizing its continuity with revivalist artistic activities, socialist art bolstered its nationalist credentials. Similar populist approaches can be found in contemporary culture as well, with some artists voicing their protests by alluding to comparable historical contexts. Last but not least, both revivalist art and socialist realism were tightly intertwined with political thinking, and much of contemporary art exhibits similar ambitions.[29] A sign of such interest in history among active Slovak artists may be found not in the borrowing of motifs but, rather, in their deconstruction and in efforts to draw connections to the present. If at times we might wonder whether Július Koller or Stano Filko are simply citing historical motifs and national symbols or, instead, are subjecting them to their own interpretations, it is clear that 21st-century artists in Slovakia are taking such elements to a new level.

Slovak artist Svätopluk Mikyta has also turned to the interpretation of historical themes. In his numerous journal drawings, we find conventional images from the Slovak rural world: the *valaška* (a long, thin, light ax used by shepherds), crosses, potatoes, sickles, and corncobs are often combined with symbols of modern times. His interest in and detachment from the past are linked to his generation (he was born in 1973). He has experience of the ideological transformation associated with 1989 but also with a cosmopolitan way of life resulting from his numerous exhibitions and long-term sojourns for work outside Slovakia. However, Mikyta is by no means a globalized being without roots. He is the type of artist whose experiences abroad have led him to explore his own identity. He identifies with the Slovak modernist artists before him who dealt with national Slovak motifs but brings new, contemporary approaches. According to Petra Hanáková, Mikyta is an artist who is paradoxically better understood abroad than at home.[30]

Svätopluk Mikyta expressed his interest in the Slovak National Revival period in his oft-reproduced *Ja Ľudevít*, for example, in which he demonstrated in a series of arranged photographs his identification with revivalist Ľudovít Štúr. The significance of the double portrait of the contemporary artist and the 19th-century intellectual transcends that of a mere striking visual similarity. In addition to juxtaposing time periods, Mikyta is interested in contrasting East and West and pitting national stereotypes, preconceptions, and realities against one another. Mikyta adopts Štúr's eccentric beard in order to provocatively embody the stereotype of a wild and crazy artist from the East. Mikyta also identifies with Štúr as though with a colleague—as the shaper of his language, in both real and figurative senses, as someone who created a cultural matrix and symbols that he himself inherited and then developed further. In the double portrait, Mikyta attempts to test the extent to which a historical ideology may be translated into a visual language, although it is unclear whether the result can be considered successful. Mikyta's references to history are imbued with contradictory values. In his works he walks a fine line between irony and nostalgia.[31] [ill. 2]

We can describe much of Svätopluk Mikyta's work as forays into the past. He collects photographs from old books or magazines, which he then draws or prints on, or incorporates into assemblage structures. The starting point is his archive, which he himself comments on, edits, and navigates based on free association.[32] In his cycle titled *Re-portréty* [Re-Portraits], which he has been working on since 2002, he has transformed gravure portraits of prewar athletes and magazine portraits by drawing on them. His interest lies in the ways both individual and social identities are formed and transformed. This transformation is the theme of works by Mikyta in which he intervenes in appropriated photographs of historic rallies, sporting events, and modernist or totalitarian architecture. He routinely works with Czech photographic sources, but his interventions have a general significance. He adds geometric forms to the source images, as if he were trying to understand and complement historic compositions and patterns composed of human bodies engaged in group activities. His interest in probing collective memory, working with historical phenomena, and decoding their hidden dimensions is reminiscent of the work of Eva Koťátková. Many of Mikyta's works can thus be categorized as totalitarian modernology, as discussed in a chapter in the present volume, "A Collage between Generations: Jiří Kolář as Witness to Modernity and His Contemporary Successors" (p. 102–136).

V.

Although Stano Filko emigrated from Czechoslovakia to Germany in 1981 and moved to New York in 1982, his work did not attract broader international interest during this period. After his return to Slovakia in 1990, his reception, first at home and later abroad, was greatly influenced by a series of intergenerational exhibitions in which his works were juxtaposed with those of a younger generation of artists.[33] Since 2000, Filko's works have been presented in the collections of major museums across the world and are often showcased in large surveys of both contemporary art and historical conceptual art.[34] International interest in the work of Július Koller was sparked by his 2003 solo exhibition at the Kölnische Kunstverein, which was organized with the assistance of younger slovak artist Roman Ondák. Since then Koller's works have been included in a number of major group exhibitions at major institutions worldwide. He exhibited at Vienna's Galerie Martin Janda and the GB Agency in Paris. Prominent theorists and critics like Jan Verwoert and Georg Schöllhammer have written about his work. The MUMOK in Vienna mounted a large-scale retrospective in 2016.

The current visibility of the work of Stano Filko and Július Koller on the world art scene conceals a paradox. Their work conforms—though not as a result of conscious efforts—to the stereotypical Orientalist idea of conceptual art from the East: irrational, emotional, rural, in some respects oddly archaic, in others irresistibly humorous. In reality, artists from Eastern Europe have extensive experience with the cultural dynamics of center and periphery. They borrowed ideas from cultural centers and tried to bring them to fruition long before their own national culture, in the modern sense, had emerged. The advent of modernism was decisive in this respect. From modernist centers in Western Europe, artists from the East appropriated various elements and imported them to their home cultures. In consequence, an ambivalent relationship to modernism was born: it was perceived as something foreign but also as something superior that artists had to come to terms with in their own way.

Relations between the center and the periphery of world art are a crucial theme in Eastern Europe over the last twenty years. Unlike other issues, local art historians, critics, and artists have returned to it again and again. Eastern Europe has felt neglected by the center: its art, often resembling that of the center, has not, in the view of numerous Eastern art historians, appropriately addressed the Western canon—and, not surprisingly, it has not been admitted to it. Explanations for this discrepancy have long been based on political considerations: socialist states restricted creative freedom. The Iron Curtain made the free exchange of people, artworks, and information impossible. When the Iron Curtain fell in 1989, many art historians and artists thought it reasonable to expect that in a short time, the free movement of people and ideas would facilitate the reception of Eastern art outside the region of its origin. The difference between the center and the periphery would surely disappear—the question was only how long the transitional period would be. Similar expectations were kindled by political rhetoric of the day, according to which the countries of Eastern Europe after 1989 were supposed to rapidly adopt a Western political system and a market economy. But it has become increasingly clear that a transitional period, after which the East would merge completely with Western Europe politically, economically, and culturally, is a complete illusion. The transitional state has become permanent.

The lasting and distinctive urgency of the issue concerning the relationship between Eastern European and world art is to a large extent based on the overall conception of identity in the Eastern European region following 1989. The fall of the totalitarian Communist regimes saw the victory of an ideology based on a "great return"—i.e., the return of Eastern Europe into the bosom of Western civilization. The ideology was described critically by Croatian philosopher Boris Buden: at its core stood the conviction that progress in Eastern Europe had come to a halt with Communism, which had disrupted its age-old ties to Western culture. The historical experience of actual Communism, including its culture, was dismissed as an anomaly imported from the Soviet Union. While socialist states were considered a deviation, Western values have become the benchmark of normality. After the collapse of the USSR and a brief period of transformation, countries such as Czechoslovakia, Poland, and Yugoslavia were set to return to Europe.[35] I believe this state of affairs is where the roots of the increased need to compare Eastern and Western art lie. However, Eastern European art before 1989 still has a long way to go before it can rid itself of the label identifying it as a flawed, immature version of Western art whose value will ultimately be determined by the East's ability to catch up with the achievements of world art and merge seamlessly with its paradigms.[36] The dream of an art that is appreciated and understood on a global scale is patently absurd. It is as utopian an idea as expecting humankind to abandon historically established languages and start to communicate in Esperanto or some other shared language.[37] In its own way, modern art created a kind of Esperanto. Impressionists and Cubists from Sweden, Argentina, and Australia speak a similar artistic language. They might not be mutually intelligible, but the family resemblances are clear. The worldwide dimension of contemporary art, which corresponds to the development of communication technologies and economic globalization, is fascinating. From the perspective of the cultural periphery, this dimension has a quasi-religious character: global art and its emphasis on multiculturalism creates the impression that art is a perfect medium through which nations can understand one another, a model of an ideal world community in the spirit of the great religions. Artists and art historians from around the world travel to various biennales and *documenta*-style exhibitions as if on religious pilgrimages to Rome or Mecca. Then, in Venice or Kassel, they all experience a sense of unity in their diversity. Much as pilgrims from Morocco and Indonesia become aware of their shared Muslimhood when they meet before the Kaaba, a mystical fellowship of contemporary art is engendered at large world exhibitions. If artists and art historians from Eastern Europe have ever experienced a "great return," then it has been at such exhibitions, where they can gaze warmheartedly at work representing their country. At such exhibitions, members of the artistic periphery receive confirmation that their work is meaningful, even when seen away from its local context; in contrast, the art from the centre gives the impression that it has universal qualities that manifest themselves through local mutations in wildly improbable and exotic locations.[38]

The visibility of Eastern European art in the world—and of peripheral art more generally—is multidimensional and often has unintended consequences. The ideal form of this visibility is made plain in major international publications and exhibitions, where, in addition to canonical artists, artists from other regions are represented. Although exhibitions like *Global Conceptualism* (1999) cover a wide geographical spectrum, their impact might not be what the artists themselves had hoped for.[39] Given the definition of conceptual art and its chronology, it may happen that the art of peripheral areas presented at such exhibitions only serves to confirm the primacy and dominance of the art of the center or, at the most, Orientalist-tinged supplements to the basic canon. It is as though such events served as evidence of objective evolutionary trends in art. If neoconstructivism and op art emerged in the Paris of the 1950s, then analogous works from Belgrade or Prague in the 1960s seem to confirm a similar evolutionary logic. Performances outside the United States that were similar in spirit to

American happenings seem to suggest that other cultures and national art scenes had to arrive at the same stages of artistic evolution. The American public might look upon such artistic expressions from the periphery with the same fascination and excitement as if they were in the presence of a living Neanderthal. The real challenge for Eastern art after 1989 was not deciding how to build on the existing traditions and genealogies of Western art. The main task of Eastern art historians was to map out their own traditions based on the internal logic, personalities, and works that local cultures produced. But it was artists who first disrupted the externally constructed history and began to go about this process in very subjective ways. In 2004, Vit Havránek and Ján Mančuška, under the sway of Nicolas Bourriaud's *Postproduction*, likened the work of historians who study art produced by different cultures to that of directors synchronizing the audio and video tracks of a film—they are trying to dub art into understandable language, an effort that Havránek and Mančuška do not necessarily regard in a negative light. The video and audio tracks of a film almost never synchronize automatically; coordinating them perfectly is an artificial process. Havránek and Mančuška also introduce a number of terms relating to the space of asynchronicity. According to them, "the arbitrary history is freedom with which the artist can move about in history and draw on the codes, theories, and historical aesthetics that are available. Freedom is limited by the accessibility of the historical accounts that are available, and its main source is constructed history."[40]

It is surprising that not only in the Czech Republic but in the rest of Eastern Europe, we have encountered entrenched resistance to the thought of examining the relations between Eastern and Western art using the findings and methods of postcolonial theories. This approach might include analysing the behavior of dominant and minority cultures—as found, for example, in the work of Edward Saïd—or using the methodologies arising from the study of situations in Ghana or Indonesia. Yet such studies probably seem exotic and far removed from the reality of Central Europe. Even so, Slovenian art historian Igor Zabel very effectively described the relationship between Eastern and Western art in postcolonialist categories—and with reference to Edward Saïd—almost 20 years ago. According to

Zabel, the art of Eastern Europe, even after 1989, found itself in the position of an unequal partner expected to unconditionally assimilate into Western art. Eastern art is recognized only when it defers to the language of the West, and even then, it is only accepted as proof of the universality of Western artistic values. According to Zabel, "The West has set itself up both as a center and as a general reference point."[41]

Although conditions in Central Europe during the last decades do not correspond to the classical colonialist conditions of the 19th and 20th centuries, the term "self-colonialization"—in the way Alexander Kiossev uses it, for example—may aptly be used to describe them.[42] According to Kiossev, Eastern Europe, though not colonial, is a periphery where the instrument of Western hegemony became not violence but social imagination. The minority cultures yearned to have the same history as the dominant culture, including its art history. Here it should be noted that this self-colonialization began long before 1989, for social imagination was most active precisely when the West represented an unattainable dream. If current works by the international avant-garde rarely found space in the galleries of Eastern European socialist countries or in contemporary art school curricula, exploring the procedures used in such works became a natural strategy for resisting socialist totalitarian regimes. Artists thus built upon other nonsocialist traditions; they measured themselves not only against local art but against the art being made west of the Iron Curtain. It was only sometime after 1989 that the West in Eastern Europe took on the role of being a force that had to be resisted for purposes of self-definition, based on the logic of enforcing and maintaining cultural identity. Thus, it is often some rather peculiar individuals who have become Eastern European art heroes. Their work might emphasize local characteristics or, instead, might even seem to come from another world. How is this otherness to be understood? It may seem like a defensive tool for self-definition with respect to the global art-historical narrative. Alternatively, might it not be a consequence of the fact that the cultural periphery has not been able to create its own globally compelling narrative of art history, and therefore, only bizarre, marginal figures who create their own closed personal worlds have been able to make their mark?

From this perspective, even viewing Július Koller and Stano Filko as cult artists of the Slovak art world becomes complicated. They are conceptualists; even under the conditions of socialist Czechoslovakia, they created works that resonated formally with global trends. At the same time, they are artists who, despite the remarkable form and scope of their work, remained rooted in their local environment. They remain exceptional; their work is difficult for us to understand without entering into a Slovak context, and even after doing so, we still do not know how they actually intended their work to be understood. The cases of the baffling nationalist works of Július Koller and Stano Filko have thus led us to more general issues, which it will only be possible to address following a broader exploration of Eastern European culture in the late 20th century. Does our desire to write ourselves into the world's art history books have roots in a revivalist mentality coupled with a need to create our own unique culture with equal rights among other cultures of the world? Or is the very concept of national art a defense mechanism against such processes? And who will play the role of the "other" that small Eastern European cultures must set themselves apart from? Modernism, socialist realism, or contemporary global art? And who are "we" in this dichotomy, anyway? The descendants of national revival movements, or ordinary Europeans who until recently had to grapple with totalitarian regimes? Is the schizophrenia —half nationalist identity, half Western cosmopolitanism— of the cultures of the East a chronic state or a passing phenomenon?

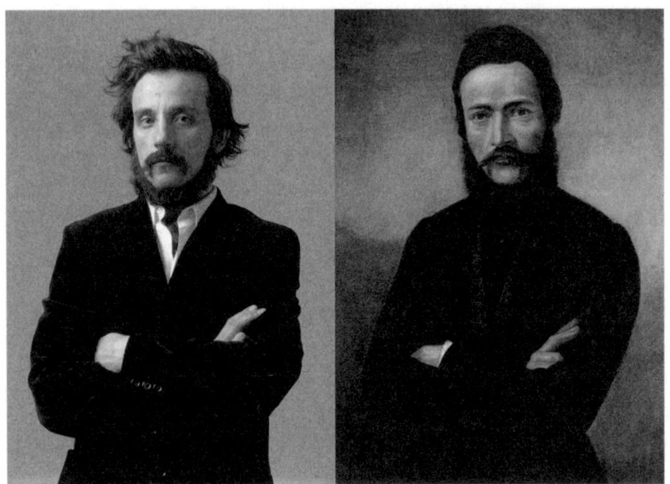

[ill.2] Svätopluk Mikyta, *Já Ľudevít* [I, Ľudevít], 2008
Color photography and reproduction, variable dimensions
Courtesy of the artist

[1] Certain artists have been reevaluated, with attempts being made to fit them into a world art context, such as Jiří Kovanda (Czech Republic), Sanja Iveković (Croatia), Miklós Erdély (Hungary), Ewa Partum (Poland), and the Gorgona group active in the former Yugoslavia.

[2] Definitions of conceptual art are often overly general or even contradictory, for one of the hallmarks of conceptual art is calling definitions into question. Conceptual art as an art movement that places ideas before aesthetic and material values arose in late 1960s New York in a circle consisting of Joseph Kosuth, Lawrence Weiner, Sol LeWitt, and others.

[3] Edit András, "Transgressing Boundaries (Even Those Marked Out by the Predecessors) in New Genre Conceptual Art," in Alexander Alberro and Sabeth Buchmann (eds.), *Art after Conceptual Art*, Generali Foundation and MIT Press, Vienna 2006.

[4] Jana Geržová, "Mýty a realita konceptu na Slovensku" [Myths and Reality of Conceptual Art in Slovakia], in *Konceptuálne umenie na zlome tisícročí* [Conceptual Art at the Turn of the Millenium], Aica Section Hungary, Slovak Section of Aica, Budapest and Bratislava 2002, p. 23.

[5] The case of a "different" conceptualism enriched by an ironic dimension is analyzed in detail by Luiza Nader in her essay "Language, Reality, Irony: The Art Books of Jarosław Kozłowski," in Alberro and Buchmann, *Art after Conceptual Art*, pp. 101–117.

[6] The first time was in the journal *A-Ya* (Paris), 1979.

[7] For the sake of completeness, I will add that Daniel Grúň labeled a certain segment of 1970s Slovak art "fantastic conceptualism" (in a lecture given at the Academy of Fine Arts in Prague, November 6, 2011). To my knowledge, the term has not gained wider acceptance.

[8] Sol LeWitt, "Paragraphs on Conceptual Art," 1969, cited in Alexander Alberro and Blake Stimson (eds.), *Conceptual Art: A Critical Anthology*, MIT Press, Cambridge and London 1999, p. 106.

[9] We might mention, for example, a 1997 group exhibition by Stano Filko and Boris Ondreička, a 2003 publication edited by Roman Ondák on Július Koller, and the 2005 Czech-Slovak contribution to the Venice Biennale, for which Stano Filko, Ján Mančuška, and Boris Ondreička organized a group exhibition.

[10] The fascination of Slovak artists with space is the topic of a study by Daniel Grúň titled "Red Planet: Cosmic Imagery of the Slovak Neo-Avant-Garde," in Lukasz Ronduda, Alex Farquharson, and Barbara Piwowarska (eds.), *Star City: The Future under Communism*, Mammal Foundation and Nottingham Contemporary, Nottingham 2011, pp. 52–68.

[11] A 2010 exhibition at the Slovak National Gallery titled *Vedecko-fantastická retrospektíva* [Scientific-Fantastic Retrospective] (with accompanying catalogue) attempted to present the work of Július Koller in the most comprehensive manner possible. See Petra Hanáková and Aurel Hrabušický, *Július Koller: Vedecko-fantastická retrospektíva* [Július Koller: Scientific-Fantastic Retrospective], Slovenská národná galéria [Slovak National Gallery], Bratislava 2010.

[12] Dílo represented a network of commercial galleries in socialist Czechoslovakia through which it asserted a monopoly over the art market. Authorized artists could only sell their works officially through branch galleries.

[13] Zora Rusinová situates Koller's flags within the context of pop art and compares them iconographically to works by Jasper Johns, for example. Zora Rusinová, "V mene syntézy umenia a života" [On Behalf of the Synthesis of Art and Life], in Zora Rusinová (ed.), *Šesťdesiate* [The Sixties], Slovak National Gallery, Bratislava 1995, p. 176.

[14] The word "all" is only a slight exaggeration. Materials from the Koller estate include long lists of periodicals he subscribed to. Others were provided by his friends. He copied out by hand the magazines he had on loan and considered particularly significant. The spectrum of foreign press (newspapers and magazines from Austria, Germany, the Soviet Union, France, etc.) in the Koller archive also relativizes our understanding of the information blockade caused by the Iron Curtain.

[15] Part of the Koller estate is owned by the Slovak National Gallery, and a significant portion is in the hands of the Július Koller Society and other private collectors.

[16] Petra Hanáková, "Kultúrna stopa JK" [The Cultural Trail of JK], in Hanáková and Hrabušický, *Július Koller: Vedecko-fantastická retrospektíva*, p. 9. We can only catch glimpses of Koller's archive—or fragments thereof—in exhibitions after his death. See, e.g., *Archiv Júliuse Kollera: Badatelna* [Július Koller Archive: Study Room], tranzitdisplay, Prague 2012.

[17] Apparently, it is no coincidence that Koller's collecting ceased the moment the Internet came along. However, he tended to ignore this new invention enabling instant access to billions of items of pictorial and textual information.

[18] *Mnemosyne Atlas* is a photographically documented series consisting of dozens of bulletin boards made in the 1920s on which Warburg juxtaposed clippings of historical art with photographs and advertisements. Juxtapositions were meant to expand the methods of existing art history and the transformations and continuities of certain forms and themes.

[19] We find analyses of the processes of national revival in the studies of Ernest Gellner, for example. See Ernest Gellner, *Nacionalismus* [Nationalism], Centrum pro stadium demokracie a kultury [Center for the Study of Democracy and Culture], Brno 2003.

[20] The most famous example of similar revivalist efforts were the medieval Czech literary hoaxes known as the Dvůr Králové and Zelená Hora manuscripts. We find analogical cases elsewhere—for example, in the counterfeit *Songs of Ossian*, meant to constitute evidence of the antiquity of Irish culture, or the continuing controversy regarding the authenticity of the Russian epic poem *The Tales of Igor's Campaign*.

[21] Aurel Hrabušický, "Počiatky alternatívneho umenia" [The Beginnings of Alternative Art], in Rusinová, *Šesťdesiate* [The Sixties], Slovak National Gallery, Bratislava 1995 p. 220.

[22] Vít Havránek, "Klonovaná realita (Stano Filko)" [Cloned Reality (Stano Filko)], *Umělec* [Artist] 3, 2001, p. 69.

[23] The first apparently involved a fall into a quarry and the second was an injury caused by electric shock.

[24] Daniel Grúň, *Archeológia výtvarnej kritiky* [Archaeology of Art Criticism], Slovart and the Academy of Fine Arts and Design, Bratislava 2009, p. 140.

[25] This had been noted by Jiří Padrta in a review of Filko's first Prague exhibition in 1967, for example. A similar concern for national Slovak art was explored in *Slovenský mýtus* [Slovak Myth], a project of the Slovak National Gallery. An exhibition was organized and a publication created for the Moravian Gallery in Brno as well. See Aurel Hrabušický, *Slovenský mýtus*, Moravian Gallery in Brno, Brno 2007.

[26] Vladimír Macura even talks of a "linguocentrism." See Vladimír Macura, *Znamení zrodu: české obrození jako kulturní typ* [Birth Sign: The Czech Revival as a Cultural Type], Československý spisovatel [Czechoslovak Writer], Prague 1983.

[27] Johan Gottfried Herder (1744-1803) was a German philosopher who significantly influenced national revival movements in Eastern Europe. Herder was one of the first to argue that language contributes to shaping the frameworks and the patterns with which each linguistic community thinks and feels. According to him, the nation is a group of people connected by a language.

[28] See the observations of Richard R. Brettell, *Modern Art, 1851–1929*, Oxford University Press, Oxford 1999, in the chapter titled "Nationalism and Internationalism in Modern Art," pp. 197–210.

[29] See Vladimír Macura, *Šťastný věk (a jiné studie o socialistické kultuře)* [A Happy Age (And Other Studies on Socialist Culture)], Academia, Prague 2008, p. 144.

[30] Petra Hanáková, untitled text, in Svätopluk Mikyta, *Pre-kresby* [Pre-Drawings], *Svätopluk Mikyta and Hikbok Culture*, Bratislava 2006, p. 6.

[31] Lenka Kukurová, Svätopluk Ľudevít Mikyta a jeho histórie [Svätopluk Ľudevít Mikyta and His History], *Umělec* [Artist] 1, 2010; accessed July 14, 2014, http: http://divus.cc/praha/en/article/new-mythology-the-work-of-svatopluk-mikyta.

[32] This working process is reminiscent of the work of Július Koller and Stano Filko.

[33] For example, *60/90. VI. Výročná výstava SCCA* [60/90 6th Annual Soros Center for Contemporary Arts Exhibition] in Bratislava in 1997, where Filko and Boris Ondreička created a shared environment.

[34] For instance, *Global Conceptualism: Points of Origin, 1950s–1980s*, Queens Museum of Art, New York 1999, *Les Promesses du passé*, Centre Pompidou, Paris 2010, or 11th Lyon Biennale of Contemporary Art, "A Terrible Beauty is Born," Lyon 2011.

[35] The social and philosophical aspects of post-Communist identity in connection with the illusion of the "great return" are explored by Croatian philosopher Boris Buden, for example. See Boris Buden, *Zone des Übergangs—Vom Ende des Postkomunismus* [Transition Zone: From the End of Communism], Suhrkamp, Frankfurt am Main 2009.

[36] The 1994 *Europa-Europa* exhibition in Bonn is most often given as an example of a similar type of project. Its goal was to showcase Eastern European art previously concealed behind the Iron Curtain, but according to critics, it presented only artists whose works resembled Western European art or artists who had been living for decades in the West and had adopted its values and aesthetics.

[37] The importance of language for the shaping of individual societies or, more exactly, their systems of sharing, is emphasized by Benedict Anderson, *Představy společenství, úvahy o původu a šíření nacionalismu* [Imagined Communities: Thoughts on the Origins and Spread of Nationalism], Karolinum, Prague 2008. Nevertheless, the cultivation of a national language is not the only sign of the creation of nation-states. Anderson sees the inability of elites from the periphery to break into the center—which impels them to create their own national and cultural identity—as one of the main reasons for the emergence of such nation-states.

[38] How, for example, are we to understand the inclusion of three Czech artists—Běla Kolářová, Jiří Kovanda, and Kateřina Šedá—in documenta 12?

[39] *Global Conceptualism: Points of Origin, 1950–1980s*, The Queens Museum of Art, New York 1999. As a recent example of a similar type of exhibition, we might mention *Dynamo* at the Jeu de Paume in Paris. As the structuring and rhythm of the exhibition of world and kinetic art suggested, the roots of this type of expression may be found in the works of the artists connected with the Galerie Denise René.

[40] Vít Havránek and Ján Mančuška, "Revoluce v asynchronním prostoru" [Revolutions in Asynchronous Space], in Jiří Ševčík, Pavlína Morganová, Terezie Nekvindová, and Dagmar Svatošová (eds.), *České umění* 1980–2010, Texty a dokumenty [Czech Art 1980–2010: Texts and Documents], the Academic Research Center of the Academy of Fine Arts, Prague 2011, p. 358.

[41] See Igor Zabel, *Contemporary Art Theory*, JRP|Ringier, Zurich 2012, p. 28.

[42] For example, Alexander Kiossev, "The Self-Colonizing Metaphor", in Zbyněk Baladrán and Vít Havránek (eds.), *Atlas of Transformation*, tranzit and JRP|Ringier, Prague 2010, pp. 567–575.

The Politics of Intimacy: Czechoslovak Performance Art in the 1970s and Its Remakes

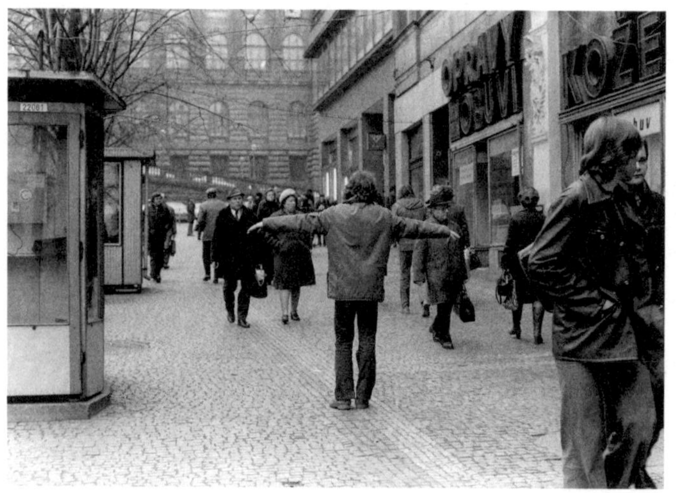

[ill. 1] Jiří Kovanda, *Untitled*, November 19, 1976, performance in Wenceslas Square, Prague
Documentary photograph
Courtesy of the artist

I.

A dialogue with history is an inherent part of any work of art. Whether this takes the form of a deliberate element of creative intent or is the result of artists negatively defining themselves in relation to historical connections, creators of a new works of art consciously—or unconsciously—become part of the whole of an existing culture, while drawing from it and, in retrospect, influencing and altering it, however slightly. Encounters with historical works of art have been facilitated by the establishment of certain important institutions and the rise of technical innovations, including public art museums at the turn of the 19th century, lithography, photography, and the mass media. It would appear that, for the fine arts, a dialogue with history becomes easier through the technical possibilities afforded by recording, reproduction, and distribution.

We no longer have to travel to see original works when access is possible through reproductions in books, magazines, or on the Internet. Artists need not reproduce existing works by hand when technology can assist them. The widespread existence of technology-based copies, however, can render creative intervention in the culture problematic. Moreover, the second half of the 20th century saw the appearance of art forms that lacked a material form and that could not be fully recorded or reproduced. In place of artistic works that end up in collections or in traditional museum exhibits, artists began to create ephemeral, nonmaterial works whose essence could not be captured or repeated. Happenings or performance art, for example, survive mainly in the memory of direct participants or through the documentation of events.

Even though, in practice, contemporary exhibits and the art trade suggest the opposite, the documentation of performance art is not equivalent to the actual performances. It would be more accurate to say that documentation has become a distinct form of artistic production. Artists and viewers both approach it in an increasingly open manner. As Boris Groys and others have noted, interest in the art world as a whole is shifting from works of art to the documentation of art.[1] Something that originally supported artistic output and had a utilitarian function has gradually assumed a character so close to that of the artwork that it has become interchangeable with it. Even artists recognize this fusion. For example, the American artist Vito Acconci recalls in retrospect that documentary photographs of performances were a tool for him to display his work in galleries and enter the world of established art:

> Once they were documented, either through words or photographs, they could be shown on the walls of a gallery or museum; but the documents were only souvenirs, after the fact, whose proper place was in the pages of a book or magazine […] I wonder if, in the back of my mind, there wasn't the urge to prove myself as an artist, prove myself a serious artist, make my place in the art world; in order to do this, I had to make a picture, since a picture was what a gallery and museum was meant to hold […] These pieces

were ways to put my work (put myself) up on the wall, these pieces were ways to push myself up against the wall.[2]

In one respect, Acconci resorted to a compromise and entered the world of institutionalized art through the medium of documentation. At the same time, he began to develop the language of documentation in a creative way. Photography, video, and film shifted from being utilitarian instruments for recording reality to being a means of artistic expression.

Acconci worked in New York, where it was difficult to ignore the world of institutionalized art or effectively shut oneself off from it. For artists who lived in Czechoslovakia during the 1970s, not only the state but also the character of the local culture precluded such dilemmas. Performance art found itself outside the realm of both official and unofficial conceptions of art; at the same time, artists did not seek the attention of art institutions. Although artists such as Karel Miler, Petr Štembera, and Jan Mlčoch managed to establish contacts with foreign artists or to exhibit abroad, they created works mainly for themselves or a narrow circle of friends. In fact, the overwhelming majority of established performance artists did not even consider what they did to be art. As Czech art historian Hana Buddeus claims, during this period the documentation of works of art by Czech performance artists functioned as a substitute for missing institutions, such as galleries, art magazines, and avenues for mediating contact with the public, whether at home or abroad.[3] Evidently, because of these factors, the format of documentation was not subject to much experimentation in the former Czechoslovakia. One reason for the interruption of the artistic work of Petr Štembera, Karel Miler, and Jan Mlčoch (in addition to other, perhaps more important, artists) at the end of the 1970s could be the discovery of how easily, in the international context of documentation, their work became art objects, sometimes in negative ways that distorted the original creative intent of the works.[4] In view of the absence of an art market and the limited possibilities of communication, the works of performance artists were for many years preserved not as individual works of art but as unique archives. In world art, what were originally documentary records increasingly became gallery art. At the same time, media used for making records became modes of artistic experimentation, whether in the form of conceptual photography or video art. Performance artists in Czechoslovakia did not concern themselves much with their image. It served no purpose in moving them forward. They saw photographs and texts depicting their performances mainly as straightforward records of what happened. Later, documentation was to serve as a means of communication with the audience. Jiří Kovanda even specifies that only through documentation did a work find its "enunciation," finalization, and closure.[5]

While documentation enables the reproduction, exhibition, and sale of art, it is beginning to take on an even more important role in the interpretation of artworks. Alongside the consideration of performance art in its own right is an analysis of the form of the documentation, its properties, and its history. Documentation also serves as the basis for restaging original works by contemporary artists. It is a logical way to link current performance art with historical art. Classic works from the field have, at least for the past twenty years, been subject to new interpretations. This does not constitute a challenge to their uniqueness; a new rendition is a way of working in the present with material that has already been enacted in a performance of the past. This approach, in which a remake cannot be summarily dismissed as a parasitical derivative of an original work, is widely acknowledged both abroad and domestically.[6]

With respect to the present, a curious discontinuity exists for the work of Czech performers active before 1980. Many original artists no longer perform, or they are developing their work by other means. In light of the continually weak art infrastructure, their historical output has only recently been transformed, or is still in a state of transition, from archival materials into works of art. For artists of the generation that began to engage with performance art after 2000, re-performances of classic works became one of the few ways of establishing a dialogue with this history. They represent an affirmative means of staking out their own creative genealogy, while serving as tools for contemplating the polemical questions that their predecessors dealt with a quarter-century ago. Contemporary artists who have recently been reperforming works from the 1970s and 1980s knew these works only from their documentation. Forty-year-old performance art speaks to them so deeply that they do not want to be mere passive observers; they want to engage in a direct dialogue with the experiences and problems mediated by documentation. Expeditions to the past, however, are not just a matter of searching for one's roots. They can also show how links to the past, as past, have been altered for younger generations. In contrast to artists of the era of modernism, contemporary artists are less interested in how art will appear in the future; they care more about its history and meaning. A creative space opens up not through a gesture of rejection of the works of an older generation but in an analysis of that which was, and what it means today.

A similar dialogue between generations can conceal numerous dangers and pitfalls. The contemporary artist works with historical documentation, mostly in the form of concise text and photographs. After the passage of time, it can acquire ambiguous meanings. A work mediated by documentation also opens up a spectrum of possibilities that have long ago transcended the artist's original intentions. These earlier goals grew out of a specific time period, which artists reflected and against which they defined themselves. They were not primarily concerned with creating photographs or verbal descriptions of situations. Instead, the subject of their efforts was the shaping of life, something that cannot be reduced to the creation of even a more and more dematerialized work of art. It is not possible to document through black-and-white pictures the shaping of personal attitudes, communities, and strategies and use the documentation to achieve similar goals, even where there is a strong will to do so. What seems to be a simple question—to what extent can we understand Czech performance art of the 1970s as political speech?—has no simple answer.

II.

Performance art in 1970s Eastern Europe developed against the background of the political system of the time. Although the specific conditions in Czechoslovakia, Poland, Yugoslavia, and the Soviet Union differed, we now perceive the art made in these countries in contrast to the repressive methods of their state apparatuses of the past. Repressive states influenced the freedom of artistic speech and the lives of individuals to varying degrees, and it is obvious that a segment of artists and society found itself thereby limited. Resistance to totalitarian regimes for the most part did not consist of an open struggle against the state apparatus.[7] Much more often it consisted of attempts to lead individual lives beyond the influence of official repression or to create small, internally free communities defying overarching domination. Conditions at the time forced citizens into "nonpolitical politics" in the spirit of Václav Havel. In the politicized world of socialism, a rejection of politics became what appeared at first glance to be a paradox, but it was, in fact, a logical gesture of resistance. [ill. 1]

Because of this, it is not surprising that many performance artists from Eastern Europe whose works initially suggest straightforwardly political or even activist interpretations emphasize instead a personal, apolitical dimension. In an iconic, unnamed performance from November 1976, Jiří Kovanda stopped in a passing crowd of people on Wenceslas Square in Prague and spread his arms out from side to side. From the contemporary perspective, this appears to be a manifestation of an individual attempting to stop the course of the surrounding world of peak normalization. But, according to the artist, the performance was not intended as a conscious expression of dissent in relation to the surrounding world. "Many people have asked me what influence the state of society at the time had on those performance pieces, and I'm not saying that it was entirely without influence. But it was decidedly not the most important element for me. The personal aspect always predominated over the societal one."[8] Even a gesture declared to be personal, however, bears a political dimension for the contemporary viewer, although one distinct from traditional perceptions of political or activist art. This is a result, among other things, of the fact that we strongly perceive the end of the 1970s and beginning of the 1980s as a distorted era. A common view among contemporary interpreters of his work was that "Kovanda proposes something else. He proposes a freedom that cannot be limited."[9] Perhaps it is time to concede that Kovanda was not actually concerned with testing social limits or even with political freedom; he was, instead, concerned with a specific and apolitical experiment involving his own shyness. In his own way, he fulfills the character and behavior of a member of the "gray zone," functioning in both the official and the unofficial worlds at the same time. The normalized setting eliminated politics from people's lives. Instead of attempting to change or correct public affairs, they retreated to the private realm to deal with their personal issues.

Although Eastern European performance artists operated in the public space, because of political control and nonexistent or inadequately functioning art institutions, most of them had neither the opportunities nor the ambition to appeal to broader audiences. Their works were mainly targeted at themselves and their circles of close friends. This represented to them a space of freedom and authenticity built on the unrepeatable experience of a given moment. Zdenka Badovinac writes about Eastern European performance artists: "They took the space on the margins as their oasis of freedom, the only space which allowed the development of artists' autonomous creativity, which elsewhere was under attack from the prevailing spirit of collectivism."[10] The existence, or nonexistence, of organized oppositional political platforms also played a role in the formation of political opinions in each country. The emergence in Czechoslovakia of civic initiative Charter 77, ferociously persecuted by the regime, transformed the relationship people had with political engagement. As Petr Štembera recalls, "The Charter, and the time after it, to a certain extent inspired the more intense politicization of my performances. On the other hand, the physical risk involved in pulling off certain performances after Charter 77 somehow became less valuable. People associated with Charter 77 risked much more, and often on a daily basis."[11]

In the eyes of some artists, open political engagement could debase the artworks themselves, as if activist readings decreased their general artistic quality. An openly apolitical stance, however, in no way indicated approval of the status quo. It was a response to it. In the politicized environment of the totalitarian state, the refusal of a socially critical context could function as a confrontational gesture. But even in the history of performance art in the former

Czechoslovakia, we find examples of works in public spaces that include direct interactions with an unsuspecting public. One of the most radical works of the Slovak artist Ľubomír Ďurček, *Rezonance* [Resonance] (1979), was aggressive in this respect. Participants agreed to move around the center of Bratislava and use their bodies to create geometric formations in synchronized shapes around random passers-by. It could appear that their intention was to impose a neutral geometry on normal social chaos. But it was more than that. The actors observed their fellow citizens while sometimes using their bodies to make it impossible for them to pass by. It was a visible and outright attack on the normal use of public space. The living formations surrounding passing pedestrians seemed like protective police units dressed in civilian clothes or—more broadly—a metaphor of the individual and society, of the other people who form the backdrop to our lives. An event of this type, involving voluntary as well as involuntary participants, brought into full view the tissue of interpersonal relationships. The performances of Jiří Kovanda and Ľubomír Ďurček seen from the perspective of the passers-by might be interpreted as being something between innocent games or controlled social experiments to forms of intentional individual provocation. I am convinced that the decidedly political readings of Kovanda and Ďurček's performances are ex post projections seen through the lens of present-day viewers and interpreters who set these works in the context of what they know about the time when they were created, and their assessment of the entire cultural and social context of the 1970s influences their conclusions.

The works of Czech performance artist Jan Mlčoch contain numerous indisputable links to violence, state control, and the deformation of life under "real socialism," albeit in abstract, metaphorical, or ironic form. In the mid-1970s he unsuccessfully attempted to smuggle live earthworms on his body across the heavily guarded border between Czechoslovakia and Hungary.[12] In a performance, titled *Bianco* from February 1977, he spat into his own face while lying on his back and then sat at a table for 30 minutes while very slowly writing his signature on a piece of white paper without completing it. If we consider that at the time a massive state-led campaign against Charter 77 was taking place and that the Czechoslovak Communist government was forcing people to sign declarations of support for the regime's policies under a variety of threats or in humiliating conditions, the performance could be seen as a straightforward portrayal of this reality. Other performances by Mlčoch contain elements referencing police methods or various practices taken directly from the Communist State Security services. In November 1977, he escaped from a window to avoid an audience in Hradec Králové. Photographic documentation of the event is highly reminiscent of a police reconstruction of a crime. In his work *Není návratu* [No Return], which he staged in 1976 at the Small Fortress in Terezín (German: Theresienstadt), Mlčoch photographed and recorded unsuspecting visitors and made them involuntarily into the subjects of an investigation. Like Petr Štembera, Jan Mlčoch became interested in broader social issues because of the rise of Charter 77: "In the beginning I dealt exclusively with myself. From the late 1970s onward, mostly because of Charter 77, the atmosphere in Czechoslovakia changed completely […] I lost interest in the self-oriented things from the early 1970s and, on the contrary, I got interested in the Salvation Army and missionary activities."[13]

Perhaps the most straightforward of Jan Mlčoch's performances in this regard is *Noc* [Night], which was staged on May 5, 1977. "An unfamiliar office in a building I'd never seen. A young woman was led into the office not knowing what is about to take place. I was waiting there for her with a tape recorder, camera, and bright lamp. After interrogating her for an hour I let her go. She left the building together with others who had been outside waiting for her."[14] The artist's explanation describes the setting of a police interrogation, which would have been either directly or indirectly familiar to at least some of participants present. This performance can be seen as a direct enactment of social reality, the restaging of a traumatic situation in which many inhabitants of Czechoslovakia found themselves, or as a sort of preparation for such an eventuality. The performance, of course, did not end with the depiction of repression. The broader social situation portrayed in the piece became even more important than the interrogation the young woman was forced to endure. The participants were divided into the individual being interrogated and the group that was waiting. Depending on the conditions, the other participants might have freed the young woman from her predicament. In any case, they had to find a way to communicate with her after the interrogation experience, to accept her back into the group, and to deal with their own inaction and pangs of conscience. We can thus see *Noc* as a sort of therapeutic play intended to prepare us for an encounter with—as well as the consequences of a conflict with—a totalitarian state apparatus.

The unspoken political readings of performance art pieces from the 1970s also inspired artists who came generations later and had no direct experience with the era. One of the very first restagings of earlier Czech performance art pieces took place in January 2005 at the Preproduction Gallery in Berlin, when the Rafani group performed a three-person remake of Jan Mlčoch's *Bianco* (1977). Rather than attempting an academic revival of an older work, the Rafani artists were interested in exploring how its meaning could be transformed. The social repression of 1977, when Mlčoch's original came out, was in no way present in Rafani's restaging. Instead, they wanted to see how, in light of its political content, the range and changing interpretation of a restaged work would play out in a context different from the original. The use of three actors, all emphatically dressed in uniforms, created a new dimension to the work. In contrast to the original work, which stressed the centrality of a personal dilemma linked to the context and era of its creation, Rafani presented its remake of *Bianco* as a work focusing on the limits of transparency and group responsibility. For the audience in Berlin, who were familiar with the circumstances of Mlčoch's original work only from documentation lacking interpretation, the act of preventive collective self-degradation took on the more general character of the relationship of the individual—here in the form of a three-person unit—to a social system. While any links to Charter 77 disappeared, the work maintained its political character.[15]

Updating the political meaning of performance works was central to the restaging of Jiří Kovanda's untitled work with outstretched hands. When Daniela Baráčková repeated the work in 2006, she chose Times Square in New York City instead of Wenceslas Square in Prague. The piece once again took the form of a premeditated experiment to see how the meaning of an artwork might vary in a different place and time. As with Kovanda's in Prague, the performance did not cause any significant incidents with passers-by. But after several minutes, the New York City police stopped it. In Baráčková's restaging, the symbolic gesture of a human individual vis-à-vis society was shifted to a plane on which the value of individual freedom under the conditions of a totalitarian society was contrasted with the same value in a post-9/11 liberal democratic setting. [ill. 2]

Barbora Klímová's 2006 project *Replaced* presented a targeted and complex exploration of social shifts in the Czech lands. New stagings of works from the 1970s and 1980s served as a means for analyzing public spaces and their transformations. Klímová selected performance art pieces that not only took place in public spaces but also simultaneously presupposed certain types of social interaction. The tension between the historical works of Vladimír Havlík, Jiří Kovanda, Karel Miler, Jan Mlčoch, and Petr Štembera, on the one hand, and the way that in Klímová's interpretation they fit into the contemporary world, on the other, revealed mechanisms and historical transformations that would otherwise have been difficult to perceive. If we look closely at Klímová's restagings of the historical performances, we see that she deliberately deviated from the original premises and meanings. Karel Miler would not likely have chosen the center of a city for his 1972 work *Buď a nebo* [Either/Or], in which he lay down at the edge of a curb and then just below it. Unlike Klímová 30 years later, he did not want to challenge his surroundings. He wanted only to demonstrate a variety of extreme contortions he could make his own body assume. Klímová did not want to slavishly repeat Miler's work but, rather, to use it in another time and in a different place to reveal the social changes that had taken place. Lying down in a heavily trafficked location during Miler's era would have been a sign that an accident had occurred, and it would probably have attracted the attention of passers-by and perhaps even of the authorities. Klímová's performance in Brno in 2006, repeated several times, met with indifference. Although the conduct, which defied the rules of normality, was noticed, it was ignored—except for one instance, when someone anonymously called an ambulance. However, no one dared to talk to the young woman lying prostrate in a public place. Klímová's interpretation of Jan Mlčoch's *Vzpomínky na P.* [In Memory of P.], originally performed in Kraków in 1975, also illustrates the radical transformation of the world over recent decades. At the time, Mlčoch was captivated by public markets in Poland, which were much more widespread than in Czechoslovakia under the "normalization" regime. He would go to a deserted market in the morning to try to sell personal belongings that reminded him of his friends. In her restaging of the earlier performance, Klímová did not need to travel to Poland, since the Czech Republic is rife with markets, where mostly Asian vendors sell their wares. The surprised vendors were curious about her invasion of their territory and of their market stalls packed with goods, but they were remarkably tolerant.

By re-situating historical performances in the present, Barbora Klímová did an important service for the creators of the originals. They themselves did not agree with those who gave their works a clearly political interpretation. *Replaced* shows that Czech performance art of the 1970s and 1980s was not only a historically rooted way of demonstrating how to give life meaning during a time of totalitarian rule. The ostensibly banal—or, on the contrary, intense—performances did not have just a therapeutic function; they also created meanings that sustain their validity today. We believe that we are not surrounded by a repressive state, as we were in the 1970s. Yet some aspects of today's society can be seen as similarly totalitarian, in that we often enter involuntarily into predetermined and strictly regulated relationships that, whether we like it or not, limit our personal freedom. *Replaced* is not simply an analysis of the mechanisms of the modern state and its transformations; it also represents the artist's attempt to forge direct links between different moments in the history of Czech art. It is no coincidence that this is precisely the kind of art that highly values authenticity. Klímová experienced firsthand the scripts of the performances she chose, and although she was conscious of the impossibility of "stepping into the same river twice," what she learned from her experiences goes beyond the knowledge she could have derived from surviving documentation. Her multifaceted experiences are conveyed to the viewer as well, within the limits of video footage, photographs, and written text, all working in conjunction. The significance of *Replaced* also lies in Klímová's careful work with historical artistic materials. Her remakes are attempts to develop a deeper understanding of the contexts of the original works, and they have led her to undertake further projects that straddle the border between art and art history.[16]

III.

The ways in which the social and political state of affairs projected itself into the work of performance artists of the 1970s can be illustrated by the various approaches to the widespread theme of police surveillance. Artists on both sides of the Iron Curtain dealt with this issue. However, in different contexts, meaning diverged. While in the East, artists made reference to official repression, to the fact that citizens informed on other citizens, and to the oppressive atmosphere of the totalitarian state, in the West, works had a more individual character or they addressed the power of the press and mass media. The degree of state surveillance and its ubiquity in socialist countries has been underestimated not only by later generations who did not experience it but also even by those who witnessed it. Jiří Kolář, for example, was under the constant surveillance of the secret police for a quarter of a century. Relentless official scrutiny of his everyday life did not cease until he emigrated in 1979.[17] It is very likely accurate to say that in Eastern Europe during the Communist era, all performance artists, and others whose work resembled performance art, attracted either the open or covert attention of the security services. This was true not only for openly provocative individuals such as Milan Knížák. In Poland the secret police kept a dossier on Tadeusz Kantor; the same thing happened in Hungary to Tamás Szentjóby.[18] The Czechoslovak secret police showed an interest in Petr Štembera and Jan Mlčoch, while Jiří Kovanda was taken in for interrogation in connection with his nonartistic activities.[19]

Secret police records from Eastern Europe have aroused interest among art historians during recent years. It is, however, necessary to proceed with great caution and recognize them as documents of the period. As sources of information, they are unreliable and often misleading. Police officers and their accomplices were often uninformed or downright dim-witted. In many cases, those being spied upon were aware that the police were interested in them, and they acted and spoke accordingly in the presence of potential informers.[20] To search secret police files for thought-provoking reflections on the work of performance artists is as absurd as expecting to find analyses of the music of the Czech underground band The Plastic People of the Universe in their dossiers. Secret police officers were, not surprisingly, generally indifferent to art. Their goal was to create a surveillance society in which everyone was watched and compromising information could be produced when needed. The secret police were interested in Jan Mlčoch not as an artist but because they hoped to make him inform on his artistic collaborators.[21] The name Petr Štembera can be found in various notes in Jiří Kolář's secret police dossier. At the end of 1977, the State Security bureau concerned itself with the "Biennale of Dissent" in Venice, against which it launched an extensive "decomposition" operation.[22] Their goal was to prevent the participation of Czech artists at the exhibit abroad—which the artists themselves often knew nothing about. The Biennale of Dissent built on earlier politically oriented projects of the Italian cultural organizer Carlo Ripa di Meana. After artists presented works reflecting on the right-wing political putsch in Chile under General Pinochet, he decided to present the works of unofficial artists from the Soviet Union and Eastern Europe. The Soviet Embassy protested against the exhibit, and in response, the USSR refused to participate in the Biennale until 1982. The exhibit was criticized, however, in both Italy and Western Europe for overly politicizing art. This was made evident, for example, in the refusal of several Western collectors to loan their works for the event.[23] Communication with artists behind the Iron Curtain was understandably minimal or nonexistent. Artists often learned from the media that their works were included in exhibitions. Jiří Kolář and Petr Štembera both protested publicly in Czechoslovakia against the political exploitation of artworks in connection with the Biennale of Dissent. They interpreted the actions of the event organizers as dragging their work into a non-artistic context.[24] If the Communist secret police took notice of art, they were mainly interested in its overlap with politics, and it was in that spirit that they interpreted the wide range of unusual art forms they sometimes came across. Tamás Szentjóby's 1966 happenings were seen as an expression of anti-youth reactionary forces, and the very notion of a happening was perceived as a manifestation of nihilism, irrationality, decadence, and a negation of healthy human conduct. According to a Hungarian police informer, the organizing of happenings led to public scandals and outrage, as well as violence, conflicts with the police, and drug abuse. Szentjóby's secret police dossier contains the recommendation that the organizers of happenings be monitored, that they be prevented from engaging in any public activities, and that their communities be broken up and dispersed. As means for achieving these goals, the police recommended surveillance, confiscation of travel documents, and threats aimed at the organizers of happenings—threats to the effect that they would be committed to psychiatric hospitals.[25]

The surveillance of artists took on a somewhat more pragmatic form in Poland during the 1970s. Art historian Łukasz Ronduda spent several months researching secret police reports at the Polish Institute for National Memory.[26] His work revealed that, during this time, the Polish secret police led several operations aimed at individuals engaged in performance art and conceptualism. Among those targeted were Jarosław Kozłowski, Zofia Kulik, and Przemysław Kwiek. Most of these artists, however, were left-leaning. They did not want to overthrow the regime but to reform it. More than anything else, they pointed out particular shortcomings of art-related institutions in Poland, specifically the *Pracownie sztuk plastycznych* [Fine Arts Workshops] (PSP), which functioned for artists as the official intermediary for orders and contracts. The artists listed above felt discriminated against by the PSP and warned of possible criminal economic activity. "Operation 'Letraset' shows that the authorities were only interested in the propagandist value of the PSP's work and not in the means the institution (and its director) used to achieve it. What mattered was its loyalty and subservience to the party's directives and the lack of ideological controversy around the fruits of its efforts."[27] The police were not interested in works of art themselves; they only cared about activities that could upset the status quo.

The work titled *Bis auf weitere gute Zusammenarbeit Nr. 7284/85* [Looking Forward to Our Further Cooperation No. 7284/85] by German artist Cornelia Schleime, has become an ex post reflection on police surveillance. The artist emigrated from Communist East Germany to West Germany in 1984. Then, at the Gauck Commission in 1992 and 1993, she studied the dossier the East German Stasi kept on her. Schleime decided to illustrate the written reports, denunciations, and analyses with staged photographs in which she appears. In retrospect, she thus filled in the image of her person to reflect the way it was first created by the East German secret police.[28]

Several authors have already noted the parallels between the documentation of Jiří Kovanda's performance art from the 1970s and photographs taken by the Communist secret police of "people of interest."[29] Upon first glance, both look very similar. Police photographs taken with hidden cameras capture the atmosphere of normalization-era Prague. An agent observes a person who does not visibly differ from any one else, and the agent photographs him or her in the course of ostensibly ordinary activities: on the way to work, while shopping, or meeting with friends. The meaning of the photographs taken from their original context is difficult to grasp for the contemporary observer. Only from the file containing the photographs and comments on them do we find out that the person being followed—while doing what appear to be everyday things—is engaged in anti-state activities. Mailing a letter, sitting down in a restaurant, or picking someone up at the airport constitute, in reality, the distribution of subversive materials, meeting for purposes of plotting a coup d'état, or making a liaison with an agent of a foreign intelligence service. Yet no criminal behavior is evident at first glance. Because of this, it becomes necessary to provide information about the time, place, and identity of other individuals in the photo and to describe what, exactly, the image has captured. A photograph becomes evidence of a crime upon an additional interpretation of facts and an analysis of the entire police file. For Communist justice, what was essential was the real or imagined intent of the person being spied on, or even his or her class or social affiliations.[30]

Some of Jiří Kovanda's performances took place at roughly the same place and time that the secret police were monitoring other people. From 1976 to 1978, Kovanda used to set out for the busy city center to perform various activities. While walking, he would bump into people, hide himself without any apparent cause, or proceed according to a prewritten script, which, of course, did not deviate from ordinary behavior. His friend Pavel Tuč documented everything with a camera while remaining relatively free in the manner in which he captured his subject. Kovanda's most important requirement was that his friend not interrupt what he was doing while photographing him. The documentation was conducted in such a way that only the artist and the photographer would be aware of it. Many people whom the secret police photographed knew that they were under surveillance. They would adjust their behavior accordingly in order to avoid persecution, or they would use various methods to confuse the police. Kovanda knew that he was being photographed, since he himself invited his friend to document his inconspicuous performances. Despite this, he acted as if he had no idea that he was being photographed. Kovanda would later affix the photographic documentation of a work to a sheet of paper, write the name of the performance, the time and place of the event, and then add the script—as if he were making a report on his own activity. Two parallel activities were thus taking place in a public space, one by the secret police, the other executed by an artist. Both were originally not available publicly and were only accessible to a narrow circle of viewers. In addition, a proper understanding of both the police shots and Kovanda's performances requires that we know the motivation behind their origins and the foundations of their language. Jiří Kovanda make no explicit reference to the work of the secret police in his method of documentation. In all probability, he had no idea what their reports looked like. Yet it is strange that today, when the State Security archives are publicly accessible, similar or identical elements shape our contemporary reading of the artist's work. We recognize them not only as individual artistic expressions arising from the internal needs of the artist but also as a compelling metaphor for personal resistance against the era of totalitarianism.

IV.

As mentioned above, artists working under other political systems did not have extensive experience with continuous surveillance by the secret police. *Following Piece* was one of the first performance artworks by American artist Vito Acconci. For an entire month in 1969, he followed a randomly chosen person on the street for as long as that person did not enter a private space from a public one. Acconci's work was documented with black-and-white photography and text descriptions of each act of monitoring. The photographs capture not only the person being followed but also the entire act of surveillance, including the artist trailing close behind the subject (a third person, documenting the performance, followed them both). The performance did not have overtly political content, in the sense of criticizing the state agencies. The artist did not want to create a metaphor of police surveillance or private snooping. What interested him much more than the abuse of power involved in one person tracking another was the search for the boundaries between the public and the private, as well as his submission to someone else's movements in an urban space. Acconci says that during *Following Piece*, he lost awareness of his own subjectivity and became the mere tool of a pattern of behavior designed in advance, mindlessly following the chosen person as long as possible.

Similarly, a few years later, French writer and artist Sophie Calle made surveillance a part of her work. Starting in 1978, she followed randomly selected people on the streets of Paris and surreptitiously photographed them. She then supplemented the photographs with journal entries. As with Acconci, Calle was concerned chiefly with the question of how to choose a direction in a paralyzing world so full of possibilities and choices: "I realized that this gave my walks a direction. I said to myself that I'd discover places and restaurants that I didn't know about. It was a way of letting myself be swept along by the energy of other people, getting them to choose my itineraries for me."[31] Calle immediately applied the theme of surveillance to several other artistic projects. In her work *Hotel* (1981), she took a job as a maid in a hotel so she could document what rooms looked like before they were cleaned up. From the various messes people left behind, she guessed at their life stories and transformed them into lyrical textual and photographic accounts. In her work *The Shadow* (1981), Calle reversed the roles of the individual following and the individual being followed. In this case, she had her mother hire a private detective to document her daughter's everyday activities. In 1983 Calle decided to abandon following and being followed, while raising questions about the limits of artistic ethics and the law. She found a notebook filled with telephone numbers that belonged to a stranger whose name was inscribed in it. She returned the notebook to him anonymously, but only after copying its contents. She then phoned the unknown man's friends, and from their descriptions, she put together a portrait of him, which she then published in the French daily *Libération*. The owner of the lost notebook recognized himself and threatened to sue Calle for violating his privacy. As a form of revenge, nude photographs of Calle were published in the press.

In works dating from the late 1970s and early 1980s, Sophie Calle may have played the role of a private detective, but she did not work for others or even for the state. Despite the legal threat against her for violation of privacy, mentioned above, Calle's work did not contain a distinctly critical, political dimension. Instead, we see a novelistic approach, on the border between visual arts and experimental literature. During this time period, Czech performance artists also displayed a strong desire to experiment. Their work, however, came out of the distorted reality of the social environment in Czechoslovakia. Informing on others under socialist regimes was not something out of a novel but an everyday reality with a tangible effect on the fates of human beings. Jan Mlčoch made this point in *Tam a zpět* [There and Back] (1976), in which he exposed himself not only to surveillance but also to the possibility of physical violence. He sent an anonymous letter in which he offered a reward for attacking a person identified in the letter—namely, Mlčoch himself. The letter was passed on by intermediaries to people who did not know the artist.[32] Mlčoch illustrated the performance—though we learn nothing about how events transpired from his depiction of it—using blurred photographs that resemble secret police surveillance photography. We do not see him in the photographs.

We see only a common urban setting where many people might find themselves. The uncertainty about where and when the attack from an external force would come was a part of everyday life in socialist countries. The secret police spied on thousands of people, and detailed information about their lives ended up in files belonging to state security services.

In Eastern Europe, we find artists who directly confronted the secret police and made spying and the intrusion of the state security services into people's private lives their explicit subject matter. Sanja Iveković's *Triangle* (1979) is a classic in this respect. While former Yugoslav president Josip Broz Tito was visiting Zagreb, a column including the Communist leader's motorcade drove by the building where the artist lived. On this occasion, she noticed that a secret police officer with binoculars was standing on the roof of a building across the street. Another officer stood on patrol in front of her building carrying a walkie-talkie. Iveković lay down on a cot and leaned back so that her concrete balcony would obscure the view of everyone except the man on the roof across the street. Lying on the cot, she drank whiskey, read a book, and made movements simulating masturbation. After a while, a policeman rang her doorbell and demanded that "all persons and objects be removed from the balcony." Four photographs and an explanatory text document the piece. The imaginary triangle, whose vertices are the two police officers with walkie-talkies and the artist, crosses the boundary between the public and private spheres. "The composition is carefully balanced, to the extent that the photographer has managed to include a fragment of the street that places the balcony at the scene of the crime."[33] The performance can be read in two conflicting ways—as an artistic act and as a criminal offense—even though in neither sense was it visible to the public. Iveković's work, in which photographs serve ambiguously as material evidence, is deliberately political. The artist voluntarily becomes the subject of police surveillance. The nature of her own photographs is also obscured. Who is the artist? The police? An assistant to the artist? Some neutral force linked to the nature of photography as a medium?[34]

The performance art–police–documentation triangle could also be found in the work of Czech artist Tomáš Ruller during the 1980s. When Ruller was prosecuted in 1985 for staging his *Mezi-tím* [Mean-While], he used the documentary photographs during his trial as material evidence in his defense. The documentation thus became part of the court record, where it served as evidence that his performance was indeed a work of art. Later, Ruller even attempted to reverse the situation and use the state apparatus as a source of his artistic documentation. In a lawsuit related to a 1988 performance in Lubenec, he attempted to have secret police video documentation entered into the court record, but he was unsuccessful in that instance.

The possibilities for surveillance have acquired new dimensions over the past decades, thanks to the evolution and expansion of advanced technology developed for the purpose. While a briefcase camera and satellite spy photography would have been among the required exotic props of a Cold War film, today we are increasingly living in an environment where security cameras and other systems keep us under constant and open scrutiny. Most of the time, we are either unaware of this surveillance or have stopped paying attention to it. The monitoring of people's movements and the tapping of phones is justified by criminal investigations or the war against terrorism. Yet more and more people are seeing such activities as violations of privacy. In the early 1970s, however, industrial cameras and closed-circuit television did not yet have the negative connotations they do today, and artists often used them as tools for playful experimentation. For example, in *Video Surveillance Piece* (1969–1970), Bruce Nauman created a simple television circuit: a television monitor sits in the corner of a small room, while a camera is located at the opposite end of the room. We see the image of the monitor on the screen. If we attempt to interact with this system, we find out that the image on the monitor is not what it should be. We realize that somewhere in the gallery, a similar room with a similar arrangement exists, and the signals have been crossed. The closed-circuit video here does not have a primarily existential or political meaning. Instead, it falls into the area of research on the self-referential nature of the medium of video, characterized at the time as narcissistic, and simultaneously inquires into the disruption of expectations.

From the 1980s onward, however, we see a growing trend in the art world that not only understands the technological capabilities of surveillance as an opportunity to create impressive visual spectacles and various perceptual paradoxes but also employs them as tools for social criticism. A central element in the installations of Julia Scher, the films of Harun Farocki, and the video work of Emily Jacir is the indictment of actual or fictional instances of restrictions of personal freedom and privacy. A similar motif has served as the basis for several thematic group exhibits. The pioneering exhibition in this regard was *ctrl[space]*, a wide-ranging 2001 event organized by ZKM in Karlsruhe.

The monitoring of and abusive intrusion into formerly private aspects of people's lives have multiplied, as a result of the nature of television and the Internet and formats developed specifically for them. *Big Brother*, which debuted in 1999, as well as countless knock-offs are built on the premise of the continual surveillance of volunteers, who are kept in a closed environment filled with hidden cameras. The survival competition format used in such reality shows, which have entertained countless millions, was exploited by Austrian director and performance artist Christoph Schlingensief in his 2000 project *Foreigners Out! Schlingensief's Container*. For the project, a "House of the Chosen," which resembled a prison from the exterior, was built in the center of Vienna. Seekers of asylum in Austria were put into containers, while members of the public voted to decide who would obtain asylum and who would not. The genesis and timing of such an experiment, which garnered enormous public acclaim, coincided with the rise in popularity of Austrian nationalist political parties and their views on immigration policy.

Even virtual movement on the Internet has its risks. Web browsing is recorded, evaluated, and potentially abused for commercial purposes, among others. The invisibility and ubiquity of Internet monitoring has led to a state of affairs in which no one is outraged anymore. We see it as part and parcel of how such technology works, as a sort of tax on its use. One of the few Czech artists who have reflected on the relationship between the medium of the Internet and the individual is Martin Kohout. In 2010 he produced a work titled *Watching Martin Kohout*, in which he filmed himself each time he watched a video on YouTube and then posted the resulting video online. In a period of one year, he posted 821 videos of himself watching a monitor that the viewer cannot see. Kohout's project turns Internet voyeurism in the opposite direction, laying bare its scale and its absurdity, which we no longer notice or have resigned ourselves to accept. In addition to its humorous aspect, the work contains an element of social criticism: it subversively takes advantage of the circumstances and the tools of Internet surveillance in order to reveal their nature and the potential dangers they pose.

V.

To this day, Communist secret police files in Eastern Europe are incendiary material. People still view them as evidence of individual guilt. The volumes of documents consist of what appear to be authentic records and reports, and few people will admit that they represent a fictitious genre in which the objects of interest were viewed through a distorted lens from the start. In her book *Police Aesthetics: Literature, Film and the Secret Police in Soviet Times*, Cristina Vatulescu, associate professor of comparative literature at New York University, attempts to understand the relationship between secret police activity and the art created in the Soviet Union and Eastern Europe based on research in the secret police archives of the former Soviet Union and Romania.[35] Vatulescu quickly realized that she did not know how to interpret the thousands of pages of wiretaps, reports, intercepted letters, denunciations, and bits of photographed manuscripts. Most of the documents had already been annotated by unknown police personnel who, like Vatulescu, were attempting to find meaning in the materials—though obviously Vatulescu was looking for meaning of a different sort. She began investigating the history of police files and the techniques used to create them. A classic police record in a democratic society documents a precisely defined crime. By contrast, in Communist societies, police records attempted to capture the entire life of the person being investigated, without overstepping the law. The biography of the person of interest, a description of his of her life, and an interpretation ascribed to it all, were key elements of a personal dossier. Ideally, they would be accompanied by an autobiography of the person of interest in his or her own hand, worked over so many times while that person was in custody that it could eventually serve as a confession of guilt. According to Vatulescu, the goals and methods of keeping police files approximated those of a modern literary genre. A police file, in her view, is a collective literary work—a sort of perverse novel typical of a totalitarian state. Although at first glance, police files may appear objective or take an autobiographical form, it would be a mistake to assume that they are truthful. Communist secret police files are calculated constructions and tools of oppression. Taking them at face value, Vatulescu argues, would be like accepting Communist propaganda as true. When we read volumes of secret police files today, we learn much more about the Communist state apparatus than we do about the characters of the individuals who were under investigation.

The documentation of performance art does not only represent an objective record of what took place; it also reflects an artist's approach to his or her own work—as the person who describes it, chooses and gives direction to the photographer, selects the most appropriate photographs, and determines how the piece will be adjusted and dealt with in the context of an exhibition. We have a good understanding of the ways in which Czech performance artists of the 1970s edited their works. As a rule, their performances were documented in numerous photographs, but in time, a single image would be chosen to represent a given work. Alternative sources of documentation in private artists' archives sometimes manage to cast additional light on performances. We may learn, for example, whether or not an audience was present or whether or not those watching were tense or in high spirits. In the case of Jan Mlčoch, we see a tendency to document works not with descriptions but more freely, with illustrative photographs that leave a lot of room for the imagination of those examining the documentation. Nonetheless, even in this case, documentation does not enter fully into the field of fiction, nor can it be considered a tool for manipulating people.

We see a more direct appropriation of the format of a police dossier or bureaucratic file in the works of 1970s Soviet conceptual artists. The Collective Actions group organized a series of performances during this era that included the distribution of pseudo-official documents. For the event titled *Revelation* (1976), viewers were summoned to a remote location, where they were distributed documents confirming that they had participated in the event. Similar confirmations were a part of *Performance* (1983). The same year, for a performance titled *Group 3*, attendees were gathered together, and a group photo was taken to document their participation. *Slogan* (1977), for which a large banner was hung in a secluded spot in the middle of a Russian forest, also displayed features of a police interrogation. It read, "I have no complaints and I like it here, although I have never been here before and know nothing about this place." The tone of a version of this piece a year later changed from a stubborn denial to a resigned confession: "I wonder why I lied to myself when I said that I had never been here and knew nothing of the place—in fact, it's just like anywhere else here, only the feeling is stronger and the incomprehension deeper."[36]

During the same period, Polish artist and cultural figure Anastazy B. Wiśniewski worked with similar, although more sharply defined, motifs. Wiśniewski (who in the early 1970s was the director of the Cultural Center in Elbląg, where he also established and ran the hoax-centered Yes Gallery) published a novel titled *Confessions of a Dissident* (1971), which contained official-looking documents mimicking the language of documents, police reports, interrogations, and denunciations.[37]

Whether the format of police or official government records was exploited unconsciously, as in the case of Jiří Kovanda, or consciously, as in the case of Collective Actions group, it emphasizes for the contemporary viewer the centrality of bureaucracy in the totalitarian state. But it would be a mistake to perceive the self-documentary elements in the work of performance artists of the 1970s as a simple indictment or parody of the methods used by the bureaucracy and the police of the era. Artists faced the problem of how to maintain and convey to a wide audience not only individual works but also their efforts in a larger sense. In a situation of state-sponsored repression, where an institutional framework for art that would have compelled artists to produce art objects did not exist, artists' efforts were naturally directed toward establishing themes, forming vital individual attitudes, and shaping congenial communities united by similar beliefs and a familiar language. The documentary archives of artists thus represent a specific autobiographical format, an attempt to capture a parallel existence that set itself apart from the broader totalitarian whole. We may see this as the real reason why in the performance art of the 1970s and 1980s—whether in the East or in the West—we so often encounter the theme of surveillance. The essential thing here is not the relationship to the police as a tangible instrument of power but, rather, the need to make records of human lives. If the production of documentation and its subsequent interpretation by viewers is the basis of such artistic projects, it makes sense that such documentation would approximate police records in form. Both are used to record certain values, although for completely different purposes. The politics of such art does not consist in adopting forms exploited by the state apparatus but, rather, in its content, in articulating alternative models for life. This would also be shown by the interest of a younger generation of artists, who return most often to works with the theme of alternative attitudes. They test them in new conditions and compare them with their own experiences. However, they are not compelled by a superficial anti-Communism, nor is it only the now-exotic reality of socialism that interests them. They want to generalize the experiences of older artists and apply them to their daily lives today.

Artists whose works are performed again after many years often resist clear categorization and comparisons. To inquire about the political dimension of their activities may, justifiably, be seen as asking the wrong type of question. The fact that such artists feel no internal need to structure and interpret their works more generally testifies to the communal character of the art scenes both back then and today, as well as the priorities of individual artists. They did not—and do not retrospectively—have a need to define the boundary where art ends and political activity begins, or where self-expression ends and attempts at vital free speech in the context of a totalitarian regime begin. As artists, they wanted to address the general issues of art rather than create from the need to highlight or explain the particular local context of a particular time. They wanted to think and work in universal, not regional, categories.[38] No artist considered illustrating his or her era to future generations to be a priority. Yet with the passage of time, the significance of the link between performance art and its local contexts continues to increase. Understanding what happened in Eastern Europe in the 1970s and 1980s will one day be possible precisely through works of performance art. Because of this, an emphasis on the political aspects of such works will increase, even though the artists themselves may continue to resist it.

Understanding the nuances of performance art of the 1970s and 1980s in Czechoslovakia and Eastern Europe, particularly with regard to its political significance, will always be a changeable endeavor. A work of art cannot be interpreted definitively, once and for all. Its meaning will vary over time. But it may be seen as a tool for bringing the past into the present. Such a process, however, can never be one-sided. That is why we can think of works of art as channels of communication between the past and present. Their meaning is different at the moment of their genesis than it is when viewers relate to them in a more distant time. Historical circumstances—be they technical, social, or personal—progressively fade, and the importance of the perspective of the contemporary viewer increases. Wanting to see Jan Mlčoch and Jiří Kovanda as political artists is, more than anything else, a sign of how the present is politicizing its relationship to the normalization period. The works of Daniela Baráčková and Barbora Klímová take up this challenge and show us that even the present has its political dimension. Their reinterpretations of performance art from the normalization period demonstrate that today, too, the public sphere is a place where the tools of social control and the unwritten rules of social conduct manifest themselves. Although their works differ from what we might have come across in similar places 30 years ago, they are nonetheless equally effective and normative. In contrast to the remakes of classical performances, which Marina Abramović has performed in recent years in a spirit of "academization," I would consider the critical relationship toward the present to be the main positive aspect of Czech reinterpretations of existing works. They are not valuable because they remind us of a difficult past or petrify the repertoire of already-famous works. They bring our attention back to the present, which is the most potent argument in their defense.

[1] Boris Groys, "Art in the Age of Biopolitics: From Artwork to Art Documentation," in Boris Groys, *Art Power*, MIT Press, Cambridge and London 2008, p. 53.

[2] Vito Acconci, "Notes on My Photographs 1968–1970 (1988)," in Douglas Fogle (ed.), *The Last Picture Show: Artists Using Photography, 1960–1982*, Walker Art Center, Minneapolis 2003, p. 183.

[3] Hana Buddeus, "Poznámky k funkci dokumentace v době normalizace" [Notes on the Function of Documentation in the Normalization Period], in Jan Krtička and Jan Prošek (eds.), *Dokumentace umění* [The Documentation of Art], Faculty of Art and Design, Jan Evangelista Purkyně University, Ústí nad Labem 2013, p. 69.

[4] In his letters Petr Štembera complains how his photographs were manipulated without his knowledge. This topic is covered in a doctoral dissertation written by Maja Fowkes, in preparation.

[5] Email communication from Jiří Kovanda to the author, May 27, 2014.

[6] In 1995 the California-based artists Mike Kelley and Paul McCarthy released a 45-minute film entitled *Fresh Acconci*, in which several performers from American B-films and soft-porn films performed works in the classical genre of Vito Acconci. The New York-based artist Clifford Owens repeats performance works of the Fluxus artist Benjamin Patterson. In 2001 curator Jens Hoffman organized an event called *A Little Bit of History Repeated* at the Kunst-Werke Gallery in Berlin. Elke Krystufek and John Bock performed works first seen 30 years earlier, when Acconci or John Baldessari performed them. In January 2005, the exhibit *Life, Once More* at the Witte de With Gallery in Rotterdam dealt with various forms of works being performed once again. A spectacular event of the same type, called *Seven East Pieces*, took place in November 2005 at the Guggenheim Museum in New York, where Marina Abramović repeated the works of her generational peers.

[7] Under conditions of "socialist democracy," it made no sense for those who disagreed with what was happening in society to attempt independently to enter parliament and try to change things "from above." If someone tried to do this, under the laws that existed then, he faced prosecution or physical liquidation. The cases of Charter 77 and Czech dissident Pavel Wonka serve as examples here. Open mass uprisings, such as those in Hungary in 1956 and in Poland in 1980, were exceptional.

[8] "Vždycky jsem měl pocit, že jsem ateliér nepotřeboval" [I always felt I didn't need a studio], a conversation between Hans Ulrich Obrist and Jiří Kovanda, in *Jiří Kovanda, 2005–1976 akce a instalace* [Jiří Kovanda 2005–1976: Performances and Installations], tranzit, Prague 2006, p. 107. The Slovak Ľubomír Ďurček is another example of an artist who avoids directly political readings of his performances. In 1979, for example, he did a performance entitled *Horizontálny a vertikálny pohyb (Transfigurácia)* [Horizontal and Vertical Movement (Transfiguration)], which closelyr esembled Kovanda's minimalist performances in public spaces. Near a stone curb he placed his hands on the sidewalk, then pinned them to the pavement with his feet in a squatting position, while trying to pull himself up. The unnatural position of his body allowed him to assume only two extreme positions without being able to straighten himself. The relationship between the artistic act and the environment in which the act took place was fundamental in this instance. The performer tests the limits of his body while simultaneously exploring the limits of a public or more generally social space in the situation during the transition from the 1970s to the 1980s.

[9] Jiří Ševčík, "Rozhovor II. Kostky cukru nemají ostré hrany, okamžitě se rozpadají, když zaprší [Interview II: Sugar Cubes Don't Have Sharp Edges; They Dissolve Immediately When It Rains]," in *Jiří Kovanda, 2005–1976 akce a instalace* [Jiří Kovanda 2005–1976: Performances and Installations], tranzit, Prague 2006, pp. 110–111.

[10] Zdenka Badovinac, "Body and the East," in Zdenka Badovinac, *Body and the East: From the 1960s to the Present*, MIT Press and Museum of Modern Art in Ljubljana, Ljubljana 1999, p. 15.

[11] "Vzpomínka na akční umění sedmdesátých let" [Memories of Action Art in the 1970s], Ludvík Hlaváček interviews Petr Štembera and Jan Mlčoch, in *Výtvarné umění* [Fine Art], 1991, no. 3, p. 66.

[12] *Mýr-nyx-týr-nyx*, Prague, Budapest, Hungary, February 27–28, 1975.

[13] "Od osobního ke společenskému" [From the Personal to the Social]. The Ládví group interviews Jan Mlčoch, in *Sešit pro umění, teorii a příbuzné zóny* [Notebook for Art, Theory and Related Zones], 2007, nos. 1–2, p. 107.

[14] As cited in *Karel Miler, Petr Štembera, Jan Mlčoch, 1970–1980*, Prague City Gallery, Prague 1997, p. 58.

[15] Rafani would return to reperformances and reinterpretations from the performance field several more times, the last instance being in the 2012 film *Dlažba nad pláží* [Paving over the Beach]. They transformed six performances, including ones by Jan Mlčoch and Jiří Kovanda, into a silent grotesque form. The resulting 13-minute film was made by Martin Ježek.

[16] Klímová's book *Navzájem*, published by tranzit in 2013, is the product of a more or less art-historical examination of performance art of the 1970s and 1980s.

[17] The Czechoslovak secret police were convinced that Kolář had organized a subversive group. His files contain reports of monitoring, interrogations, a list of Kolář's friends and their characteristics, a floor plan of his apartment, and transcripts of telephone conversations, which police wiretapped for years. These files are held in the Security Services Archive at the Institute for the Study of Totalitarian Regimes in Prague.

[18] For excerpts from the dossiers of artists working under Communism, including police characterizations of the artistic activities of those under investigation, see Klara Kemp-Welch, *Antipolitics in Central European Art*, I. B. Tauris, London and New York 2014, pp. 30, 111.

[19] The isolation of performance artists in Czechoslovakia during the Communist era can be seen by the fact that Jiří Kovanda met Petr Štembera and other artists belonging to his Prague circle only through the Polish artistic duo known as KwieKulik.

[20] To give an idea of the quality of surveillance reports, in the mid-1960s, one informant reported that Jiří Kolář was acquainted with the long dead artist František Kupka and that he was linked with "a certain Guggenheim" in the United States.

[21] Jan Mlčoch avoided collaborating with the secret police using a common strategy. In response to the offer that he become an informer, he would tell a State Security officer that he had already announced at his workplace that he had had a meeting with an employee of the Ministry of Interior, which immediately made him unsuitable as a reporter of information. A similar method worked in particular with people the secret police considered less relevant or useful.

[22] The so-called Biennale of Dissent took place in Venice from November 15 to December 17, 1977, which was an off year between the main Biennale exhibitions. Three thematically linked exhibits, organized by Carlo Ripa di Meana, the socialist politician and longstanding president of the Biennale, were staged at the Palasport Stadium not far from the Arsenale. The first exhibit was devoted to film. Vojtěch Jasný, who lived in the United States, presented

Czechoslovak cinematography. The second exhibit covered samizdat underground literature, while the third explored fine art. Artists from the USSR played a major role in the third exhibit, which also reflected the label they adopted, "New Soviet Art: An Unofficial Perspective." The event served to define the unofficial and exile art scene in the former USSR. Artists from other Communist countries in Eastern Europe participated as well, but to a lesser degree.

[23] Major collector Meda Mládková, for example, refused to loan works from her collection to the exhibit.

[24] State Security interpreted Kolář as expecting the easing of his situation in Czechoslovakia, which had become complicated by his signing of Charter 77, as the result of a similar public statement.

[25] Kemp-Welch, *Antipolitics in Central European Art*, pp. 111–112.

[26] See Łukasz Ronduda, "Neo-Avant-Garde Movement in the Security Service Files," *Piktogram*, 2007–2008, no. 9/10, pp. 28–97.

[27] Łukasz Ronduda, *Polish Art of the 70s*, Polski Western and the Center for Contemporary Art—Ujazdowski Castle, Jelení Hora and Warsaw 2009, p. 249.

[28] See Hans D. Christ and Iris Dressler (eds.), *Subversive Praktiken/Practices*, Württembergischer Kunstverein Stuttgart and Hatje Cantz, Stuttgart 2010, pp. 513–514.

[29] See, for example, Sébastien Pluot, "Include me out," in *Voids: A Retrospective*, Centre Pompidou, Kunsthalle Bern, Centre Pompidou—Metz, JRP|Ringier, Zurich 2009, p. 272; Tomáš Pospiszyl, "Look Who Is Watching: Photographic Documentation of Happenings and Performances in Czechoslovakia," in Claire Bishop and Marta Dziewańska (eds.), *1968–1989: Political Upheaval and Artistic Change*, Museum of Modern Art in Warsaw, Warsaw 2009; and Claire Bishop, *Artificial Hells: Participatory Art and the Politics of Spectatorship*, Verso, New York and London 2012, p. 149.

[30] A more detailed study of secret police photography does not yet exist. In the Czech Republic, the Institute for the Study of Totalitarian Regimes (ÚSTR) in Prague has published a selection of surveillance photography. See Patrik Virkner and Štěpán Černoušek (eds.), *Praha objektivem tajné policie* [Prague through the Lens of the Secret Police], ÚSTR, Prague 2008. A view into the topographic archives of the East German Stasi in an entertaining light is provided by Simon Menner, *Top Secret, Bilder aus den Archiven der Staatssicherheit* [Top Secret: Images from the Archives of the State Security Service], Hatje Cantz, Ostfildern 2013.

[31] Christine Macel, "Biographical Interview with Sophie Calle," in *Sophie Calle: M'as-tu vue*, Prestel, Munich, Berlin, London, and New York 2003, p. 77.

[32] According to Mlčoch, the planned act failed because the unreliable intermediary who was chosen never delivered the letter and kept the money. Therefore, no attack ever took place.

[33] Ruth Noack, *Sanja Iveković*, Triangle, Afterall Books, London 2013, p. 6.

[34] We also find the element of surveillance and the nonlinear, mediated relationship between participants of an action—in this case, a completely private one—in Jiří Kovanda's *Pokus o seznámení* [Attempted Acquaintance] from October 19, 1977. The artist invited a group of his friends to the Old Town Square in Prague to observe him at a distance as he tried to make the acquaintance of an unknown girl. Friends observed Kovanda, who knew he was being watched. The girl, of course, knew nothing about the scenario, although the artist could have informed her. Several of Kovanda's publicly staged works in the second half of the 1970s contain the similar element of a hidden scenario, which ordinary passers-by cannot discern. They only learn by being let in on it or by reading Kovanda's ex post documentation of the event. The possibility of photography or video to capture the invisible or, conversely, the inability of these media to portray banal reality are the subject of a series of works by Sanja Iveković from the second half of the 1970s. See, for example, her video performance work entitled *Monument* (1976) or her work of photography *Artist Working in a Studio on a New Work* (1977).

[35] Cristina Vatulescu, *Police Aesthetics: Literature, Film and the Secret Police in Soviet Times*, Stanford University Press, Stanford 2010.

[36] As cited in *Empty Zones: Andrei Monastyrski and "Collective Actions,"* Black Dog Publishing, London 2011, pp. 28, 38.

[37] Łukasz Ronduda, "Soc Art, or the Attempt at Revitalizing Avant-Garde Strategies," in Łukasz Ronduda and Florian Zeyfang (eds.), *1, 2, 3 … Avant-Gardes, Film/Art between Experiment and Archive*, CCA Ujazdowski Castle and Sternberg Press, Warsaw and Berlin 2007, pp. 52–53.

[38] Piotr Piotrowski, *In the Shadow of Yalta: Art and the Avant-Garde in Eastern Europe, 1945–1989*, Reaktion Books, London 2009, pp. 241–242.

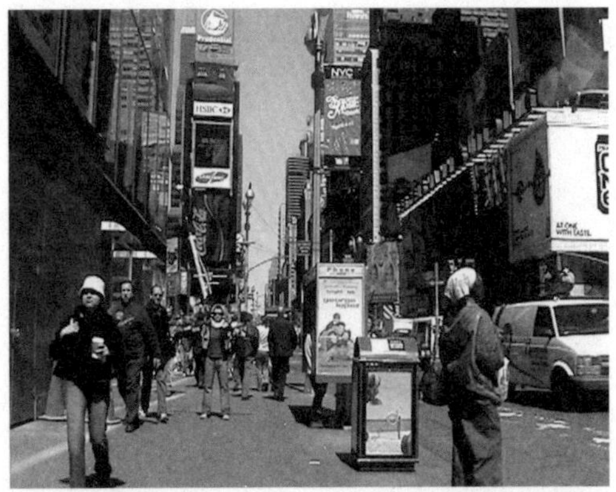

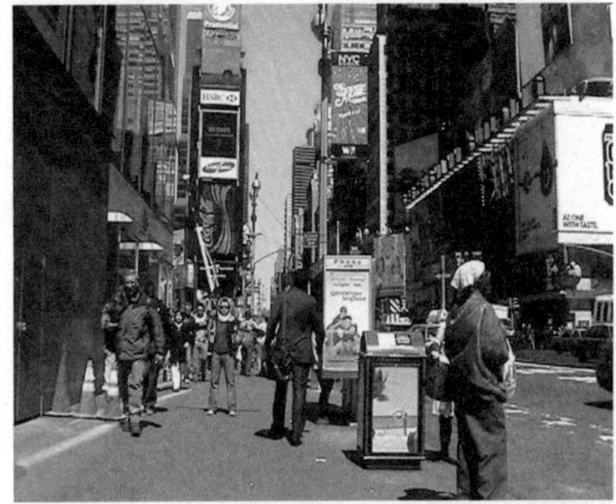

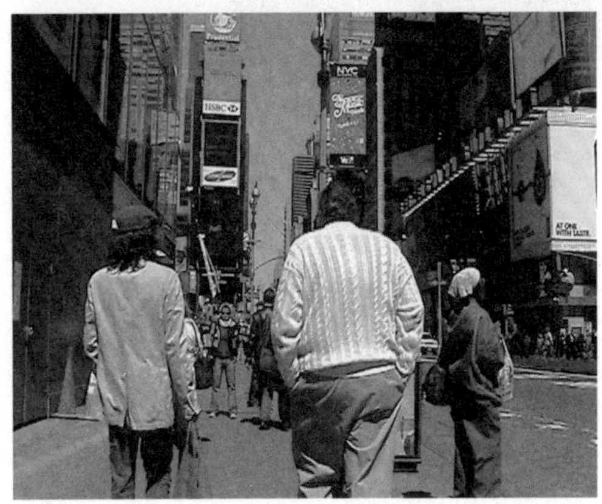

[ill. 2] Daniela Baráčková, *Times Square*, 2006, remake in Times Square, New York, of a performance by Jiří Kovanda originally staged in 1976 in Wenceslas Square, Prague
Video, color, sound, 2:10 min, video stills
Courtesy of the artist

Visual Art in a Moving Frame: Ján Mančuška between Art, Film, and Literature

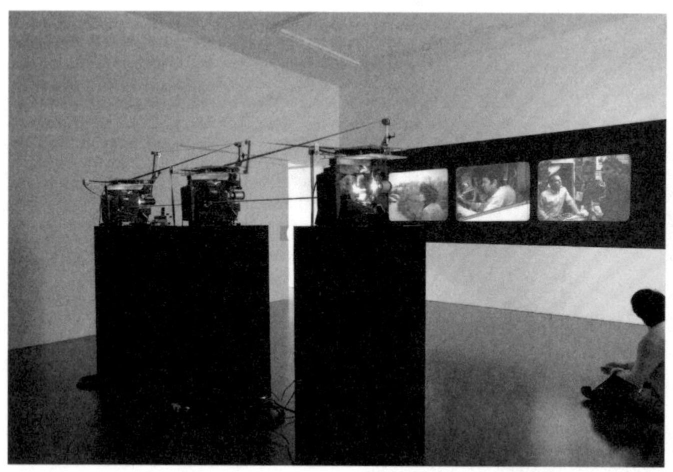

[ill. 1] Ján Mančuška, *Lost Memory (Postcatastrophic Story)*, 2010, installation view, Meyer Riegger Berlin, 2010
Three 16mm film projectors, 16mm film loop, wall painting, construction made of wood and metal
Courtesy of the Ján Mančuška Estate, Meyer Riegger Berlin/Karlsruhe, and Andrew Kreps Gallery, New York

I.

Film and the visual arts have engaged in a rich dialogue since the moment film emerged as a distinct medium at the end of the 19th century.[1] As the texts and manifestos of the historical avant-garde indicate, to artists and theorists during the first half of the 20th century, film became an ideal—albeit in most cases a technically and financially unattainable—expressive medium.[2] Since at least the late 1960s, in connection with the abandonment of the modernist idea of medium specificity, film—and later video—has come to be an important tool in the visual arts in a global context. Particularly since the advent of video in the 1970s, of widely available projection technologies in the 1990s, and of digitization at the end of the 20th century, museums and galleries have begun to fill up with a broad range of projections and other audiovisual pieces. These works are often collectively referred to as "art of the moving image," a term that encompasses a wide and heterogeneous range of works of an often hybrid nature, including classic films, video art, animated films, and works falling into the categories of traditional experimental films, light installations, new media works, and Web projects. In the context of art institutions, the umbrella term "art of the moving image" denotes more than works presented in a traditional film-based context; the designation also reflects their characteristics of increasingly powerful hybridity, intermediality, and remediation.[3]

The convergence of visual art and film is a phenomenon that is not confined to what the latest technological advances have made possible in recent years. In fact, ideological and practical incentives have linked the worlds of film and art throughout the entire 20th century. It is thus natural that many contemporary artists are building on that historical tradition. As British historian Michael Newman notes, "it is striking how much of the best recent moving image work draws on models that were established in the 1960s and 1970s, and technology that is obsolete."[4] Outdated and seemingly impractical technical equipment as well as decades-old experiments pose a challenge to contemporary artists who want to establish a historical dialogue and make use of certain technologies bearing a cachet of uniqueness. Such technologies may also represent tools for coming to terms with the thinking of their predecessors—at least in instances where this type of history is within reach.

In contrast with artists working in Western Europe and the United States, those on the eastern side of the Iron Curtain often had to deal with less favorable technical conditions as well as restricted channels of communication. Yet even in the East, we find numerous works operating at the intersection of film and the visual arts—with the exception of Czechoslovakia, where the tradition was noticeably weaker. The 1999 survey exhibition titled *Akce slovo pohyb prostor* [Action Word Movement Space] at the Prague City Gallery presented Czechoslovak experimental art from the 1960s as a whole that comprised various forms of visual art, literature, music, and architecture. Film, however, was represented only minimally.[5] For artists coming of age around the year 2000, the exhibition provided an overview of the hitherto-uncontextualized historical precursors to their own efforts and inspired their relationship to domestic art traditions. The exhibition's curator, Vít Havránek, noted that there was almost nothing from the field of Czechoslovak film suitable to include. In contrast, experimental film in Poland, Hungary, and Yugoslavia in the 1960s joined the repertoire of artistic media, though not without encountering various difficulties. In these countries, experimental film evolved in contact with other forms of art, and as a result, it bore a legacy upon which contemporary local artists in their respective countries could build.[6]

Two reasons can be offered to explain Czechoslovakia's exceptionally weak contribution to the field of postwar experimental film—and, in turn, experimental film's feeble influence on the visual arts in the Czech lands. First, after World War II, film and film equipment were effectively nationalized, centralized, and monitored. The same was true of film education. Second, the official national cultural sphere had suppressed the tradition of the avant-garde since at least 1948 and instead clung to the formal traditions and qualities of the established artistic disciplines. In contrast with the interwar period, during postwar years the mixing of genres was only reluctantly permitted.[7] The nationalization of the Czechoslovak film industry cannot be seen simply as a political decision related to the rise of the Communist regime, since it had already been under discussion during the war. Instead, it was motivated by efforts to raise the film industry's artistic standards and rid it of its dependence on commercial interests. Several recent studies have examined the relationship between filmmaking and the Czechoslovak state.[8] Although nationalization made achieving and maintaining a high level of professionalism possible, it also effectively suppressed an entire range of alternative productions and artistic exploration—and independent development and distribution have been shown to be key requirements for experimental film.[9] Without the famous Film School of Academy of Performing Arts in Prague (Czech acronym: FAMU), the phenomenon of the 1960s Czechoslovak New Wave would likely not have occurred. Within the system of state-run filmmaking, this movement reflected the times with originality and artistic integrity. For New Wave filmmakers, formal experiments served mainly as a means to portray social themes. After the golden era of the 1960s, FAMU would continue to teach the most time-proven and practice-based filmmaking skills effectively. This, however, made it very difficult or even impossible to set out in new directions of independent experimentation.[10]

Although the former Yugoslavia had a film school in Belgrade, it did not have the monopoly or the influence enjoyed by the Prague-based FAMU. It was a broad network of film lovers' clubs that propelled the extraordinary development of experimental film in Yugoslavia. From the 1950s onward, the creators of films that were nonconformist in both form and content were recruited from their ranks. Many of them were oriented toward "structural" film, which may be understood in connection with the domestic development of modernist and avant-garde visual art.[11] It is remarkable that the individual clubs produced their own specific styles. The Zagreb club developed structural film techniques and gave birth to the original concept of the anti-film. The club in Split was known for works made on the basis of a predefined compositional structure. In Belgrade, amateur filmmakers produced the expressive and socially oriented works of the Black Wave.[12] Yugoslav experimental filmmakers were not restricted by professional standards, and state supervision of their activities was relatively lax.[13] In addition to the right technical and bureaucratic conditions, opportunities for filmmakers to show their work to the public are essential. In this, the film clubs played a critical role. From the film clubs emerged a wide range of personalities, such as Tomislav Gotovac, who is best known as a performance artist but began as an amateur filmmaker. The lively experimental film scene in Yugoslavia left its mark on the methods of individuals working in other fields of art. For example, Yugoslav performance and conceptual artists did not limit themselves to the use of photography for purposes of documentation. Neša Paripović and the OHO Group worked with 8mm film during the 1970s. In the same period, Dalibor Martinis, Sanja Iveković, and Marina Abramović had already started using video.

The tradition of experimental film in Poland presents an unusual continuum of development from the prewar avant-garde up to the present. Despite various difficulties, there was always at least some trace of it on the cultural scene. The Łódź Film School played an important role in the Polish context, although one quite different from that of FAMU in Czechoslovakia. The Film Forms Workshop (Warsztat Formy Filmowej) operated there from 1970 to 1977, producing works by filmmakers and artists such as Ryszard Waśko, Józef Robakowski, Wojciech Bruszewski, and Paweł Kwiek. While association with the film school was unrestricted, the workshop received financial support from the school, and its members were able to use its equipment and supplies. The community that emerged focused on structural and conceptual film and set itself apart from the mainstream of Polish cinema, with its formal approaches and production techniques. Even in socialist Poland they thought it necessary to emphasize the noncommercial nature of their work. In contrast with the environment in Czechoslovakia at the time, members of the Film Forms Workshop conscientiously refused any economic or social privileges arising from their work in the film or television industries.

The majority of the films produced by the Film Forms Workshop were characterized by a pared-down cinematographic language. Individuals associated with the workshop rejected the expressiveness of narrative film. Instead, they wanted to build on the tradition of formal analytical art and took an interest in contemporary conceptual trends in both film and the visual arts. More than any other figure, Józef Robakowski cultivated contact with a broad range of personalities linked to the global avant-garde movement.[14] Representatives of the Film Forms Workshop did not work in isolation from the international context; in 1977 they managed to get their works exhibited at documenta 6 in Kassel.[15] On the Polish scene, however, their work was either ignored or rejected outright by both the film world and, in part, the visual-art world.[16] Furthermore, for foreign experimental filmmakers, works from the Film Forms Workshop sometimes seemed ponderous in their exaggerated need to emphasize the craft of filmmaking, making them reminiscent of student exercises. Yet at the same time, the technical abilities of their Polish colleagues, particularly their use of 35mm film, surprised them.[17]

In Hungary the Béla Balázs Studio functioned as a refuge for unconventional filmmaking. Originally created in 1959 as an organization of film lovers, by 1961 it had become part of the Hungarian state film industry, initially as a studio for recent film school graduates. The Béla Balázs Studio represented a unique system of production: state funds provided to it were apportioned at the discretion of directors themselves. The films produced there were not motivated or influenced by considerations of profit or dissemination but exclusively by a general ambition to achieve a high level of cinematic quality.

The Béla Balázs Studio produced a wide range of films, from documentaries and feature films to a diverse variety of experimental works. Directors Miklós Jancsó, István Szabó, Béla Tarr, and Gábor Bódy all created works there. In addition to producing lyrical documentaries, sociological investigations, and feature films, the studio management became interested in exploring the language of film. During the 1970s the Béla Balázs Studio began to cooperate with artists in the visual- and conceptual-art scenes who had not previously worked in filmmaking. Works by Tamás Szentjóby, Tibor Hajas, and Miklós Erdély resulted from this collaboration.[18]

II.

For Czech visual artists who began working with the moving image during the 1990s, there were very few cinematic paradigms that they could readily build on at home. The concept of experimental film could be applied to a rather narrow chapter of prewar cinema or to a group of young filmmakers asserting themselves at roughly the same time that visual artists were attracted to the moving image. Experimental film from the interwar period seemed like a long-closed chapter, and those experimenting with film in the 1990s were working in their own relatively closed community.[19] In Czechoslovakia, and later in the Czech Republic, we find an art scene in which the different forms of art commingle far less frequently than in neighboring countries. Artistic media are not juxtaposed with one another, and we do not often see intermedial reflexivity—i.e., artworks whose content involves making obvious the structural differences between individual media.[20] We can view this state of affairs as the paradoxical consequence of the cultivation and institutionalization of the domestic cultural milieu. Artists and filmmakers have worked exclusively with predetermined means of expression and have not expanded beyond those borders. They have made use of their own institutions and appealed to specific audiences. This was even the case during the liberal experimentalism of the 1960s.[21] Such a general assertion, of course, does not take into account exceptional individuals like Jan Švankmajer. His case is unusual in that he had not studied to be a filmmaker and was able to produce his works largely at the outskirts of mainstream state-sponsored cinema, or even completely independently of it.

And yet experimental tendencies may also be found squarely within the Czechoslovak film industry of the 1960s. Cinematographer Jaroslav Kučera of the Barrandov Studio, for example, achieved remarkable results, particularly in films he shot for the director Věra Chytilová and her collaborator Ester Krumbachová, the leading light of the Czech New Wave. Films such as *Automat Svět* [Vending Machine World] from the anthology film *Perličky na dně* [Pearls of the Deep] (1965), *Sedmikrásky* [Daisies] (1966), and *Ovoce stromů rajských jíme* [Fruit of Paradise] (1969) stand out even in the context of world cinema because of their unique forms of artistic expression. This formal dimension serves not as an end in itself but is, rather, an integral part of each film. It would be interesting, for example, to imagine the opening minutes of *Fruit of Paradise* as an experimental film in itself. In view of the visual power of Kučera's spellbinding technique, the sequence might conceivably stand on its own. This impressive visual foreshadowing of the film, however, only arose afterward, based on the requirements of a musical sequence by Zdeněk Liška that had not been originally planned. Only in a small number of films in which he worked as camera operator was Kučera able to use experimental techniques like those in the films he shot for Věra Chytilová. He never ventured beyond the compass of the Czechoslovak film industry into the realm of independent filmmaking.[22]

During the normalization period, Jaroslav Kučera vented his need for creative experimentation with a photographic camera. His photographic oeuvre, which began in the 1960s and continued until his death in early 1991, could easily be considered only a sideshow in relation to his work as a cinematographer. Kučera's photographs provide detailed documentation of his family, architectural phenomena, nature, works of art, and other motifs that would not be outside the scope of the typical amateur's approach to photography. Despite this, we can find traces of experimental techniques developed over the long term in his photographic work. Kučera returned obsessively to certain themes that he subsequently captured in an enormous number of images.[23] Such themes included plastic sheets billowing in the wind covering facades of buildings under repair, scaffolding on historical buildings (the normalization period offered much of interest in this regard), and engineered structures like stadiums and flagpoles. He considered the objects and tableaux in the world around him to be works of art. He photographed wrecked cars, the remains of agricultural equipment, cracked walls and the patterns they made, quarries, cliffs, layers of sediment, and various other subjects. Judging by the number of photographs, we can guess that if a visual motif interested Kučera, as a rule he would spend an entire roll of film on it. In some cases, it is apparent that he used his still camera as if it were a film camera. In other cases, the number of photographs of an individual subject indicates a more analytical approach—as in, for example, a series of 29 photographs of the facade of the KOVO office building in Prague's Holešovice district. In this case, Kučera apparently wanted to capture the organic and ever-changing cloud formations reflected in the repeating grid of the modernist glass surface. The reflection of the sun off the glass building and the reflected light in nearby streets also attracted his attention as a photographer.

One of the largest collections of photographs by Kučera consists of several hundred images shot on slide film in the center of Prague, chiefly in Wenceslas Square, the Old Town Square, and Národní třída (National Avenue). Judging from the images, we can deduce that they were taken over an extended period in the late 1970s.[24] Photographs from the upper end of Wenceslas Square appear to be the most numerous. Kučera most frequently photographed in the area between Vodičkova and Krakovská Streets. From this position, he photographed the buildings opposite as well as views of the monument of Saint Wenceslas and pedestrians walking up and down the square. By coincidence, Kučera was once in the square at the same time and place that Jiří Kovanda was staging one of his performances.[25] We almost expect to catch sight of Kovanda's silhouette with outstretched arms among the passing pedestrians. In some of Kučera's photographs we find the motif of light reflecting off the windows of buildings opposite, as in the photographs of the KOVO building. But in most of them, we hesitate to say what the artist was trying capture in the streets of Prague. Unlike professionals photographing architectural phenomena, for example, Kučera did not use a tripod. He preferred to roam freely with camera in hand. He was indifferent to parked cars that blocked his view of the square and was unconcerned with the precise spatial composition of his images. Perhaps what interested him was the pure color and light in his surroundings. Perhaps he sought to document the everyday reality and infinitesimal changeability of the city at the time. In any case, Kučera pursued his photographic research interests with the meticulous care normally seen in photographic typologies from the field of conceptual photography.[26] Kučera's photography, however, remained a strictly private affair, one he did not share with the public. Today we can only speculate as to the motivations behind the creation of his various photographic series. Given that Kučera's photographic work has, to this day, never been showcased in a comprehensive exhibition, it cannot be said to serve as a reference point for newer generations of artists.

The situation in Slovakia, when compared with Bohemia and Moravia, differs mainly in the details. We find attempts to mingle the visual arts and film there as well, even more so than in Bohemia and Moravia. But such efforts took place mostly in the realm of unofficial art and had only a limited impact on the public. In addition to the formally ambitious works of artists of the New Wave, which arose within the local film industry in the late 1960s and early 1970s, in Slovakia we find artists who worked with television, film, and video. As early as the late 1960s, we can see operating televisions as audiovisual objects in Stano Filko's assemblages. *Kozmos* [Cosmos] and *Katedrála humanizmu* [Cathedral of Humanism] (both 1968), his large installations and environments from the end of the decade, included slide projections and switched-on radios. We may consider Stano Filko to be the pioneer of expanded cinema, at least in the context of Central Europe.[27] Vladimír Havrilla's short 8mm films from the 1970s continued the tradition of the international film avant-garde by virtue of their use of technology, including pixellation. In the 1980s Ľubomír Ďurček recorded his performances on 16mm film. Several of them—for example, *Informácia ... o rukách a ľuďoch* [Information about People and Hands] (1982)—have, thanks to their meticulous composition, more of a pictorial character than that of performance works. By 1985 Peter Rónai was working with video in Slovakia. His anti-videos (the name has nothing to do with the Yugoslav concept of anti-film but refers instead to the Dadaist tradition of negation) work with the paradoxes involved in video images and often take the form of spatial and object-based installations.[28]

The technology enabling Czech artists since the 1990s to work with the moving image has not been film but chiefly video. For most of the public and the art community, video arrived after a 20-year delay. But it was also possible to find artists in socialist Czechoslovakia who worked with video. After 1989, however, the majority of their work seemed to be out of sync not only with the history of global video art but also with the efforts of emerging young artists. Radek Pilař and Petr Skala are generally recognized as the founders of video art in Czechoslovakia. The unique characteristics of their work prefigured their roles as pioneers in the field of experimental film, which was almost nonexistent in the public sphere. In the late 1960s, they began making hand-painted films inspired by classic works of the genre. These experiments were of a purely private nature and only received exposure to a broader audience several decades later. Pilař and Skala both started working with video relatively late, during the first half of 1980s. By that time, both already had years of experience working in the areas of animated and documentary films for the Czechoslovak film and television industries.

Petr Skala began using video technology in 1982, initially as a medium for completing his studies in the field of experimental film.[29] Since he had no other way to gain access to the relevant technology, he secretly used equipment belonging to Czechoslovak Television and the Central

Industrial School of Telecommunications in Prague. Radek Pilař, a painter, illustrator, and creator of animated films, purchased his first video camera and recorder while abroad in 1983. He also had access to a communications truck belonging to record company Supraphon, with whom he collaborated on a series of mainstream musical films. Pilař and Skala did not approach the video medium analytically; they exploited its expressive possibilities to create emotive visual collages of a metaphorical nature. Beginning in the late 1980s, they also tried to establish the field of video art at an institutional level.[30]

Tomáš Ruller, who had worked with video since the early 1980s, occupied a special position in the Czech scene. Before 1989 he worked at the intersection not only of the visual arts and theater but also of officialdom and unofficialdom. Ruller used video as a multifaceted tool that had no fixed essence. He used it primarily to record performance art, but relatively quickly, he also began to employ it to investigate the interaction between live events and the audiovisual medium. However, works such as *Živá smyčka* [Live Loop] (1983) and *Mezi-tím* [In-Between] (1983–1984) had only limited audiences and only survive in the form of written descriptions and rudimentary photographic and technical documentation.

III.

It seems that over the past 20 years, many world artists working with the moving image have been building upon works of experimental film. More precisely, they have been developing the principles hinted at in the video works of artists of the expanded cinema movement. This has been made possible in part by advances in video technology that, for example, simplify working with multiple synchronized projection systems. With artists such as Eija-Liisa Ahtila and Doug Aitken, we see the expansion of film-based narratives into gallery spaces or even public spaces. At the same time, many contemporary artists are, despite technical challenges, making a conscious return to film materials and gallery installations that involve film projection equipment. The traditional cinematographic mechanism by which moving images are mediated not only makes it possible to watch a film but is also used by these artists to make an impression on the viewer. We see this, for example, in the film installations of the duo João Maria Gusmão + Pedro Paiva. For some artists, the fact of working with a film projector, film stock, or magnetic tape is even more important than the projected images themselves, which are sometime entirely absent. Such works—like those by Rosa Barba and Žilvinas Kempinas—are closer to kinetic sculpture than to film.

Ján Mančuška is one of the first Czech artists whose work dealt with the apparatus of film and whose methods can be compared to those used in expanded cinema. He belonged to a generation of Czech artists who, with the new millennium approaching, strongly connected with world conceptual art as well as with the tradition of domestic experimental art showcased in *Akce slovo pohyb prostor* [Action Word Movement Space]. Mančuška first worked with video in 2000, but his literary and sculptural installations from 2004 to 2006 were more important to the development of his mature works in the field of the moving image. In them, he tried out alternative approaches to narration, which we later find in different forms in his mature film works. For the installation *While I Walked* (2004), a text written on flexible rubber is stretched between the walls of the gallery space. As we read the text, we must move around the space the way the artist did—which he describes on the piece of stretched rubber. In the installation *True Story* (2005), Mančuška worked with several lines of text spelled out in metal letters that cross the exhibition space in several directions. The texts all relate to a single story, but each line of text corresponds to a different narrator. The individual narratives intersect at particular places both in the story itself and in the metal text extending throughout the space, before each moves on in its own direction. This gives rise to a distinctive, multilinear hypertext that comes to life as the viewer reads and moves around the space.

The first work by Ján Mančuška dealing with film equipment is *Killer without a Cause* (2006). The installation engages the viewer with its scale, volume, and robust character. Two massive 35mm film projectors stand across from one another in a dark space, projecting a joint film loop. After a moment, we realize that one of the machines is projecting a miniature moving image on the same spot where a strip of film is passing through the second projector. In order to fit the image onto its unusual projection surface —the strip of film—the resulting projection cannot be wider than 35mm. In lieu of a screen, the artist has placed a small, semitransparent plate between the strip of film and the projection. Despite its small size, the image can be clearly discerned, although it can be viewed by only one person at a time. The actors in the film do not speak; however, the action is accompanied by a spoken commentary that competes with the noise made by the projectors.[31]

At first glance, the main purpose of *Killer without a Cause* seems to be a reflection on the technical parameters of film. The overall dominant impression is that of an enormous projection apparatus projecting images onto itself. The technology required for film projection illuminates itself. The circle is closed, and the image returns quite literally to a strip of film. Yet, in addition to considering the three-dimensional, technological aspect of the installation, we ought not forget to analyze the film itself that is being projected.

The film's spoken commentary recalls techniques of experimental literature, writing for the theater of the 1950s and 1960s, the French *Nouveau roman*, and the Theater of the Absurd. An indifferent voice introduces a room occupied by a young man identified as "V." We learn nothing more about him, however. By contrast, a great deal of attention is devoted to a description of the space V. occupies. It seems that V. is struggling to orient himself within his apartment and, by doing so, in his life. He does not go outside and barely communicates with others. After long periods in the room, he notices the relationship between the time of day and the geometric patterns the sun creates on the floor as it passes behind the multipaned window. He starts to measure time according to the moving pattern reflected from the window onto the floor. When the light reaches a certain section of the floor or an object in the room, he knows it's time to wake up or to eat. Time measured this way provides him a source of certainty and a fundamental system of orientation.[32]

In addition to measuring time according to the movement of light across the floor, V. also engages in other unusual activities. He arranges various geometric configurations using tablets and pills he has collected over the years. "At first he proceeded based on their more obvious aesthetic qualities. First color, then shape. Then other attributes began to play a role, such as complicated symbols, chemical ingredients, uses, the country of origin of the medicine, etc. When he had exhausted most of the combinations, he began to consider the composition of the medicines on the table, of the table vis-à-vis the room, etc. Then even the placement of the parquet slabs began to play a role,"[33] according to the voice of the narrator. In closing, V. begins to consume the pills with the same systematic approach. In the final frames of the film, it remains uncertain whether or not he has survived the suicide attempt or not. V. lies slumped on the table. Gathered around him are those closest to him—including his mother, who we already know is dead—who are trying to understand what has driven him to such an act.

The relationship between the room and the light entering it—and particularly the systematic shifting and organizing of the pills—recalls certain works by post-minimalist and conceptual artists of the 1960s and 1970s. If we did not know the tragic outcome of the story, we might consider the figure of V. to be a creator of temporary sculptural installations on a kitchen table. Mančuška's protagonist, however, is not interested in an analysis of possible combinations. In his case, the impulse to organize things into patterns seems more to represent a diagnosis, an activity that is the product of a pathological mental state. V.'s need to organize pills and his efforts to orient himself within the spatiotemporal coordinates of an apartment are, despite the dispassionate tone of the narrator's voice, the desperate reactions of a man searching for a set of reference points in his life. What at first appears to be a rational and dryly analytical activity is, in reality, fraught with emotion, the expression of a deepening mental crisis.

According to Karel Císař, with regard to thematic content, Ján Mančuška's work is limited in scope to a few issues, among which the possibility of mutual understanding and individual self-reflection are centrally important.[34] In *Killer without a Cause*, he narrates a story of hopeless desperation and suicide, themes we do not normally associate with the conceptual art of the late 1960s, which took shape by setting itself apart from the subjectivity, aesthetics, and emotionality of previous movements.[35] Instead of revealing the artist's inner core, conceptual art in its classic phase analyzed the ways perception operates; it was directed toward examining functioning systems, be they linguistic, social, communication-based, or economic. It is only later that we detect a conscious shift in conceptual art from detached analyses of impersonal systems toward emotional subjects. The cause of this shift is evident in the works by Mančuška we have been discussing, which restore personal narratives and artistic subjectivity to conceptual art.

In Mančuška's works we find not only experimentation with forms of narration but also a repeated interest in thresholds and tragic events in life. In *A Gap* (2007), a video installation that immediately followed *Killer without a Cause*, we watch two parallel stories unfold on four projectors positioned at various points in the gallery. The first portrays the history of a love triangle. We follow the narration from three different angles, corresponding to the three participants. A man and a woman take a common friend, a woman, on a trip. Several months later, the man leaves the first woman and moves in with the second. In addition to a description of the events and hints at the internal motives of the protagonists, we glean a lot of information about the settings in which individual parts of the story transpire, the positions of objects, the compositions, and the patterns that the items and the participants in the story create among themselves. After some time, the man who has moved in with his new girlfriend suffers a serious accident. Unconscious, he is taken to the hospital, and when he comes to, he wants to see his first partner. His memory loss causes him to forget his decision to live with the other woman, as if it had never happened.

The second story in *A Gap* introduces us to a second space and situation similar to that of *Killer without a Cause*. A man in a kitchen is increasingly obsessed with recording banal events and searching for their rhythms and connections. He makes precise records of a refrigerator switching on and off, and analyzes his own movements in detail. The documentation of meaningless events becomes the meaning of his life, and he is paralyzed by the need to arrange random and unimportant events around him in order to grasp their hidden logic. His desire to record the switching on and off of a refrigerator as precisely as possible means he cannot get up from the table, since doing so could cause him to fall behind in his record keeping. All four projections are related in character. The footage illustrates the story, which is narrated primarily with the help of a text that is read out loud. At the level of expressive structure, *A Gap* recapitulates the principle of the installation *A True Story* in a different format. The basis of the work is a text consisting of a multilinear story. The textual script is enacted once in the form of a spatial installation intended to be read—and then a second time in the form of a film. For Mančuška, the film script was not simply a set of instructions that when carried out would bring the final work into being but an element of the work taken as a whole, in which the text and its spatial and cinematographic enactments participated equally. His series of filmscripts can be considered independent works of literature that, by virtue of the processes used in them, build on the tradition of experimental literature of the 1960s.

IV.

Most of Ján Mančuška's "film" works have a strong sculptural presence. More than simply through projected images, the artist expresses himself through his spatial installations. This applies to his *Lost Memory* (*Postcatastrophic Story*) (2010) as well. Three film projectors with loopers through which a single length of film passes are the basis of the piece. The film loop contains a sequence of fragments of an approximately eight-minute narration with precisely calculated pauses. We watch the story on three screens in front of the projectors. It is not straightforwardly linear but circular, providing delayed commentary about itself. The story "overflows" from the first screen onto the second and third. However, the individual storylines are synchronized. Shots are often composed in such a way that the characters look in the direction of the next screen and react to what is going on there. Thus, new combinations and new meanings arise. The entire film loop lasts about half an hour. [ill. 1]

The film was shot with a moving Steadicam that continually follows one of the protagonists. If it encounters someone else, the camera then begins to follow the new person. In this way, we experience an imaginary baton being passed. The constantly repeating world is full of misunderstandings. In the basic storyline, we follow several characters who gradually reveal the peculiar situations in which they find themselves. In the introduction, a conversation between a man and a woman outlines the state of affairs, "Have you read the newspaper today? It says a minor catastrophe has occurred in the city, but that the city's inhabitants won't be affected in any way. Interesting. In reality, there are no facts here; the editor just writes that he can't remember the rest of the information. How is that possible? Can a newspaper really print something like this?"[36] We then witness the gradual memory loss of all the characters. Although they know they were supposed to do something, they cannot remember what, and they search confusedly for meaning in what is happening around them. The memory loss speaks to the end of the normal sequential character of life. Events can no longer flow into one another, since we do not remember them. Participants are caught in a time loop, forced to constantly repeat what they were doing just a moment earlier. They then lose their capacity for language as well. Finally, the protagonist of the story utters a series of chaotically arranged words that make no sense.

Mančuška presented several versions of *Lost Memory*. The basic description applies to the installation as it was first shown at the 2010 opening in Berlin's Meyer Riegger Gallery. For an exhibition at the Kunstverein Braunschweig in late 2010 and early 2011, the artist presented the work in three different ways—first, as a three-part projection, as it was shown in Berlin, with the use of synchronized digital projectors. After that, he presented it in the form of a single-channel projection in which the story was narrated in a linear manner. The third presentation used only a frame corresponding to a specially designed projection screen. In this instance, nothing was projected onto it; it served instead to frame the view from the gallery onto the surrounding landscape.

Film attracted Ján Mančuška not only as a means of narration but also as a source of conceptually rich material capable of generating meaning. As the following example shows, his works may be considered "film sculptures."

In *Tatlinova věž* [Tatlin Tower] (2009) the shape of a work of Soviet constructivist art that was designed but never built is reproduced in film stock. The choice of material has no functional justification; it serves as a metaphor for the sequentiality, dialectics, and utopian ethos of the avant-garde. Such work with the material of film, however, is only illustrative in character. A strip of film itself represents something akin to a model of temporal progression and causal evolution. The recorded sequential images are related in a natural way, depending on their position in the strip of film. Here, "forward" and "backward" indicate not only spatial locations but a temporal dimension as well. First and foremost, Mančuška's film works became tools for exploring the relationship between space and time. His work situates him among a broader group of artists who use film and the moving image in a similar way, bringing the temporality of film to museums and gallery spaces and thereby providing a framework in which narration becomes important once again. Narrative works make it possible to work more efficiently with time than more traditional works of visual art.[37]

The foundational element of Mančuška's works in the area of the moving image was often the loop or, more precisely, an imaginary or actual strip of film with images corresponding to a span of time or a sequence of moments. This can also be seen in an untitled drawing from the artist's estate in which he depicts a projector on a tripod with a piece of film passing through it, extending from both sides of the device. In front of the lens, we see a pitcher and a glass arranged in four different ways, representing the phases of the action of pouring water. We cannot tell from the drawing whether or not we are looking at four simultaneously existing pitchers. We also cannot tell if the infinite loop of film in the camera is moving or if the composition is static. The drawing and, more generally, the idea of a piece of film as an object can help us understand Mančuška's restrained approach to the resources provided by the language of film, for most of his works in the field of the moving image ignore the conventional expressive possibilities of film editing and composition as they are employed in traditional cinematic works. Instead, Mančuška works with spatial and temporal arrangements derived from the specific qualities and possibilities of the film medium.

Mančuška's installation *Sorry for Being So Late* (2007) deals effectively with the way time and space are interconnected through a piece of cinematic or photographic film. The artist superimposed an imaginary square grid consisting of 64 points over Prague's Stromovka Park. Over the course of a single day, from sunrise to sunset, he proceeded to move from point to point according to a precise timetable. He documented his route with a camera on 64 rolls of color film, each containing 48 exposures. The artist must therefore have taken one picture roughly every 12 seconds. The gallery installation consists of free-hanging strips of developed film forming a geometrical grid against the background of a large lightbox. The result is a record of the artist's existence within a well-defined set of spatiotemporal parameters, an image map of a single day.

The concept of a length of film bearing a record of time served Mančuška as a model that could be applied to other forms of art as well. A strip representing a segment of fluid time could be run not only forward but also in reverse, as he showed in his theater piece *Reverse Play* (2008). *Reverse Play* involves a rather simple but nonetheless effective trick from the early days of cinema: a piece of film is run backward, so that a demolished wall suddenly rises up from a cloud of dust and once again stands miraculously erect, and a swimmer emerges from the water after a dive, completely dry. Transposing this principle to a live theater performance, however, entails a subtle paradox. The inverted time of the play, which proceeds from the end to the beginning, nevertheless unfolds in time from beginning to end. While the actors on the stage do everything in reverse order, the voice of the narrator comments on their actions in ordinary chronological time. Audience members and protagonists alike are thus confronted with two "filmstrips of time" that are running in opposite directions. At some point, they will have to intersect. In some of his works, as in *A Gap* (2007) or *True Story* (2005), Mančuška took a similar imaginary piece of film-time and played it in turns, depending on who the narrator was, thereby splitting it into different perspectives that he then combined with one another, or he organized it into completely random sequences, as in the video installation *Nude Descending a Staircase* (2007).

An interest in experimenting with the development of narration in time and the rules governing the process link the work of Ján Mančuška and Filip Cenek. The investigation of nonlinear narrative has, for the past 15 years, been a decisive element in Cenek's work in the field of the moving image. It was originally inspired by the possibilities of computer technology and digital postproduction that facilitate the construction of nonlinear narratives.[38] In contrast to Mančuška, Cenek is critical of the effects of sequential narration on the spectator's mind. We automatically combine items that are juxtaposed or follow in succession, into higher units of meaning. We become convinced that what we see on a film or TV screen constitutes a single semantic arc, a linearly constructed narrative belonging to a tradition that dates back to ancient Greek drama. Many of Cenek's works attempt, on the contrary, to show that the moving image need not—or simply does not—have any such higher meaning. Instead, it is the viewer who creates connections among random items and combines them into a meaningful narrative. In order to demonstrate this propensity, instead of examining analytically the language of motion pictures, Cenek has increasingly resorted to working with chance. His works do not bring to mind the clearly presented, albeit branching, sequential elements of Ján Mančuška's work. Rather, they have the character of a disorderly archive that we can sift through in an unlimited number of ways. Installations like *Třpytka* [Shiner] (2010), *Vratké kino* [Wonky Cinema] (2011), and others revolve around two Carousel slide projectors—one containing photographs, the other containing lines of text. Images from both projectors merge on a single screen, where they create a changing, asynchronous time loop. The slide projectors, operating automatically, link random images with random lines of text, covering the full range of possible combinations. The viewer, however, reads the resulting projection as a unique story based on a prepared script. Only after a certain amount of time and after inspecting the projection apparatus does the viewer realize that the story told through the juxtaposition of images and text is a product of his or her own mind. The work's impact is created not only by the photographic quality of the black-and-white slides but also by other elements of the installation that impinge upon the viewer's attention—the rhythmic clicking of the slide projectors, the light emanating from them, and the distinctive smell of warm plastic. Also refreshing—and essential for interpreting the work—is the analog mechanism of the apparatus combining images and text. [ill. 2]

While Cenek generally creates his nonlinear narratives using the expressive resources of film, such as random montages of photographs, sequences of images, and subtitles, Ján Mančuška often begins from a story mediated by verbal narration that he subsequently transforms into film or spatial installations. Unlike Cenek, Mančuška believes that the meaning of a story can also be depicted with nonlinear narration—or at any rate, the protagonists of his films or plays are constantly searching for such meaning. In a world of fragmentary, multilinear and backward-running stories, they search for their unique meanings among the possibilities that lie along their relevant story lines. They want to know how things played out and what that means.

V.

This chapter opened by exploring the relationship between experimental film and the works of contemporary Czech artists who employ the moving image. The example of Ján Mančuška, however, might point to the conclusion that his relationship to film—though it was mediated by an international rather than a purely domestic context—was no more important than his relationship to experimental literary techniques. Textual elements, or, rather, the audio means through which spoken words were manifested, played a key role in shaping Mančuška's cinematographic works. It was only in his second phase, which during his last years mainly consisted of collaborations with film editor Ondřej Vavrečka, that Mančuška added a pictorial component to his scripts, breaking down images and concerning himself with the artistic design of his works. Mančuška did not narrate using images or even the language of film. Images in his works do not create contrasts or associational links. His point of departure was the written narrative. That is why his films might come across as literary and even mildly mechanical: the pictorial element in them often serves to illustrate what has already been communicated verbally.

Had Mančuška's written materials been published separately—and it is no accident that he tried to publish many of his scripts in exhibition catalogues—they would certainly suggest a collection of texts in the spirit of 1960s experimental literature or the tradition of the *Nouveau roman*. As was the case with French writer (and later filmmaker) Alain Robbe-Grillet, Mančuška's texts focus first and foremost on descriptions of settings or people's behavior. He did not use conventional means to portray the mental states of his characters; he would uncover their psychological frame of mind despite an absence of direct description. Mančuška experimented with other techniques that we find not only in film but also in literature, including shifting narrators, chronological leaps, and the multilinearity discussed above. But it was not only abroad that he found literary inspiration for his experimentation; he was also a careful reader of the prose works of Czech experimental novelist Věra Linhartová and the writings of Josef Hiršal and Bohumila Grögerová.

A look at Czech art over the last 15 years would appear to affirm the significance of such interests. In addition to the emergence of artists working to great effect with the moving image, we find a parallel and demonstrable—if somewhat less conspicuous—shift in focus toward literary forms. Many contemporary artists are creating two-dimensional or spatial texts, writing scripts, or even producing literary works. Working with text is fundamental to the inscriptions of Jan Nálevka, the projections of Jan Šerých, the diagrams of Zbyňek Baladrán, and the primarily acoustic collages of Roman Štětina. While the works of Tomáš Svoboda, Adéla Babanová, Adéla Svobodová, and Johana Švarcová may ultimately be presented in the format of digital projection, it is the way they work with written language that is fundamental. Jiří Skála and Aleš Čermák even use the traditional format of the printed book. Not only are many Czech visual artists working increasingly with texts and even becoming writers of texts, but some literary figures—the most famous among them being Ondřej Buddeus—are producing works that seem more like the written notes of conceptual artists than classical poetry.

If we were to transpose the opening question of this chapter into the field of literature, we would probably ask: what links, if any, do these artists have to the tradition of Czech experimental literature of the 1960s? From the multiplicity of approaches discussed above and their varied trajectories, it is evident that if any such influences have been at play, they must have been quite circuitous. Instead, different individuals seem to have been using similar elements and techniques but developing them in parallel fields and applying them in different contexts at different times. In contrast with the priorities of artists in the 1960s, making use of literary resources does not seem essential to artists today. The generation of Czech artists coming to prominence after 2000 had to forge their own paths to the written word. However, this did not involve a complete crossing-over to a different medium, as some writers of experimental literature or visual poetry have done. More important to them than the legacy of the 1960s are the prospects and experiences made available by digital technology—free access to a wellspring of existing written works organized in a hypertext structure and, more generally, growing experience with personal computers as a tool to facilitate the convergence of textual, image-based, and audiovisual techniques.

Paradoxically, it appears that the individual who bridged the generation gap with the most reverence and has built most authentically upon the Czech experimental literature of the 1960s is filmmaker Martin Ježek. In 2004 he shot *Tanec* [Dance], a 14-minute film whose soundtrack was a recording of Milan Nápravník's poem *Předmoucha* [Pre-Fly], from the record set *Fragmenty 1963/1964* [Fragments 1963/1964]. Ježek's masterwork *Dům daleko* [A House Far Away] (2007) is not a direct cinematic adaptation of Věra Linhartová's eponymous prose work but, rather, a work crafted through the use of similar creative principles. In this film, as in others by Ježek, a rigid, predetermined system clashes with an improvisational approach that welcomes any and all random and even directly destructive interpolations, thereby countering the classical conception of the figure of the artist.

The genesis of *A House Far Away* can be divided into several stages that illustrate the artist's approach to his work. In the first stage, Ježek and his collaborator, camera operator Jakub Halousek, chose the city Most as an appropriate place for exterior shots. In the mining city that had been relocated—it is in a different location today than it was several decades ago—they chose the best starting point on a map. They then walked around that point (located in a field) in an increasing spiral and read passages from *A House Far Away* out loud. The length of each text corresponded to the distance they covered, and on the spot thus determined, they shot footage with an 8mm camera.[39] In the second stage, they reshot the material already filmed with 16mm film. Ježek projected the 8mm footage onto a screen while Halousek filmed the screen with a 16mm camera; both were under the influence of hallucinogenic mushrooms as they did so. By mistake, Halousek repeatedly loaded film into the camera that had already been exposed and thus ended up with four layers of recorded footage. In the third stage, Ježek cut the resulting 16mm footage into one-meter strips. He then asked the Barrandov Film Lab to splice the strips together in an arbitrary order. The fourth and final stage consisted of adding sound to the images. Ježek chose all of the tracks from an audio archive recorded in the mid-1960s, during the time period when Věra Linhartová's first prose works originated. He then arranged them, not according to the dictates of normal sound design but on the basis of a graphic score. The entire film lasts 25 minutes, which according to the artist, corresponds to the time it takes to read *A House Far Away* at a normal pace.

It is remarkable that Věra Linhartová herself had already recognized in 1964 the need to analyze—at least on a theoretical level—the relationships between different artistic media and the ways they are interwoven, particularly in connection with the visual arts of the day: "This consideration [of the character of poetry] is necessary, mainly because the problem of specification or merging, or at least possible comparison of particular types of artistic creation, is one of the current problems which contemporary artistic output in some of its manifestations affirms."[40] She considered speech to be one of the basic materials of literature and thought a writer should approach it in the same way that a visual artist approaches materials in nonfigurative art. Similarly, Martin Ježek seized upon the prose of *A House Far Away* as his starting material and used the medium of film to convey it in space and time.

This excursion into the interrelationships among contemporary visual arts, literature, and film did not aim to expand indefinitely the partial connections between artistic disciplines but, rather, to show the limits of inquiries conducted in this way. The importance of Ján Mančuška's work does not lie in a reflection of the binary relationship between the visual arts and film or between the visual arts and literature, nor does it seek to build on specific forms of inspiration from the 1960s in the fields of literature and experimental film. Instead, the importance of Mančuška's work can be seen in the artist's ability to span artistic disciplines. The critical boundary between the visual arts and literature, undoubtedly essential to modernist thinking, no longer played a significant role for Mančuška. He crossed this boundary with the same ease with which he combined his selected narrative and formal content into a single whole. The film installation *Lost Memory* may serve as an example here. Cyclically closed events are narrated with the aid of projectors joined by a single strip of film. The story and the way it is narrated join in a direct, reciprocal relationship. We find a similar interconnectedness in most of Mančuška's works. His choice of artistic methods submitted to the semantic requirements of mirroring form and content. The ability to transfer the principles of one type of art to another would not have been possible for Mančuška if he had not had deep-rooted experiences of a post-media condition. He was not concerned with reflecting on the medium of film or on any other medium and its ostensibly essential properties. He wanted instead to use his chosen tools to paint a portrait of human thinking. The workings of the mind and the ways those workings are materialized are Mančuška's most private "media"; at the same time they are the signs that define him as a conceptual artist.[41]

VI.

If we accept their internal differences, experimental film and the art of the moving image represent broad areas whose histories may be described in a number of ways. While the language of both art forms may be similar, every artist adapts it to his or her purposes. Artists from both areas sometimes work with the same materials and technologies, and almost without exception, they set themselves apart from the film industry. For purists in the field of experimental film, conventional film materials and cinema projection are of paramount importance. Artists of the moving image can be more open to using different types of materials; their works are usually adapted specifically for presentation in a gallery setting and emphasize the relationship between the viewer and the projected image. After 1990, museums and galleries that had originally focused solely on the visual arts became the common ground where the two worlds would encounter each other. This meeting need not be seen as antagonistic but as an opportunity to open up new avenues of understanding.

At the most general level, experimental film and the art of the moving image have a common ability to create meaningful connections between images. This is also true, in part, of the visual arts and even of art history. These disciplines put images into shared contexts and, in thus combining them, attempt to derive something that could not be read into the images on their own. French film historian Philippe-Alain Michaud has even concluded that the methods of the eminent German art historian Aby Warburg anticipated or developed in parallel several principles of cinematography during the 1920s. His *Mnemosyne Atlas*, left unfinished upon his death in 1929, represented an attempt to construct visual text without words by exploiting the relationships between pictorial works. By pinning reproductions from around the world as well as images from the areas of advertising and ethnographic research onto panels covered with black cloth, he created a diachronic and transgeographic tool that highlighted cinematic principles. What was most important here was the creation of relationships that produced a greater whole. Philippe-Alain Michaud goes so far as to associate *Mnemosyne Atlas* with Eisenstein's method of film montage. Certain filmmakers "sought […] to bring disparate things together and work the material of film as Warburg worked that of art history, mixing personal and collective memory, going beyond the limits between the production and interpretation of works, between language and metalanguage, drawing the meaning of an actualization of images from reciprocal revelations possible only through montage."[42]

A discussion of figures who played an important role in the genealogy of the art of the moving image would be incomplete without mentioning Jiří Kolář and Július Koller as well. Kolář's collages from the late 1940s and early 1950s demonstrate the Kuleshov Effect, involving the sequential juxtaposition of shots of film.[43] He combined geographically, temporally, and contextually dissimilar clippings in such a way that the viewer is made to see their interaction as part of a single, unified sequence. Kolář's compositions are a discontinuous sequence of images that conveys the artist's meaning only when combined, allowing the viewer to take into account all the possible relationships in the web of elements. Nonetheless, most of the time, these collages do not articulate precise meanings that could be put into words but instead suggest to the viewer a multiplicity of meanings. Similar conclusions apply to the body of Július Koller's work, whose enormously complex network of connections eludes human comprehension.

The existence of such fresh ways of viewing or even of reflecting upon the history of art is the result, among other things, of changes in the civilization. The second half of the 20th century saw a proliferation of art forms that intentionally blur traditional borders and bridge different types of art, including collage, performance art, forms of experimental literature, and a wide variety of multimedia performances. Over the past 20 years, this process has reached a qualitatively new level. The main basis for dealing with the world today—whether we realize it consciously or not—is our experience of digital convergence. Computers are not just used to create specialized art forms; they impact all areas of life. A computer is able to convert content in any medium—image, sound, or film—into a numerical "common denominator." At the same time, computers influence how we create, store, and distribute elements of culture. Visual artists, filmmakers, writers, and musicians in the digital age all use structurally similar means to create and distribute their work, though this may not be clear at first glance.

Art historian Claire Bishop writes about an interesting paradox in this regard:

> In fact, the most prevalent trends in contemporary art since the 1990s seem united in their apparent eschewal of the digital and the virtual. Performance art, social practice, assemblage-based sculpture, painting on canvas, the "archival impulse," analog film, and the fascination with modernist design and architecture: At first glance, none of these formats appear to have anything to do with digital media, and when they are discussed, it is typically in relation to previous artistic practices across the 20th century. But when we examine these dominant forms of contemporary art more closely, their operational logic and systems of spectatorship prove intimately connected to the technological revolution we are undergoing.[44]

Even though it may not be immediately obvious, computers and the way we work with them fundamentally influence our perception of the present day—including the collapse of traditional media structures and the linking of seemingly unrelated and temporally distant products of culture.[45]

The dream of the avant-garde was to combine art and life into a single whole, making one indistinguishable from the other. This, unfortunately, proved to be nothing but a utopian fantasy. Although the goal of avant-garde art was spectacular self-destruction in the name of life, the works themselves remained art. By contrast, we can observe how life itself became aestheticized in the 20th century by means of pop culture, advertising, mass media, and, in recent years, the Internet.[46] The prewar avant-garde managed to connect different types of art, but the contemporary convergence has obviously exceeded even their boldest imaginings. Similarly, as media in contemporary art flow into one other, the past is becoming indistinguishable from the present. The old and the new are commingling. The erosion of dividing lines between the present and the past is now taken for granted in curatorial work. Important international art exhibitions like documenta, Manifesta, and the Venice Biennale were traditionally seen as a means of showcasing current developments in the art world. Over the past decade, such exhibitions have unveiled not only explorations across geographic areas in various artistic disciplines but, increasingly, historical ventures as well. Works from different times and different contexts are being brought together to coexist in the present and create new combinations of values.[47] On the resulting way of perceiving temporality, philosopher of art Peter Osborne writes, "We do not just live or exist together 'in time' with our contemporaries—as if time itself is indifferent to this existing together—but rather the present is increasingly characterised by a coming together of different but equally 'present' temporalities or 'times,' a temporal unity in disjunction, or a disjunctive unity of present times."[48]

Such a state of affairs must be understood as a challenge to art history as a scholarly field. In contrast to traditional methodologies revolving around endorsable findings and logical argumentation, interdisciplinarity and the linking of temporal planes are conducive to freer associations and more polyvalent conclusions. They do not lead to single interpretations but to a whole network of possible connections and meanings. The purpose of drawing interdisciplinary and intergenerational connections is not to claim that contemporary artists are building directly on experimental poetry or the film of the 1960s. I am, however, convinced that if we set these layers side by side, an otherwise invisible face of cultural history—one that is new and illuminating—will reveal itself to us.

[1] Film is understood here in the conventional sense, as a sequential series of images created by a photochemical process, which cause the illusion of movement when projected. If we adopt a looser definition of film as any sequential audiovisual work, the points of contact with other artistic disciplines would be more numerous.

[2] Among the many artists who sought to use film as a means of expression, we find Kazimir Malevich, László Moholy-Nagy, Marcel Duchamp, and Zdeněk Pešánek. Theorists like Karel Teige and Walter Benjamin saw film as the most important artistic form of the modern era.

[3] With the advent of digitization, many works are not clearly anchored in a given medium, including film or video, but more often represent a "journey" between them. This does not indicate the arbitrariness or interchangeability of distinct technical and expressive methods but, instead, serves as evidence of the enormous possibilities that are available to every artist working today.

[4] Michael Newman, "Moving Image in the Gallery since the 1990s," in Stuart Comer (ed.), *Film and Video Art*, Tate Publishing, London 2009, p. 95.

[5] This included a film by composer Alois Piňos and visual artist Dalibor Chatrný entitled *Mříže* [Grids] (1970), as well as a film entitled *Underground* (1972) by Jan Ságl.

[6] Austria remains beyond the scope of this text. A close, but inaccessible, neighbor of Czechoslovakia, that country produced works by several world-renowned experimental filmmakers. By the late 1950s, for example, Peter Kubelka and Kurt Kren were already working with film in innovative ways, in which we find parallels to the thinking of neo-avant-garde and conceptual artists. They began to influence Czech artists only after 1989.

[7] The Czech interwar avant-garde from the circles of poetism and Surrealism were theoretically, and to a somewhat lesser extent in practice, open to linking artistic styles.

[8] See, for example, Pavel Skopal (ed.), *Naplánovaná kinematografie, Český filmový průmysl 1945–1960* [Planned Cinematography: The Czech Film Industry 1945–1960], Academia, Prague 2012; and Štěpán Hulík, *Kinematografie zapomnění, Počátky normalizace ve Filmovém studiu Barrandov (1968–1973)* [The Cinematography of Forgetting: The Beginnings of Normalization at the Barrandov Film Studio (1968–1973)], Academia, Prague 2011.

[9] During the interwar period, the work of Čeněk Zahradníček was representative of the quality of experimental independent filmmaking. In contrast to several other Eastern Bloc countries that had stricter conditions, so-called amateur filmmaking was not banned in socialist Czechoslovakia. Film festivals played an important role here, including *Mladá kamera* [Young Camera] in Uničov, The Rychnov Eight, and the Brno Sixteen. The Brno Sixteen festival shaped the works of several artists associated with contemporary Czech experimental film after 1989.

[10] Noteworthy in this respect are the memoirs of Bohuslav Vašulka, a graduate in documentary filmmaking of FAMU. In order to become the video-art pioneer Woody Vasulka, he had to forget everything he learned during his studies in the early 1960s and start working with media other than film.

[11] See Pavle Levi, *Cinema by Other Means*, Oxford University Press, Oxford and New York 2012, p. 114.

[12] For more on experimental film in Yugoslavia during the 1960s, see, for example, Ana Janevski (ed.), *As Soon as I Open My Eyes I See a Film: Experiment in the Art of Yugoslavia in the 1960s and 1970s*, Museum of Modern Art in Warsaw, Warsaw 2010.

[13] Political and economic policies in Yugoslavia diverged significantly from those of the rest of the Eastern Bloc. Regarding the context of individual experimental films, it is interesting to note that such works were entirely financed by their creators. Bank loans, for example, enabled this.

[14] Among others, this included Paul Sharits and Davis Curtis. During the 1970s, films that came out of the Film Forms Workshop were part of the famous Exprmntl festival in Knokke, Belgium, and were (along with films from the Béla Balázs Studio) the subject of an independent exhibit at De Appel in Amsterdam.

[15] A massive part of documenta 6 was the section of experimental film, which included the works of Józef Robakowski, Ryszard Waśko, and Wojciech Bruszewski.

[16] Łukasz Ronduda, *Polish Art of the 70s*, Polski Western and the Center for Contemporary Art—Ujazdowski Castle, Jelenia Góra and Warsaw 2009, p. 267. The late Polish director Andrzej Wajda, for example, took a bold stand against the workshop.

[17] Steven Ball and David Curtis, "Poles and Angles," in Łukasz Ronduda and Florian Zeyfang (eds.), *1, 2, 3 … Avant-Gardes: Film/Art between Experiment and Archive*, CCA Ujazdowski Castle and Sternberg Press, Warsaw and Berlin 2007, p. 60.

[18] The Béla Balázs Studio has not yet been the subject of an extensive monograph. In 2009 the Mücsarnok Gallery in Budapest organized an exhibit that was accompanied by an anthology of texts in English. See Gábor Gelencsér (ed.), *BBS 50. Essays for the 50th Anniversary of Balázs Béla Studio*, Mücsarnok, Budapest 2009. In 2014 the director Gyula Nemes defended a dissertation on the Béla Balázs Studio, in which he borrowed liberally from this publication.

[19] The importance of avant-garde pioneers such as Alexander Hackenschmied and Zdeněk Pešánek only became established in the 1990s. It is possible to read about the modest range of contemporary Czech experimental film, for example, in a thematic issue of the magazine *Cinepur*. See the special issue no. 17, from September 2001, which was devoted to experimental film. One of the main conclusions here is that experimental filmmaking during the 1990s was primarily an undertaking of several individuals who had a camaraderie with one another.

[20] On the concept of intermedial reflexivity, see Petr Szczepanik, "Intermedialita a (inter) mediální reflexivita v současném filmu [Intermediality and (Inter)Medial Reflexivity in Contemporary Film]," in *Sborník prací Filozofické fakulty brněnské univerzity* [Anthology of Works from the Philosophical Faculty of Brno University], FF MU, Brno O I /2002.

[21] Such an argument understandably requires confirmation through relevant research. American art historian Rosalind E. Krauss considers the environment of the avant-garde cinema Anthology Film Archives, where filmmakers and visual artists alike come together to present and find support for their own works, to be important when describing the transformation of the relationship of artists of the 1970s vis-à-vis the concept of media. The post-media state, as Krauss writes, is characterized, however, by a decline in the understanding of the individual arts as areas defined by a specific medium. See Rosalind E. Krauss, *A Voyage on the North Sea*, Thames & Hudson, New York 1999.

[22] In the context of the Soviet-Czechoslovak comedy *Cirkus v cirkuse* [Circus at the Circus] (1975), Kučera composed an artistically conceived title scene in a style that was not only unusual but, despite its doubtless quality, almost ridiculous. Jaroslav Kučera also shot a series of casual family films in which he sometimes uses experimental techniques. However, these are not works that aspire to be independent experimental works.

[23] The contents of Kučera's estate have not been fully examined, but he left behind tens of thousands of negatives.

[24] According to public transport management and magazines on the newsstands, we can specify that at least part of the group of images of Wenceslas Square are from the first half of 1978. They thus appear to come from the time when Jaroslav Kučera worked as a cinematographer on the films *Malá mořská víla* [The Little Mermaid] and *Adéla ještě nevečeřela* [Dinner for Adele].

[25] Kučera also coincidentally found himself, camera in hand, in the same place at the same time that Jan Ságl was shooting his experimental film *Underground* in 1972.

[26] Bernd and Hilla Becher, as well as Edward Ruscha, belong to the classic group of individuals doing this sort of photography. They would exhaustively document a definite, predefined type of place or style of architecture, as we see in Ruscha's project *Every Building on the Sunset Strip* (1966), or in series of industrial buildings photographed by the Bechers.

[27] The term *expanded cinema* refers to a movement that, beginning in the 1960s, experimented with film outside of its traditional form as a medium projected in a cinema. Artists of expanded cinema made projection equipment a visible part of their performances. They experimented with multiple film and slide projections or a combination of film, theater, and visual arts. They also quickly accepted video and other technological innovations.

[28] There have been attempts to treat the history of Slovak media arts as a whole. See, for example, Katarína Rusnáková, *História a teória mediálneho umenia na Slovensku* [History and Theory of Media Art in Slovakia], Vysoká škola výtvarných umení v Bratislave [Academy of Fine Arts and Design], Bratislava 2006.

[29] Bohdana Kerbachová, *Utajený experimentátor Petr Skala* [Petr Skala, Secret Experimenter], Národní filmový archiv [National Film Archive], Prague 2005, p. 13.

[30] For more on the genesis of the works of Radek Pilař and Petr Skala, see Bohdana Kerbachová, "Počátky českého videoartu" [The Beginnings of Czech Video Art], *Iluminace* [Illumination], vol. 18, no. 2, 2006, pp. 133–158.

[31] The installation *Killer without a Cause* might remind us of a variation of *Two Sides to Every Story* by Michael Snow (1974), one of the classic works of expanded cinema. In this work, the artist filmed a single scene with two cameras placed in opposite positions. The resulting films are projected onto a two-sided screen placed in the middle of a space, where viewers can circle around it. Both images cannot be seen at once, so the viewer must choose which to watch and when to watch it. Viewer becomes artist as he or she is forced to change position in the space in order to create a unique narrative reading of the two works.

[32] A similar theme, freed from narration, can be found in the British experimental film *Angles of Incidence* (1973) by William Raban. During a 24-hour period a camera traces a semicircle in front of a window framed variously by the light behind it.

[33] Quoted from a text entitled *Vrah bez příčiny* [Killer without a Cause], reprinted in Ján Mančuška's publication *Chybění* [Being Absent], tranzit, Prague 2007.

[34] Karel Císař, "Conceptual Personae," in Ján Mančuška, *Against Interpretation*, Hatje Cantz, Ostfildern 2011, p. 133.

[35] Conceptual art was, of course, never completely devoid of emotion, even during the era of its birth. Jörg Heiser used the term "romantic conceptualism" to describe the area of conceptual art containing subjectivity, aesthetics, and emotionality; accessed July 14, 2014, https://frieze.com/article/emotional-rescue.

[36] As cited in Mančuška, *Against Interpretation*, p. 77.

[37] See Erika Balsom, *Exhibiting Cinema in Contemporary Art*, Amsterdam University Press, Amsterdam 2013, p. 157.

[38] Filip Cenek was, in fact, trained as a film projectionist. In hindsight, he describes his experience showing classic films as formative. He realized in the projection booth that film was not only a moving image on a screen, as most viewers see it, but also a more complicated spatial phenomenon.

[39] This is essentially the same technique Ján Mančuška used in his work *Sorry for Being So Late*. It differed insofar as Martin Ježek and Martin Halousek walked in a spiral instead of moving around points on a grid, and they used an 8mm camera instead of a photographic camera.

[40] Věra Linhartová, *Vnitřní model a vnitřní monolog* [Interior Model and Interior Monologue], in Věra Linhartová, *Soustředné kruhy* [Concentric Circles], Torst, Prague 2010, p. 114.

[41] Císař, "Conceptual Personae," p. 134ff.

[42] Philippe-Alain Michaud, *Aby Warburg and the Image in Motion*, Zone Books, New York 2007, p. 262.

[43] The Kuleshov Effect, named for the Soviet filmmaker Lev Kuleshov, illustrates the fundamental principle of film editing: the viewer combines consecutive moving images into a causal connection. Kuleshov allegedly demonstrated this with a simple experiment. He filmed the face of the actor Ivan Mozzhukhin and interspersed the image with steaming soup, an open coffin, and a woman on a couch. An uninformed viewer of the resulting montage could then admire the mastery with which Mozzhukhin's "plays" hunger, grief, and desire.

[44] Claire Bishop, "Digital Divide," *Artforum*, September 2012, pp. 434–442.

[45] For art that comes from a similar way of thinking, the term "post-Internet art" has taken hold during recent years. In the same way that modernity inspired the development of collage at the onset of the 20th century, the Internet presents a certain formal logic that artists apply, even in their work that is not directly related to it.

[46] For more on this topic, see Václav Magid, "Od estetizace politiky k politizaci umění a zpět" [From the Aesthetization of Politics to the Politicization of Art and Back], in *Kritika depolitizovaného rozumu: úvahy (nejen) o nové normalizaci* [Critique of Depoliticized Reason: Considerations (and More) on the New Normalization], Grimmus, Prague 2010.

[47] The exhibition *Paintings and Prototypes* at the City Library in Prague in 2013, organized by curator Karel Císař, is an example of a similar project whose basis was the relationship between the old and the new.

[48] Peter Osborne, *Anywhere or Not at All: Philosophy of Contemporary Art*, Verso, London and New York 2013, p. 17.

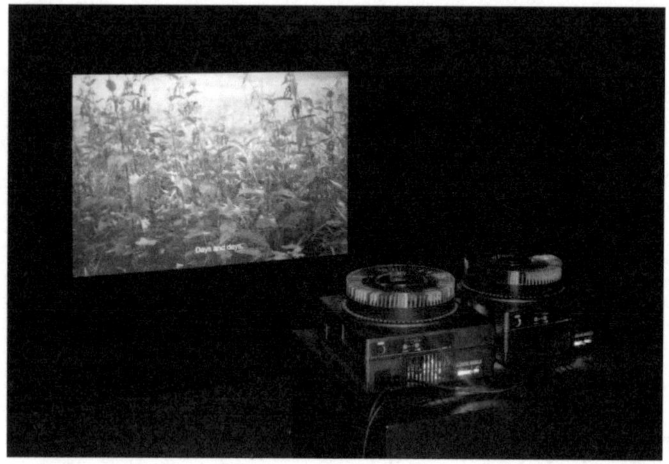

[ill. 2] Filip Cenek and Tereza Sochorová, *Before the Sea*, 2008, installation view, Brot Kunsthalle, Vienna, 2010
Two programmable 35mm Carousel slide projectors, black-and-white slides projected in asynchronous loop
Courtesy of the artists

Editorial Note

The text of "A Modernist Crossroads: Jindřich Chalupecký versus Clement Greenberg" originated as the basis for a lecture at the University of Texas at Austin in 1999. It was then adapted for presentation at České umění 1939–1999 [Czech Art 1939–1999], a conference organized by the Academic Research Centre of the Academy of Fine Arts in Prague, and subsequently printed in the conference proceedings, titled *České umění 1939–1999. Programy a impulsy* [Czech Art 1939–1999: Programs and Impulses], Prague, Academy of Fine Arts 2000, pp. 21–26. The author reworked and expanded the text for inclusion in *Srovnávací studie* [Comparative Studies], a collection published in 2004 by Agite/Fra in Prague.

The essay "Paxism, Explosionism, and Aktual in the Struggle for Peace: Jan Lukeš, Vladimír Boudník, and Milan Knížák" was published in *Revolver Revue*, no. 54, 2003, pp. 259–295.

The text was edited in some areas and included in *Srovnávací studie* [Comparative Studies].

The essay "The Fates of the Free Artists: Czechs and the Situationists" was written in 2002–2005 and was part of *Srovnávací studie* [Comparative Studies].

Fragments of the text of "Eastern and Western Cubes: Minimalism in Dispute" appeared in an article titled "Dva póly lability" [The Two Poles of Lability] in the journal *Atelier*, no. 2, 2004, p. 2, as well as in "Místo Evy Kmentové" [The Place of Eva Kmentová], a contribution to *Eva Kmentová*, a collection published by the North Bohemian Gallery of Visual Arts in Litoměřice in 2004. Another part of this text was included in the proceedings for The Post-Communist Condition, a conference that took place in Berlin in June 2004, and Authentic Structures, a conference in Prague in December 2004. It was included in *Srovnávací studie* [Comparative Studies].

The essay "A Collage between Generations: Jiří Kolář as Witness to Modernity and His Contemporary Successors" was published in *Asociativní dějepis umění* [An Associative Art History], published in 2014 by tranzit.cz in Prague.

A fragment of the first section of the chapter "Fluxus in the Czech Lands and Czechs in Flux: Communication Networks, Information Services, and the Art World Hierarchy" was presented at the SocialEast Seminar on Art and Empire in Manchester in 2006. It was subsequently fundamentally reworked and presented the following year at a conference organized by the Academic Research Centre of the Academy of Fine Arts in 2007. It was published under the title "The Golden Sixties" in *(A)symetrické historie—zamlčené rámce a vytěsněné problémy* [(A)symmetrical History: Concealed Frameworks and Displaced Problems], an anthology published by the Academic Research Centre of the Academy of Fine Arts in 2008. The chapter's second and third sections were presented in February 2014 at *Hranice experimentu* [The Frontiers of Experimentation], a conference organized by the Academy of Arts, Architecture, and Design in Prague. They are being prepared for individual publication in the 16th issue of the journal *Sešit pro umění, teorii a příbuzné zóny* [Notebook for Art, Theory, and Related Zones]. The fourth section of the chapter was written for *Post*, a Web magazine of the Museum of Modern Art in New York, and was published in *Asociativní dějepis umění* [An Associative Art History].

The chapter "National Conceptualism: Czech National Revival Motifs in the Work of Stano Filko and Július Koller" contains a fragment of an unpublished text on the work of Stano Filko from late 2009 to early 2010. National revival motifs in the work of Filko and Koller were the subject of a lecture given at the Institut für Slawistik at the Humboldt University of Berlin. The two final sections of the chapter contain certain motifs from "Sochy, které nikomu nepatří" [Sculptures that Do Not Belong to Anyone], a text written for Pavel Karous's *Vetřelci a volavky. Atlas výtvarného umění ve veřejném prostoru v Československu v období normalizace (1968–1989)* [Intruders and Decoys: An Atlas of Visual Art in Public Spaces in Czechoslovakia during the Period of Normalization (1968–1989)]. In 2013 it was published by the Arbor Vitae publishing house and the Academy of Arts, Architecture, and Design in Prague.

The genealogy of the chapter "The Politics of Intimacy: Czechoslovak Performance Art in the 1970s and Its Remakes" dates back to 2006, when the article "Replika neznamená jen kopii, ale i součást dialogu" [A Replica Is Not Just a Copy but Part of a Dialogue] was published in *Replaced*, a publication marking the presentation of Barbora Klímová's eponymous project. Another source for this chapter was material first presented in 2008 at a seminar titled "1968–1989" at the Museum of Modern Art in Warsaw. A year later the revised conference paper was published under the title "Look Who's Watching: Photographic Documentation of Happenings and Performances in Czechoslovakia" in *Political Upheaval and Artistic Change*, edited by Claire Bishop and Marta Dziewańska for the Warsaw Museum of Modern Art. Passages in the chapter dedicated to the interpretation of the work of Jiří Kovanda were published under the title "Etude" in 2011 for the 13th issue of the *Manifesta Journal*. Parallels between the work of the Prague performers and secret police photographs were pointed out in "Perverzní neorealismus StB" [The Perverse Neo-Realism of the State Security], published January 8, 2011, in the "Orientace" supplement of the newspaper *Lidové noviny*. The chapter also contains certain ideas from "Umění z druhé ruky" [Secondhand Art], published in *Dokumentace* [Documentation], an anthology edited by Jan Krtička and Jan Prošek. In 2013 it was published by the Faculty of Art and Design at the Jan Evangelista Purkyně University in Ústí nad Labem.

Part of the chapter "Visual Art in a Moving Frame: Ján Mančuška between Art, Film, and Literature" is a fragment of "Trojí reflexe Jána Mančušky" [Threefold Reflection on Ján Mančuška], an article published in the 52nd issue of *Cinepur* in July 2007.

Index

A

B

C

D

E

Imprint

EDITORS
Clément Dirié, Vít Havránek, Tomáš Pospiszyl

EDITORIAL COORDINATION
Věra Janíčková

COPY EDITING AND PROOFREADING
Ivan Gutierrez, Maria King, Clare Manchester,
Sylvia Tidwell

TRANSLATIONS FROM CZECH TO ENGLISH
Ivan Gutierrez

DESIGN CONCEPT
Gavillet & Rust, Geneva

DESIGN
Jaroslav Vlček

PRINT AND BINDING
Musumeci S.p.A., Quart (Aosta)

TYPEFACE
Genath (www.optimo.ch)

PHOTO CREDITS
Radek Brousil (p. 65); Daniel Grúň for the Július Koller society in 2011 (p. 180); Hana Hamplová (p. 90); Institute of Art History, Czech Academy of Sciences (p. 66); Estate of Jiří Kolář, 2017, c/o DILIA (p. 110); Karel Kuklík (p. 108); Martin Polák (p. 280); Filip Vančo (p. 212)

PUBLISHED BY
JRP|Ringier
Limmatstrasse 270
CH–8005 Zurich
T +41 (0) 43 311 27 50
E info@jrp-ringier.com
www.jrp-ringier.com

IN CO-EDITION WITH
Les presses du réel
35, rue Colson
F–21000 Dijon
T +33 3 80 30 75 23
E info@lespressesdureel.com
www.lespressesdureel.com

AND
tranzit.cz
www.tranzit.org
tranzit is an initiative in the field of contemporary art.
Its main partner is ERSTE Foundation.

ERSTE Stiftung

This book was published with the support of the Ministry of Culture of the Czech Republic.

ISBN 978-3-03764-517-8 (JRP | Ringier)
ISBN 978-2-84066-982-1 (Les presses du réel)
ISBN 978-80-87259-40-5 (tranzit.cz)

Distribution

JRP | Ringier publications are available internationally at selected bookstores and from the following distribution partners:

SWITZERLAND
AVA Verlagsauslieferung AG
www.ava.ch

FRANCE
Les presses du réel
www.lespressesdureel.com

GERMANY AND AUSTRIA
Vice Versa Distribution
www.viceversaartbooks.com

UK AND OTHER EUROPEAN COUNTRIES
Cornerhouse Publications HOME
www.cornerhousepublications.org

USA, CANADA, ASIA, AND AUSTRALIA
ARTBOOK | D. A. P.
www.artbook.com

For a list of our partner bookshops or for any general questions, please contact JRP | Ringier directly at info@jrp-ringier.com, or visit our homepage www.jrp-ringier.com for further information about our program.

Documents Series 26:
Tomáš Pospiszyl
An Associative Art History
Comparative Studies
of Neo-Avant-Gardes
in a Bipolar World

This book is the twenty-sixth volume in the "Documents" series, dedicated to critics' writings.

The series was founded by Lionel Bovier and Xavier Douroux.

Also available

DOCUMENTS SERIES (IN ENGLISH)

John Baldessari, *More Than You Wanted to Know About John Baldessari*
ISBN 978-3-03764-192-7 (JRP | Ringier) [*Vol. 1*]
ISBN 978-3-03764-256-6 (JRP | Ringier) [*Vol. 2*]

Sarah Burkhalter & Laurence Schmidlin, *Spacescapes. Dance & Drawing since 1962*
ISBN 978-3-03764-469-0 (JRP | Ringier)
ISBN 978-2-84066-917-3 (Les presses du réel)

Gabriele Detterer & Maurizio Nannucci, *Artist-Run Spaces*
ISBN 978-3-03764-191-0 (JRP | Ringier)
ISBN 978-2-84066-512-0 (Les presses du réel)

Hans Ulrich Obrist, *A Brief History of Curating*
ISBN 978-3-905829-55-6 (JRP | Ringier)
ISBN 978-2-84066-287-7 (Les presses du réel)

Hans Ulrich Obrist, *A Brief History of New Music*
ISBN 978-3-905829-190-3 (JRP | Ringier)
ISBN 978-2-84066-619-6 (Les presses du réel)

Hans Ulrich Obrist, *The Czech Files*
ISBN 978-3-03764-387-7 (JRP | Ringier)
ISBN 978-2-84066-760-6 (Les presses du réel)

Igor Zabel, *Contemporary Art Theory*
ISBN 978-3-03764-238-2 (JRP | Ringier)
ISBN 978-2-84066-573-1 (Les presses du réel)